LAW AND SOCIAL CHANGE IN THE U.S.S.R.

LAW AND SOCIAL CHANGE
IN
THE U.S.S.R.

BY

JOHN N. HAZARD
of the New York Bar; Professor of Public Law, Columbia University

HYPERION PRESS, INC.
Westport, Connecticut

Published in 1953 by Stevens, London
Hyperion reprint edition 1979
Library of Congress Catalog Number 79-1608
ISBN 0-88355-911-0
Printed in the United States of America.

Library of Congress Cataloging in Publication Data

Hazard, John Newbold, 1909-

Law and social change in the U.S.S.R.

Reprint of the 1953 ed. published under the auspices of the London Institute of World Affairs by Stevens, London, which was issued as 23 of the Library of world affairs.

Bibliography: p.

Includes index.

1. Law—Russia—History and criticism. 2. Russia—Social conditions—1917- I. Title. II. Series: Library of world affairs; 23.

[Law] 340'.0947 79-1608

ISBN 0-88355-911-0

CONTENTS

PREFACE

Much has been written about Soviet law. Sufficient material exists even in western European languages to permit examination of its theoretical base, of its history, and of the texts of its codes. There is little material, however, relating the Soviet system of law as an entirety to the power process, to the avowed aim of moulding a new society.

This small volume has emerged from the author's long-standing desire to place in brief compass a consideration of the manner in which the formulae of the law and the institutions of the lawyer have been utilised to achieve political ends. It is in no sense an effort to determine in philosophical terms whether there is an institution in operation within the U.S.S.R. which can properly be called ' law '. Nor is it an evaluation of the Soviet system to determine whether justice is meted out to the peoples of the Soviet Union. It constitutes but some reflections on law and social change. They are the reflections of an American lawyer who availed himself of the rather unusual opportunity offered by the Institute of Current World Affairs in New York of studying Soviet law at a Soviet law school and of seeing Soviet law in operation.

The opportunity of meditation on nearly two decades of experience with Soviet law was offered by an invitation from the Faculty of Law of the University of Cambridge to spend the better part of a year with it and to develop some of the ideas in this volume in a series of lectures before the Faculty. The provision of funds by a Fulbright grant for maintenance in England made acceptance of the Cambridge invitation possible. To all who have been concerned, the most heartfelt appreciation is due.

J.N.H.

University of Cambridge
January 1953

TABLE OF CONSTITUTIONS

TABLE OF STATUTES AND ORDERS

TABLE OF CASES

ABBREVIATIONS

Arbitrazh	Arbitrazh, Organ Gosarbitrazha pri SNK SSSR
Byull.Fin. i Khoz.Zak.	Byulleten Finansovogo i Khozyaistvennogo Zakonodatelstva
Fin.i Khoz.Zak.	Finansovoe i Khozyaistvennoe Zakonodatelstvo
Izv.Ak.Nauk SSSR, otd.ek. i prava	Izvestiya Akademii Nauk SSSR, otdelenie ekonomiki i prava
LNTS	League of Nations Treaty Series
Sbornik Deistv.Dog.	Sbornik Deistvuyushchikh Dogovorov, Soglashenii i Konventsii Zaklyuchennykh s Inostrannymi Gosudarstvami
Sbornik Deistv.Post.Plenuma i Direkt.Pisem Verkh.Suda SSSR	Sbornik Deistvuyushchikh Postanovlenii Plenuma i Direktivnykh Pisem Verkhovnogo Suda SSSR 1924–1944 g.g., pod redaktsiei I.T. Golyakova (Moscow, 1946)
Sbornik Post.Pl. i Opr.Koll. Verkh.Suda SSSR	Sbornik Postanovlenii Plenuma i Opredelenii Kollegii Verkhovnogo Suda SSSR
Sbornik Post., Raz., i Direktiv Verkh.Suda SSSR	Sbornik Postanovlenii Razyasnenii i Direktiv Verkhovnogo Suda SSSR, desitvuyushchikh na 1 Aprelya 1935 g. pod redaktsiei A.N. Vinokurova (Moscow, 1935)
Sbornik Raz.Verkh.Suda RSFSR	Sbornik Razyasnenii Verkhovnogo Suda RSFSR, izdanie 4 (Moscow, 1935)
Sbornik Tsirk.N.K.Yust. RSFSR	Sbornik Tsirkulyarov i Razyasnenii Narodnogo Komissariata Yustitsii RSFSR, deistvuyushchikh na 1 Maya 1935 g. (Moscow, 1934)
Sbornik Zak.SSSR	Sbornik Zakonov SSSR i Ukazov Prezidiuma Verkhovnogo Soveta SSSR
Sezdy Sovetov RSFSR v Post. i Rez.	Sezdy Sovetov RSFSR v Postanovleniyakh i Rezolyutsiyakh, pod obshchei redaktsiei akademika A.Ya. Vyshinskogo (Moscow, 1939)
Sob.Post.RSFSR	Sobranie Postanovlenii i Rasporyazhenii Pravitelstva Rossiiskoi Sovetskoi Federativnoi Sotsialisticheskoi Respubliki
Sob.Post.SSSR	Sobranie Postanovlenii i Rasporyazhenii Pravitelstva Soyuza Sovetskikh Sotsialisticheskikh Respublik. (With issue No. 5 for the year 1946 the title was changed to read: Sobranie Postanovlenii i Rasporyazhenii Soveta Ministrov Soyuza Sovetskikh Sotsialisticheskikh Respublik)
Sob.Uzak.RSFSR	Sobranie Uzakonenii i Rasporyazhenii Rabochego i Krestyanskogo Pravitelstva. (With issue No. 1 for the year 1925 the title was changed by adding the words, Rossiiskoi Sotsialisticheskoi Federativnoi Sovetskoi Respubliki)

Sob.Uzak.Ukrainian SSR	Sobranie Uzakonenii i Rasporyazhenii Raboche-Krestyanskogo Pravitelstva Ukrainy
Sob.Zak.SSSR	Sobranie Zakonov i Rasporyazhenii Raboche-Krestyanskogo Pravitelstva Soyuza Sovetskikh Sotsialisticheskikh Respublik
Sots.Zak.	Sotsialisticheskaya Zakonnost
Sov.Gos. i Pravo	Sovetskoe Gosudarstvo i Pravo
Sov.Yust.	Sovetskaya Yustitsiya
Spravochnik po Zak.	Spravochnik po Zakonodatelstvu dlya Sudebno-Prokurorskikh Rabotnikov, pod obshchei redaktsiei G.N.Safonova. Izdanie 2 (Moscow, 1949)
Sud.Prak.RSFSR	Sudebnaya Praktika RSFSR pod redaktsiei Predsedatelya Verkhsuda RSFSR
Sud.Prak.SSSR	Sudebnaya Praktika Verkhovnogo Suda SSSR
Uch.Zap. (Trudy Yurid.Fak.)	Uchenye Zapisky (Trudy Yuridicheskogo Fakulteta)
UNTS	United Nations Treaty Series
Ved.Verkh.Sov.SSSR	Vedomosti Verkhovnogo Soveta Soyuza Sovetskikh Sotsialisticheskikh Respublik
VKP (b) v Rez. i Resh.	Vsesoyuznaya Kommunisticheskaya Partiya (bolshevikov) v Rezolyutsiyakh i Resheniyakh Sezdov, Konferentsii i Plenumov Ts.K. (1898–1939)

Chapter I

PROPERTY IS THE KEY

No branch of law has seemed more important to Soviet leaders than that which concerns property relationships. While the subject has been treated traditionally in other countries as the very heart of 'private law', it has always seemed to Soviet authors to contain a 'public' quality. It has been looked upon as the key to power.

Shortly after the Russian revolution Lenin had occasion to consider whether any branch of the law could rightly be called 'private' under the Soviet system of government. He wrote to a colleague in 1922 that all law must now be considered 'public', and he turned his eyes particularly to property relationships.[1] It was the property sphere which seemed to him to offer an important area in which the State could further its own purposes.

Lenin was not the first of those from whom the Soviet leaders of today derive their inspiration to argue that law has a public character, regardless of the subject with which it deals. All Marxist literature had related law to power even before the Russian revolution. From the single sentence of the Communist Manifesto that the law of the mid-nineteenth century was but the will of the bourgeoisie made into a law for all to the more detailed analysis of the origin of the state and law provided by Engels,[2] the theme had been that law was an instrument of government. Lenin was but the first to be very blunt. He said simply, 'Law is politics'.[3] To Lenin, practical man that he was, law including the norms relating to property ownership was an instrument with which to effect social change.

It is not surprising that property law attracted the attention of the Soviet leadership at the outset of the Russian revolution. It was in the development of the concept of private ownership of property that Engels thought he had found the principle which made possible the emergence of the state as an apparatus of compulsion. It was in the character of the property relationships

1 Lenin, 29 *Sochineniya* [*Collected Works*] (3rd ed. 1928–1937) p. 419.
2 Engels, *The Origin of the Family, Private Property and the State* (1884).
3 Lenin, 14 *Sochineniya* [*Collected Works*] (3rd ed. 1928–1937) p. 212.

of a given society that Engels placed the factor which seemed to determine which class might hope to rule. He traced the rise and fall of those who ruled to the rise and fall in the productive quality of types of property. Those who owned the most productive property at a given period in history held the power until deposed by a new class which had gained its economic strength with the slowly developing ascendency of the productive forces it controlled.

It was argued that the course of history had demonstrated beyond doubt that those with dominant economic power created by the ownership of the most productive form of wealth obtained control of the apparatus of compulsion, the State. Thus, history was thought to prove that economic power must be equated with political power, and all else was secondary. To those who have studied and worked with the educated Soviet man, it is evident beyond question that those individuals who are reached by the Soviet educational process continue to relate economic and political power. Conclusions of western anthropologists tending to refute the thesis upon which Engels constructed his study pass unnoticed.[4] What Engels believed is accepted as the beginning point for all Soviet research in anthropology. Proof of the lingering qualities of the Engels thesis can be found in unexpected quarters. One need but look at the conclusions of Leon Trotsky in his *Revolution Betrayed*[5] written after his expulsion from the ranks of Soviet leadership. One might have expected him to have had some second thoughts on the seat of power, yet he was able to say that in spite of the concentration of power which Stalin had achieved, the Soviet Union could not be expected to remain permanently subverted for one primary reason—the Stalin group had never denationalised productive resources to its own advantage. Stalin and his associates had never acquired for themselves the private ownership of productive wealth.

The mass of studies in the west tending towards the conclusion that the ownership of wealth no longer spells power seems to have made little impression upon the mind of the Soviet intellectual. There is no acceptance of the thesis that management has replaced the shareowner as the seat of power in

[4] R. H. Lowie, 'Incorporeal Property in Primitive Society' (1928) 37 *Yale Law Journal* 551.

[5] Trotsky, *The Revolution Betrayed* (1937) pp. 248–252.

capitalist societies.[6] Managers are still considered mere 'lackeys' of capitalists, subject to their beck and call and manipulating property in the interests of the owners. The argument that organised groups of relatively poor persons, such as war veterans or labourers, now have influence equal to manufacturing associations and real estate lobbies is simply not believed by the Soviet intellectual. He accepts as dogma that the property owner has first place among those who shape policy, and the others are believed to be but second-rate associates duped and influenced by those who lead so that they will accept at least the basic principles if not the details of a social order beneficial to the capitalists.[7] Property ownership seems to the Soviet intellectual to be fundamental to the acquisition and preservation of power.

NATIONALISATION OF KEY PRODUCTIVE PROPERTY

Emphasis upon property ownership suggests that there could be no better place to begin an examination of the influence of Soviet law upon social change than with the law concerning property. It is in this area that the Soviet leaders have sought to solidify their power position and to lay the base for a new pattern of social organisation.

No matter, other than the mechanical necessity of setting up a new apparatus of government, was higher on the agenda of the leadership following the revolution. Just after Lenin rose on the platform of the Second Congress of Soviets to proclaim that its task was to begin constructing socialism, a decree was issued annulling without indemnification rights to large landed property, and the land was placed at the disposal of regional agricultural committees and district Soviets until a Constituent Assembly might determine the permanent government of the new Russia.[8]

[6] Berle and Means, *The Modern Corporation and Private Property* (1932). Burnham, *The Managerial Revolution* (1941).

[7] Stalin, 'Interview with H. G. Wells', *Voprosy Leninizma* [*Questions of Leninism*] (10th ed. 1935) p. 605. English translation, *Stalin-Wells Talk –The Verbatim Record and Discussion* (1934).

[8] Decree of October 28, 1917, [1917] 1 Sob.Uzak. RSFSR, No. 1, item 3. All dates through January 31, 1918, are given in accordance with the Julian calendar in force in Russia at the time. By decree published January 26, 1918, [1918] 1 Sob.Uzak. RSFSR, No. 19, item 289, the Gregorian calendar was adopted for all dates beginning with February 14, 1918, which would have been February 1, 1918, under the Julian calendar.

Lenin had wanted to go farther. He explained at the time that he felt himself retarded in his attack upon private ownership of the principal productive source, the land; because his Bolshevik faction of the Russian Social Democratic Labour Party was not yet strong enough to stand alone.[9] It shared power with the left wing members of the Socialist Revolutionary Party, comprised primarily of peasants. Not until after the necessity of compromising with the more conservative elements had passed with the dispersal of the delegates called to vote at a Constituent Assembly was Lenin able to proceed as he wished. On February 19, 1918, a decree[10] abolished for all time all property rights in land, sub-soil, waters, forests and livestock and transferred it without direct or indirect indemnification to the use of the whole toiling population.

Private ownership of other forms of wealth was attacked in like fashion. Banking was declared a State monopoly and all private banks except those of the co-operatives were merged with the State Bank on December 14, 1917.[11] Yet interests of small depositors were guaranteed in their entirety. Trading in the stock of private corporations was forbidden on December 29, 1917, and the payment of dividends and coupon interest of these corporations was forbidden.[12] The principle was extended within a month to bonds issued by former governments of Russia,[13] so that the obligations were annulled, and the December, 1917, coupons were not paid. All government guarantees of private obligations were likewise annulled. Exceptions were created for short term obligations and banknotes, and for holders of government bonds not exceeding 10,000 rubles in face value. The latter could be exchanged for obligations of the new government in like denomination.

Nationalisation measures struck at other forms of large-scale wealth. The merchant fleet corporations were nationalised on January 26, 1918,[14] together with their fleets of vessels. Small

[9] For English translation, see Bunyan and Fisher, *The Bolshevik Revolution, 1917–1918* (1934) p. 128.
[10] [1918] 1 Sob.Uzak. RSFSR, No. 25, item 346.
[11] [1917] 1 Sob.Uzak. RSFSR, No. 10, item 150. The fate of the co-operatives is discussed in Chap. 6.
[12] [1917] 1 Sob.Uzak. RSFSR, No. 13, item 185.
[13] Decree of January 28, 1918, [1918] 1 Sob.Uzak. RSFSR, No. 27, item 353.
[14] [1918] 1 Sob.Uzak. RSFSR, No. 19, item 290.

private owners of fishing boats and small co-operatives which used their vessels solely to provide a living for the members of the co-operatives were not molested. The multiple dwellings which brought their owners considerable wealth were made the subject of a decree. On August 20, 1918,[15] a decree repeated the fact that land had been nationalised earlier and indicated that this concerned urban land as well as agricultural land. It then declared that title to houses on that land should pass to the State, but only if the city in which they stood numbered more than 10,000 inhabitants and the number of apartments in the dwelling exceeded a figure to be established for each city independently. Finally the great insurance companies were nationalised with their investments, and insurance was declared a State monopoly.[16]

Industry had been looked upon by Lenin in his preliminary studies as the primary source of economic power, and the bulwark of imperialism, together with the banks which financed it.[17] Yet industry because of its complex character presented a stumbling-block in the programme of nationalisation. It could not be operated by the bench workmen who had no managerial training or experience. Unlike the land, which could be farmed by the peasant even without the estate manager, the industrial plant was but a lifeless enterprise without the skill of the manager in the front office. In most cases this manager was the owner and, therefore, a part of the class to be expropriated in the revolution, but in some cases he was an employee of the owner. The fact that the manager was an employee did not facilitate the Soviet leaders' task, for they had no faith in men who had long been associated with industrial ownership. The plant managers were considered to have been perverted beyond hope of rehabilitation in the fire of revolution.

The steps taken with industrial ownership indicate no faltering in the leadership's purposes if one appreciates the complexity of the managerial problem. It was impossible to sweep private owners aside as had been done with the land, the merchant vessels, the banks, the insurance companies, and the multiple dwellings. The industrial complex was believed to be the heart of the capitalist system, and action was thought to be necessary

15 [1918] 1 Sob.Uzak. RSFSR, No. 62, item 674.
16 Decree of November 28, 1918, [1918] 1 Sob.Uzak. RSFSR, No. 86, item 904.
17 Lenin, *Imperialism, The Highest Stage of Capitalism* (1917).

as fast as possible. Yet it was felt that there must be little disruption of the production so necessary to retention of power during the early months when much of the population waited to see whether the revolution could do better in satisfying their needs than the Tsarist regime had done. The solution was a compromise.

To prepare the way, owners were required to register their holdings by a decree of April 18, 1918,[18] and a controlling hand was maintained over management by workers' committees established in the plants under a decree of November 14, 1917.[19] Certain very large industries were nationalised by name, but no concerted action was taken against private owners until June 28, 1918. On that date a decree [20] listed the basic fields of endeavour which were considered as the commanding heights and declared that all enterprises within those fields were nationalised without compensation to the owners. Former owners who have since taken refuge in the west, have reported that in many cases possession was not taken by the State officials for some time.[21]

Smaller enterprises were left to their private owners for more than two years longer, but finally on November 29, 1920, a decree [22] nationalised all industries having more than five workmen with mechanical tools or ten workmen without mechanical tools. Although the precision with which the size of the industry was defined suggests a careful determination of which industries created sufficient economic power to threaten the new Soviet political power, this was not the case. The lower limit happened to be the one at which the factory inspection laws of the Russian Empire applied. The limit was, therefore, but an administrative convenience, and its application in the nationalisation scheme meant simply that the government had lists of industries down to this level and no lower. Nationalisation, even if it had been desired, of smaller enterprises would have required a possibly wasteful use of the scanty administrative personnel available to the new State.

By late 1920 the record indicates that the commanding heights had been taken, and these heights were not only the lofty

18 [1918] 1 Sob.Uzak. RSFSR, No. 32, item 420.
19 [1917] 1 Sob.Uzak. RSFSR, No. 3, item 35.
20 [1918] 1 Sob.Uzak. RSFSR, No. 47, item 559.
21 Reference to such testimony is to be found in Gsovski, 1 *Soviet Civil Law* (1948) pp. 293–294.
22 [1920] 1 Sob.Uzak. RSFSR, No. 93, item 512.

peaks but the low hills as well. Private enterprise had been reduced to such a point that only the small businessman survived. The first goal of the Soviet leaders had been achieved. Economic power in so far as it stemmed from the ownership of productive wealth had been eliminated.

A STRATEGIC RETREAT

It was already becoming apparent, however, that the damper had been closed too far on the productive machine. The leaders had pressed their doctrine farther than the situation permitted, considering the economic destitution of the country following the world war and the revolution itself. Managerial talent was limited. Economic chaos was the result. The step Lenin then took is known to all who have glanced even casually at the history of the Russian revolution. In the early months of 1921 Lenin decided that it was necessary to lift the controls of the early period, to start the fires of industry again and to stimulate agricultural production. He took a bold step. He called for a policy which seemed to require a reversal of direction in terms of his doctrine.[23] He hoped that individual initiative might be utilised for a time, at least, in restoring the economy. The new programme was called the New Economic Policy. To many it was thought to mark the beginning of the end of the Bolshevik experiment.

Private trade was permitted in March of 1921.[24] Soon thereafter citizens were authorised to establish new small scale enterprises[25] and to lease from the Provincial Councils of

[23] Speech of May 26, 1921, at All-Russian Conference of the Communist Party, Lenin, 26 Sochineniya [*Collected Works*] (3rd ed. 1928–1937) p. 388.

[24] Decree of March 28, 1921, [1921] 1 Sob.Uzak. RSFSR, No. 26, item 149. The decree followed by one week a decree abolishing the system of agricultural assessments and substituting a tax in kind, computed as a percentage of production, thus assuring the peasantry that only a fixed part of their produce would be appropriated and the balance left to their own use. Decree of March 21, 1921, [1921] 1 Sob.Uzak. RSFSR, No. 26, item 147.

[25] Decree of July 7, 1921, [1921] 1 Sob.Uzak. RSFSR, No. 53, item 323. The owners were authorised to employ not more than 10 or 20 persons, the maximum to be fixed between these limits for each type of industry by the Supreme Council of National Economy. If more employees were desired, it was necessary to obtain a special licence or concession. Civil Code RSFSR, Art. 55.

National Economy such of the nationalised industries as were offered for exploitation on a leasehold basis.[26] Within a month a decree set forth the official justification for the introduction of the New Economic Policy and outlined the general policies to be followed.[27] In December some small enterprises which had fallen technically within the nationalisation decrees were ordered to be restored to their original owners.[28] Thus, the basis was laid for private enterprise, albeit of small size.

In spite of the steps taken to restore private enterprise rather little in relation to the entire national economy was returned to private hands. The statistics indicate that four thousand industrial enterprises had been leased to private persons by September, 1922, but these accounted for only 5 per cent of the total industrial production of the new Russia and employed only some 70,000 workmen, as against the 1,300,000 employees in State-owned industry.[29] The major development in the plan of restoration of private enterprise was in the field of commerce. It is said that private activity dominated the retail trade, reaching a peak of 58.6 per cent in the total exchange of goods in 1923–4, and including 608,300 licensed private traders by 1925–6.[30]

In spite of the step backward in industry and trade, there was no such compromise with the land or the natural resources. While concessions were granted for their utilisation, and in some cases these went even to foreign firms, title remained in the State, as the concessionaires were to appreciate later when the contracts were terminated.

By 1927 the pump had been primed, and the Stalinists had reached the conclusion that it had become possible to move forward along different lines. The Congress of Soviets in April and the Congress of the Communist Party in December ordered the preparation of a five year plan for presentation to the next

[26] Decree of July 5, 1921, [1921] 1 Sob.Uzak. RSFSR, No. 53, item 313.
[27] Decree of August 9, 1921, [1921] 1 Sob.Uzak. RSFSR, No. 59, item 403.
[28] Decree of December 10, 1921, [1921] 1 Sob.Uzak. RSFSR, No. 79, item 684. The decree declared that industry which had not been nationalised in fact by the taking of possession, by the naming of a State manager, or by the payment of State funds to its use remained the property of the original owner.
[29] R. Schlesinger, *Soviet Legal Theory* (1945) pp. 88–89. The private enterprises are said to have employed only two persons on the average. See A. Baykov, *The Development of the Soviet Economic System* (1947) p. 107.
[30] R. Schlesinger, *ibid.*, at p. 131.

meeting of the Congress of Soviets.[31] The five year plan started the new Soviet system upon the road to complete socialisation of industry and commerce.[32]

While the five year plan became effective in 1928, formal measures to discourage and finally to eliminate the private entrepreneurs and merchants were taken somewhat later. A business tax upon private producers and merchants was introduced in 1930,[33] together with an income tax discriminating against them.[34] In 1932 the criminal code was amended to make the conduct of commerce criminal.[35]

Doctrine had triumphed, in a situation which has seemed to some socialist observers to require no such triumph. To such eyes the economic power of the private owners and traders would not have been sufficiently strong to imperil the government's programme had it been left at the level of the strategic retreat. Be that as it may, the Soviet leadership thought otherwise, and the attack upon the private entrepreneur continued. To them it seemed, apparently, that the property owner, even on a very small scale, was a potential threat to their programme and their concentration of power.

CONTROLLING THE SMALL SCALE PRODUCER

While a policy of discouragement of the private small scale producer was clearly indicated, there was no general legal prohibition of such activity in the 1930's, nor is such activity completely forbidden even today. Yet the private producer is severely circumscribed. Even before the discriminatory tax laws to which reference has been made, the private producer who employed labour was denied the right to vote and to be elected to office.[36] In March of 1936 a licensing act reduced the number

[31] Resolution of IV Congress of Soviets USSR, s. 31 [1927] 1 Sob.Zak. SSSR, No. 21, item 239; Resolution of the XV Communist Party Congress, 2 *VKP (b) v Rezolyutsyakh i Resheniyakh* [The All Union Communist Party (bolsheviks) in Resolutions and Decisions] (6th ed. 1940) p. 247.

[32] The plan was adopted by the V Congress of Soviets USSR on May 28, 1929, but dated back to October 1, 1928. [1929] 1 Sob.Zak. SSSR, No. 35, item 311.

[33] Decree of September 2, 1930, [1930] 1 Sob.Zak. SSSR, No. 46, item 481.

[34] Decree of September 2, 1930, [1930] 1 Sob.Zak. SSSR, No. 46, item 482.

[35] Decree of November 10, 1932, [1932] 1 Sob.Uzak. RSFSR, No. 87, item 385.

[36] Constitution of the RSFSR, adopted May 11, 1925, Art. 69. The franchise restriction was removed by the Constitution of the USSR, adopted December 5, 1936, Art. 135, but at the same time the employment of labour was prohibited.

of employees permitted a private producer to one.[37] In December of the same year a new constitution of the U.S.S.R. forbade the employment of any labour whatever in privately owned handicraft enterprises.[38]

Well before the constitutional prohibition the private entrepreneur who employed labour must have been almost unknown on the Soviet scene. Soviet statistics indicate that all disfranchised persons (and the group included priests, members of the Tsarist police, and serious criminals as well as persons employing labour for profit) constituted but 4.9 per cent of the adult population in 1929, 3.9 per cent in 1931 and 2.5 per cent in 1934.[39]

While the licensing act now prohibits the licensing of enterprises employing labour, it sets no formal limit upon the size of an enterprise itself. A judicial decision suggests the possibilities.[40] The facts emerged in a prosecution of four persons for violating the licensing act. The report of the court indicates that a woman had been arrested while selling barley sugar in a public bazaar from a hawker's tray. The woman had been licensed to manufacture and sell, but investigation disclosed that not only the hawker but a female friend and Chinese husbands of both women had been engaged in manufacturing the sweets. All four persons shared equally in the profits, and they were partners in the enterprise. While the trial court had convicted and the Provincial and Kazakh Republic Supreme Court had affirmed the conviction, the Supreme Court of the U.S.S.R. set aside the conviction on the ground that the activity was not illegal by virtue of a special provision of the licensing act permitting the manufacture of barley sugar upon obtaining a licence. The Supreme Court held that there had occurred only a violation of the licensing act, for which a fine was prescribed, and that the fine should have been exacted without criminal prosecution. From the case it appears that private enterprise in a permitted field of endeavour may continue, provided that the

37 The decree of July 7, 1921, *cit. supra,* note 25, appears to have remained in effect until superseded by the licensing act of March 26, 1936, published in [1936] Fin. i Khoz.Zak. No. 17, and as an annotation to Civil Code RSFSR, Art. 54 (editions dated 1943 and subsequently).

38 Art. 9.

39 See N. Denisov, *Sovety-Politicheskaya Osnova SSSR* [The Soviets–The Political Foundation of the USSR] (1940) p. 37.

40 *Case of Nikiforova and others* [1944] 6 Sud.Prak. SSSR 23.

persons engaged in the activity are co-owners and not in a relationship of employer and employee.

The licensing act suggests in its provisions that there are varying grades of political danger to be found in various types of economic activity, even when conducted on the small scale authorised generally under the act. Some activities are forbidden completely, even to the individual working alone or in partnership. Thus, an individual may not obtain a licence to conduct a print shop or to operate duplicating machines or to make stamping or printing machines. Such a prohibition seems to indicate a fear lest ideas and information be disseminated outside the channels subject to the censorship law.

Some of the prohibitions are more difficult to understand. A licence will be granted to a person who wishes to process grain, hemp, wool, including flax and woollen thread and yarn (excepting carpet threads), but only if the processor receives his raw materials from his customer. The processor may not purchase the raw materials on the market. Likewise, food may be cooked or prepared, but only if the service is performed with products provided by the person placing the order. An exception for the manufacture of berry paste, barley sugar, poppy seed cake and kvas is permitted, and it was under this exception that the woman and her Chinese husband and friends referred to above was operating.

A reason for the distinction indicated in the limitation of production to that which is possible with the raw materials provided by the customer is suggested by Soviet reluctance to permit individuals to buy commodities for resale at a profit. Although it is hard to distinguish what part of the resale price of a manufactured product represents the contribution of the artisan's labour, and what part represents a mark-up on the value of the raw materials as raw materials and without considering their new form, it would seem to be theoretically possible for an artisan to make a profit on the transaction, and Soviet doctrine forbids it. If this is the rationale, then one wonders why there is an exception made for the barley sugar, the kvas and the other items. Can it be that these items are subject to physical limitations on the quantity that a single cook may prepare, and hence far from likely to produce economic wealth in sufficient quantities to permit competition with the State for economic leadership, or is the exception made only because the State has found it impossible as yet to meet the needs of the population in this field, which has universal importance in preserving the morale of the people? It is possible that the exception will exist only so long as the State is not preoccupied with matters of greater political importance than barley sugar. Unfortunately for our study, no clues are to be found in Soviet literature.

Some processing activities are forbidden even if the customer provides the raw materials. Some of the prohibitions are readily understandable because danger is involved to the population. Thus, no problem in understanding the reason for prohibition exists for the refusal to license the processing of acids, lacquers, drying oil, vitriol, soda, indigo dyes, poisonous substances, perfumes, cosmetics, soaps, explosives and inflammable materials, including fireworks. But what is the reason for the prohibition of the processing of tobacco and its cheaper Russian substitute 'makhorka', or oil seeds, cotton and cotton fibres, silk cocoons and silk thread, leather and linings for sheepskin coats. The restriction on some of these items seems remarkable because tailors and seamstresses may be licensed to make clothing even if the customer does not provide the cloth, provided that a specific order is placed in advance.

Restrictions of the sort indicated may stem from a desire to control the source of supplies of tailors and seamstresses so that they may be regulated apart from the licensing system by controlling their source of supply. Perhaps the processing of tobacco and seeds reflects an appreciation that such substances may be the subject of enormous profits in black markets. Certainly the difficulty in controlling the distribution of cigarettes in occupied areas after the war suggests the possibilities. It must be remembered that oil seeds are to the eastern European what chewing gum is to the American.

While the specification of the Communist Manifesto indicating that only bourgeois property is to be confiscated has been made very precise and nearly all-embracing by the march of legislation concerning production, there is the area of commerce which has received more selective treatment.

PROHIBITING PRIVATE COMMERCE

From the days of the completion of the first five year plan the private trader has fallen under a ban, but it has been necessary to define the term. Trade and commerce within the definition of Soviet law have a technical meaning. Commerce, or trade, is defined as 'purchase and resale'. The private producer, to the extent that he is permitted to produce under the licensing act or under the agricultural laws may sell his own wares, but the professional merchant may not operate. The only exception listed in the licensing instruction is the bootblack, who may be licensed to purchase and resell accessories for shoes.

It is in the middleman, the private merchant, that Soviet doctrine has seen not only political danger, but anti-social activity. To the Soviet critic the merchant adds nothing to 'value', and is therefore, like the parasitic mistletoe in the tree. He sucks the life blood of the productive process and thrives to the detriment of the community. Those who know the Marxist explanation of the elements which contribute to 'value' will recognise the foundation for this view.

The facts of a concrete situation will indicate the attitude taken in the statutes. The attitude was disclosed in a suit brought by two salesmen against a co-operative society to recover a commission.[41] Under an agreement executed by the salesmen and the society, a commission of 12 per cent of the receipts for the products of the society sold by the two men was to be paid. For two months during the summer of 1939 the men travelled throughout the country-side and obtained orders for which the compensation at the contract rate would have been 18,077 roubles and 88 kopeks. To assure payment of their fee, the men withheld part of the proceeds when remitting to the society, but they did not withhold enough to cover their fee. When the balance was denied them, they brought suit. Although they obtained a judgment in their favour in the trial court, the Provincial Court reversed, and on review by the College for Civil Cases of the Supreme Court of the U.S.S.R the Provincial Court was upheld.

The relationship established by the agreement between the salesman and the co-operative society was found by the Supreme Court's College to be in a category forbidden by the licensing act. The men were said to have been working not under an employ-

[41] *Golubchik and Gakman* v. *Rasnoprom,* Sb.Post.PlenumaVerkh.Suda SSSR (1940) p. 220. Also reported in [1940] 16 Sov.Yust. 44.

ment agreement but a commission contract, typical of the travelling salesman agreement. To the Supreme Court this type of contract seemed to be illegal as being against the policy of the State as defined in the licensing act and violating a 1936 order[42] restricting the commercial middleman function to special State agencies. The salesmen were ordered to pay over to the State the amount withheld by them on the ground that it was an unjust enrichment, and the co-operative society was denied thereby any benefit at the salesman's expense under the illegal contract.

Presumably the salesmen and the co-operative society would have been within the law if the men had been placed on the pay roll of the society. Under the piece-rate system of payment everywhere in vogue in the U.S.S.R., their wages might have been made to vary in accordance with their sales. It looks to the outsider like an instance where the form was given importance beyond its real substantive possibilities. Doctrine seems to have triumphed over reason in a case indicative of the extent to which private enterprise is restricted.

The judicial decisions of the Soviet courts indicate the very minor proportions to which commerce of the prohibited variety has fallen. One finds no prosecution of large scale commercial operations and it can be assumed that there are none. Only small scale merchants have tried to do business. A few cases will indicate the nature of the current attempts to make a profit in a manner prohibited by the State. They arise under Article 107 of the criminal code, as it was amended in 1932[43] to prohibit the 'purchase or resale by private persons, for gain (*i.e.*, as a speculation) of any agricultural produce or of any article of mass consumption'. The narrow definition has been expanded beyond agricultural products and articles of mass consumption by a series of administrative orders, and even some interpretative decisions of the Supreme Courts of the R.S.F.S.R. and of the U.S.S.R.

A review of the matters included by the orders within the prohibited area suggests the type of activity attempted by private traders, and the Soviet leadership's feeling that there was latent in these activities a threat to their power. The orders expand the offence of speculation to include failure to take up ration books

[42] Order of May 4, 1936, [1936] 1 Sob.Zak. SSSR, No. 24, item 231.
[43] See note 35, *supra*.

from a dismissed employee or illegal issue of books if speculation in the goods obtained thereby occurred[44]; failure by *kulaks* to make grain deliveries to the State within the period set[45]; resale of wine, liquors and other spirits at prices in excess of fixed prices[46]; the buying up of collective farmers' expectancies in future distribution of produce ('labour days'), if done systematically[47]; the buying up of State bonds at less than face amount[48]; the production of flour by a secret mill if conducted as a business and for the purpose of making a profit[49]; and the pounding up of State metal money into metal sheets and objects for sale.[50]

PROOF OF SPECULATIVE INTENT

While many of the activities covered by the administrative orders and court interpretations would be considered illegal in non-Soviet economics, there is a type of activity which would hardly be banned outside the U.S.S.R. It is exemplified in a series of judicial decisions which indicate the type of illegal activity into which enterprising seekers for profit have flowed. The cases arose under an interpretation of the Supreme Court issued in 1940 on the eve of World War II stating that if a court could find no direct evidence of purchase for resale as a business, the crime of speculation might still be found if there were reason to impute a speculative intent from the circumstantial evidence offered by stores of goods in the possession of the accused in excess of the needs of the accused and his family.[51]

A few of the decisions will indicate the activity which excited the Supreme Court. A man was convicted of speculation in the

44 Order of the Presidium of the Supreme Court RSFSR, December 31, 1932, printed as an annotation to the Criminal Code RSFSR (1934 ed.) p. 110.
45 Order of the People's Commissariat of Justice, July 8, 1933, printed in *ibid.*, at p. 20.
46 Order of Presidium of the Supreme Court RSFSR, March 3–5, 1934, printed in *ibid.*, at p. 130.
47 Order of Presidium of the Supreme Court RSFSR, November 3–4, 1934, printed in *ibid.*, at p. 152.
48 Order of Presidium of the Supreme Court RSFSR, June 3, 1935, printed in Criminal Code RSFSR (1935 ed.) p. 129.
49 Order of Presidium of Supreme Court RSFSR, April 14, 1934, printed in Criminal Code RSFSR (1938 ed.) p. 142.
50 Sbornik Deistv.Post.Plenuma i Direkt.Pisem Verkh.Suda, SSSR, 1924–1944 (1946) p. 47.
51 Order of Plenum of the Supreme Court USSR, February 10, 1940, printed as an annotation to Criminal Code RSFSR (1943 ed.) p. 176.

Georgian Republic because he was found in possession of 1,090 pairs of women's stockings, and there was some testimony that he had planned to sell them on the day they had been discovered by the police. He was sentenced to five years' imprisonment and deprived of his electoral rights, but the sentence was reduced on appeal. The Supreme Court of the U.S.S.R. reviewed the case at the request of the Prosecutor and accepted the lätter's contention that there was no reason for reducing the term, particularly in view of the fact that the defendant had been engaged at the time in no socially useful work. A new trial was ordered.[52]

An argument that large purchases had been made for friends was found incredible in a subsequent prosecution.[53] The evidence produced at the trial indicated that the accused had travelled to a distant Republic after release from prison for another offence. At his destination he had purchased in the open market in two small cities a large quantity of consumers' goods, including 400 jars of makhorka tobacco, 15 packages of turkish tobacco, 15 bottles of liquor, 14 pocket mirrors and a large quantity of cigarette papers. He then entrained for another city and on his arrival began selling the goods at prices above their cost to him. When apprehended he still had a part of them in his possession and also 12,000 roubles. The defendant argued that he had made the purchases to permit him to make gifts, and had had no intention of reselling them. While the trial court accepted the defence and found no speculation but only violation of trade regulations, which involved a much smaller penalty, the College for Criminal Cases of the Supreme Court of the U.S.S.R. set aside the sentence and ordered retrial for speculation.

Large stocks of goods in the possession of a person having no apparent need for so much caused the undoing of several persons. In one case[54] conviction for speculation followed the finding of 8 men's overcoats, 11 women's overcoats, 270 metres of cloth and 115 spools of thread in a family with but two male members. In another case[55] a brigade leader of a Ukrainian sugar factory was found in possession of 209 metres of cloth,

52 *Case of Eligulashvili* [1940] 9 Sots.Zak. 72, also reported in [1940] 23–24 Sov.Yust. 47.
53 *Case of Mintsberg* [1942] 1 Sud.Prak. SSSR 12.
54 *Case of Kaveshnikov* [1940] 12 Sots.Zak. 85.
55 *Case of I. M. Levin, ibid.*, at p. 86.

8 pairs of new rubbers, 19 pieces of leather for shoe repairing, 57 spools of thread, 16 kilogrammes of sugar and 7,761 roubles. Witnesses at the trial testified that they had seen the accused standing in queues often to buy such commodities, and that he systematically bought such commodities in quantities exceeding the requirements of his family of three.

A woman explained the possession of a large quantity of goods to the satisfaction of the court when charged with speculation.[56] It was argued that she had purchased live sheep on the market, slaughtered them and resold the meat at high prices, with the proceeds of which she had purchased kitchen utensils for resale to her neighbours on the farm. A search of her cottage had disclosed 18 buckets, 10 saucepans, a basin and 5 cups. While the trial court convicted her of speculation, the appellate court set aside the verdict because it believed her story that she had not bought the sheep for slaughter and sale, but had killed her own sheep which were of no value for breeding purposes. She had used the proceeds of the sale to buy two pedigree sheep for breeding purposes. An affidavit of her village soviet confirmed her ownership of the sheep. Further evidence was introduced to support her contention that she had received about 300 roubles from her neighbours to buy kitchen ware for them in the city.

Several defendants escaped conviction when they proved that articles sold on the market had been purchased originally for their personal use and not for resale. Thus a woman who sold items on the market was released by the College for Criminal Cases of the Supreme Court of the U.S.S.R. when it was proved that the items sold had been the defendant's own, and when she argued that the sale had been necessitated to meet the expenses incurred by an ill child.[57] Likewise a collective farmer with a family of ten who had exchanged 246 metres of cloth, 20 head coverings and 7 table napkins for wool was released by the Supreme Court because it believed that such quantities were not in excess of those required by a large family, that the wool was required to make felt boots for the family and that there were no sales above cost price.[58] A defendant also obtained her release

[56] *Case of Milyaeva* [1945] 7 Sud.Prak. SSSR 10.
[57] *Case of Matveeva* [1942] 1 Sud.Prak. SSSR 13.
[58] *Case of Maltsev, ibid.*, at p. 14.

when accused of speculation because she had disposed on the market of several packages of makhorka tobacco brought home by her husband when he came on leave. One of the packages had been exchanged for bread, and two of them had been sold on the open market. The court believed that the items had been purchased with the original intent of personal consumption and not for resale at a profit.[59]

Facts indicating that a defendant is a good citizen may also help to rebut the presumption that a large stock of goods was purchased for the purpose of speculation.[60] The Supreme Court of the U.S.S.R. found it possible in 1949 to set aside a conviction of a man for speculation who had been apprehended on return to Tashkent from a business trip to Moscow with 22 pairs of children's overshoes. The evidence indicated that he had made an exemplary record at his factory as shop foreman; that he had been elected communist party organiser of his shop subsequent to his return from Moscow and before trial; and that his friends in Tashkent had asked him to bring them the overshoes since the Tashkent stores rarely carried them. The defendant had pleaded 'not guilty'.

These judicial decisions concerning speculation indicate how the courts have been utilised in cases where the evidence is unclear to determine whether a given citizen is a casual seller of goods or a professional engaged in business as a middleman. It is for the courts to apply to each individual case the basic policy directive which has been set forth in the code to give effect to the dogmatic approach to the activity of the merchant.

Not all reliance is placed upon the criminal code to prevent disposition of property in a manner creating an income for the seller. The profits of speculators were said to be the subject of primary attack in the decree of December 14, 1947, requiring an exchange of old roubles for new.[61] Its preamble declared that war rationing was to be abolished and under such conditions, 'It was impossible to permit the speculating elements who had profited during the period of the war and who had accumulated a considerable sum of money to buy commodities with this money after the abolition of rationing'.

59 *Case of Semenova* [1943] 1 Sud.Prak. SSSR 13.
60 *Case of Kartsov* [1950] 1 Sots.Zak. 58.
61 [1948] Sob.Post. SSSR, No. 1, item 1.

The decree was drafted on the assumption that the merchants had not banked their profits and that, therefore, they could be penalised if the exchange rates for the rouble were varied in accordance with the place in which the roubles were kept and also in accordance with the amounts involved. Thus, roubles in banks were to be exchanged rouble for rouble on accounts up to 3,000 roubles, and at the rate of two new roubles for three old roubles on any excess on the account up to 10,000 roubles. The exchange rate for roubles in bank accounts in excess of 10,000 was set at one new rouble for two old roubles. If the money was not in a bank account, the exchange was effected at the discriminatory rate of one new rouble for ten old roubles.

CONSUMERS' GOODS AS AN INCENTIVE

While Marxist doctrine as interpreted by Soviet leaders, has required, apparently, the elimination of private ownership of large scale productive resources, and the abolition of the private merchant, a completely different attitude has been evidenced toward private ownership of non-productive resources and those productive resources which have a limited potential in the creation of wealth. Soviet leaders find their credo on consumers' goods in the sentence of the Communist Manifesto, to which reference has been made, 'The distinguishing feature of communism is not the abolition of property generally, but the abolition of bourgeois property'. Such property as does not fall within the definition of 'bourgeois', as it has been developed over the years, is not only countenanced. Its accumulation is encouraged.

Accumulation of wealth in the form of bank balances, State bonds, private residences, motor cars, furnishings, clothing, libraries and musical instruments is a commonplace today. Gone are the years when Soviet spokesmen talked in terms of egalitarianism. Today the Soviet dictionary says that egalitarianism is a bourgeois Utopian social theory.[62] The whole emphasis of the incentive schemes devised to increase the productiveness of the individual workman has been upon the wage pattern differentiated in accordance with quality and quantity of production. The so-called 'Stakhanov' movement to rationalise

[62] 4 *Tolkovyi Slovar Russkogo Yazyka,* D. N. Ushakov, editor (1940) p. 1393.

production and thus increase the quantity produced each hour has been encouraged by the piece work system of wage payment, as well as by the praise of the press and the awarding of medals.

The extent to which the encouragement of production by differentiated wage scales has been developed is indicated by statistics brought out of the U.S.S.R. by a British economist who attended the Economic Congress in Moscow in 1952.[63] His figures, given to him by Soviet officials, indicate that wages in the Moskvich motor factory extended from a minimum of 700 roubles a month for unskilled labour to 2,500 roubles a month for the skilled Stakhanovites, and 7,000 to 8,000 roubles a month for the manager. A professor of science was said to earn as much as 30,000 roubles a month from several appointments. A year earlier a British delegation of Quakers had been informed that the average wage for the country was 500 roubles a month. Clearly it is possible to accumulate considerable wealth when one earns well above the average, for it must be presumed that the average is adequate to meet at least the minimum requirements of life in a planned economy.

The increasing importance given to consumer's goods in the Soviet economy was indicated dramatically at the time of the adoption of a new Constitution for the U.S.S.R. in 1936. Articles 7 and 10 guaranteed to the peasant and to the city dweller the right to own their own dwellings, to keep their personal savings, to use and dispose of articles of personal use and convenience even to the transmission of such property to their heirs by way of inheritance.

Bank accounts may be opened in the State Savings Banks, which are authorised by statute to accept deposits and to pay interest to the depositor at an amount fixed by the Council of Ministers of the U.S.S.R.[64] In 1952 the rate of interest stood at 5 per cent on deposits left for a minimum of six months.[65] Depositors are encouraged further by the exemption of the deposits from taxation, and from execution in satisfaction of debts, unless there be a court order requiring payment of damages arising out of criminal activity of the person who owns the deposit.

63 A. Cairncross, 'The Moscow Economic Conference' (1952) 6 *Soviet Studies* 113 at p. 131.
64 Decree of November 20, 1948, [1948] Sob.Post. SSSR, No. 7, item 89.
65 A. Cairncross, *op. cit., supra,* note 63 at p. 126.

State bonds are also exempt from taxation.[66] While the mass loans no longer bear interest in the conventional sense, they are issued subject to a lottery provision under which the owner stands to receive prior to the date of termination of the loan not only the full face value of the bond but as much as 500 times the face value if his bond's number is drawn in any of the annual drawings. The lottery winnings are planned to require a sum of money equal to 4 per cent per year on the average amount of the loan outstanding over twenty years. One third of the debentures are drawn in the lottery, the rest being paid at maturity and without any interest.

JUDICIAL PROTECTION OF PROPERTY OWNERSHIP

Enjoyment of such property as may be privately owned is promised by the Civil Code of the R.S.F.S.R. Its article 58 adopts the conventional language of Continental codes to say that 'Within the limits set by law, the owner has the right to possess, use and dispose of his property'. Examination of the subsequent provisions of the code and of judicial decisions and administrative regulations indicates the character of the limitations.

An owner is authorised by the code to recover his property which is unlawfully in the possession of another, except that he may recover from a bona fide purchaser only that property which was lost by or stolen from the owner.[67] Even lost or stolen property is not recoverable from a bona fide holder if it is bank notes or other bearer securities permitted to circulate within the U.S.S.R. The necessities of the open market seem to be felt in the U.S.S.R. quite as much as elsewhere.

A series of tests of the extent to which these provisions of the code protect an owner found their way into the courts after World War II. The cases chosen by the Supreme Court of the U.S.S.R. to be reported as guidance to lower courts concerned individual cows of which the owners had been deprived of possession in unusual circumstances not foreseen by the code. In one instance a woman of Orlov Province had transferred her cow to the army for evacuation to the rear as the Germans advanced.[68]

66 Statutes authorising specific loans are exemplified by that of May 3, 1948, [1948] Sob.Post. SSSR, No. 3, item 36.

67 Civil Code RSFSR, Art. 60.

68 *Susoeva* v. *Avekieva*, decision of October 7, 1943, reported in P. E.

The army had not evacuated the cow but had exchanged it for meat with a peasant woman who planned to stay behind as the village was overrun. The cow survived the German occupation and was found by the owner on her return with the Soviet army during the German retreat. Being unable to obtain it from the peasant in possession, she brought suit, but without success as the trial court held that the possessor had obtained it in good faith and it had not been lost or stolen from the original owner. The Supreme Court held that the principle of the code should be extended to cover cases in which an owner had been deprived of possession under circumstances of *force majeure,* and the military situation was such a circumstance.

Another cow owner was allowed to trace title through an even more complicated chain of events.[69] His cow had been taken from him by the German occupation troops, who had later lost it to a Soviet army unit. This unit had delivered it to a collective farm as a trophy of war, and the owner sued the collective farm to recover it. While the lower court held for the farm, the Supreme Court said that the cow must be returned to the owner, if on the retrial the alleged facts were proved. A third case[70] involving a cow concerned one which had been taken from the owner by the President of a collective farm on the ground that she had forfeited it because her son had worked for the Germans during the occupation. The trial court accepted the farm president's statement, but on review, the Supreme Court set aside the judgment and ordered retrial on the ground that the record did not support the conclusion that the owner's son had worked for the Germans.

While all of these cases concerned but single cows they went through the various stages permitted by Soviet civil procedure and reached the Supreme Court. Finally the decisions were published, which follows only when the Supreme Court believes it to be desirable to indicate a policy as a guide to the lower courts. Since none of the cases seems of particular national importance in itself, the Supreme Court's action may be inter-

Orlovsky, *Praktika Verkhovnogo Suda SSSR Po Grazhdanskim Delam v Usloviyakh Otechestvennoi Voiny* [The Practice of the Supreme Court of the USSR in Civil Cases under Conditions of the War for the Fatherland] (1944) p. 17.

69 *Shirayaev* v. *Collective Farm,* decision of December 22, 1943, reported in *ibid.,* at p. 18.

70 *Reznikova* v. *Koval* [1948] 1 Sud.Prak. SSSR 29.

preted as indicative of the Soviet leadership's war-time desire to emphasise the protection to be given the private property owner, even as against favoured communities such as collective farms, when the owner has been deprived of his property under circumstances not specifically covered by the provisions of the civil code. It is clear that the leadership felt at the time that the national welfare required dramatic reaffirmation of personal property rights.

The conclusion that the leadership has wished to draw greater attention to the protection afforded private ownership, in those areas in which it is to be permitted, is supported further by a decree of June 4, 1947.[71] The penalty for larceny of privately owned property was raised markedly. While the criminal code had provided prior to 1947 a moderate penalty of from three month's instalment fine payable from wages to one year's imprisonment, the 1947 decree raised the penalty to from five to six years' internment in a correctional labour camp. If the offence was that of a second offender or committed by a gang of thieves, the penalty was to be set at from six to ten years' internment. If force was used in the process upon the person of the owner, the penalty might be raised to from ten to fifteen years' internment, and the offender's property confiscated. If the force was dangerous to the life or health of the victim or accompanied by a threat of death or grievous bodily injury, the penalty might be set at from fifteen to twenty years' internment with confiscation of the offender's property.

Two 1950 cases suggest that while the policy of the leaders is to protect private property owners, the courts are expected to be quite careful in ascertaining that the offence has been adequately proved. In one case[72] a citizen was accused of stealing an overcoat from a flat and of selling it on the bazaar in Daugavpils in the Latvian Republic. The trial court convicted, and the Latvian Supreme Court affirmed the conviction. The conviction was then protested by the Prosecutor General of the U.S.S.R., and the protest was accepted by the Supreme Court's college for criminal cases with a finding that the evidence in support of the conviction was inadequate.

71 Ved.Verkh.Sov. SSSR, No. 19, June 11, 1947. This decree amended Criminal Code RSFSR, Art. 162.

72 *Case of Sergeev* [1950] 9 Sots.Zak. 85.

The conviction had been gained primarily on the testimony of a man apprehended with the coat who claimed that he had purchased it from the accused in the bazaar. The Supreme Court noted that the accused had not admitted his guilt and had presented an alibi, which had not been verified. Further, the accused had been characterised as having no socially useful occupation, when the record showed that he had just obtained a position, having been released from a labour camp only shortly before. Finally, the evidence to support the claim of the man apprehended with the coat did not confirm adequately the claim which he had made.

A second case [73] involved allegations of theft of chickens, a pig, felt boots and a door from some collective farmers. Three citizens had been convicted of the offences by a court in the Altai Province. The Supreme Court's college for criminal cases agreed with the Prosecutor General of the U.S.S.R. that the conviction could not stand. As to one of the parties, he had not been present at the trial, not having been notified of the date of the trial, nor had he been given a copy of the indictment. As to the others, the Supreme Court's college thought the evidence inadequate as there was no one who had testified that he had seen the things taken, nor had the missing party been available for questioning. There had been no exact accounting of the number of chickens claimed to have been stolen. Further, there was evidence that the door had not been stolen. On the contrary, the record suggested that it had been removed from a dilapidated house at the request of the collective farm management. Finally, one of the parties had stated in her separate action for divorce that she was applying because her husband and her husband's brother had been stealing chickens from the farm on a systematic basis. This allegation in the divorce action had not been investigated by the criminal court.

The rights of owners of private homes have been the subject of various law suits. The cases suggest the limitations on use and disposition excepted by the code in its guarantee of protection to the private owner. A house owner was held to be able to recover possession of his home after years of absence during which time his tenant had been ousted by the Village Soviet without reason and the house had been sold by the Soviet to

[73] *Case of M. Duplinsky, A. Duplinsky and Bashkireva, ibid.,* at p. 86.

one Rybalko, who had subsequently sold it to one Chernobaya. The Supreme Court ordered retrial merely to prove the facts suggested in the record after a trial court had refused to oust the occupant, and indicated that the issue of law was clear.[74]

An heir to a deceased former house owner was permitted to recover a dwelling which had been purchased by defendant during the period of German occupation of Kharkov for a few poods of grain and a small cash outlay.[75] The court found that the conditions indicated that advantage had been taken of the plaintiff's father who was starving at the time of the sale, and that under the provisions of the code permitting the setting aside of contracts executed under conditions of 'extreme want' the contract should be abrogated.

Such a case as the last is, however, the exception under present Soviet conditions, according to a commentator.[76] He points out that the article was incorporated in the civil code in 1922 to avoid the possibility that the entrepreneurs of the period of the New Economic Policy might take advantage of poor workmen and peasants. Since the days of the New Economic Policy have passed and have been replaced with what is officially defined as 'the abolition of the antagonism between classes and the increasing well being of the Soviet populace', the need for the application of the article is to be found, in the opinion of the commentator, only in the most exceptional situations. The commentator notes that it has been applied in recent years in circumstances which depart sharply from the normal relationships of a socialist society. He cites as proof of his statement the cases concerning Soviet citizens who executed contracts while in occupied territory under conditions of extreme poverty.

While protection of an owner was extended quite far in the hardship case referred to, there are to be found some limitations on protection similar to those which have recently appeared in some western systems of law. Thus, an owner had difficulty in establishing her right to oust a tenant from her cottage in the country on the ground that she had also an apartment in Moscow. The trial court held for the tenant on the theory that

[74] *Kolodyazhnyi* v. *Staro-Saltov Village Soviet* [1939] 6 Sov.Yust. 78.
[75] *Vitkevich* v. *Dzyuba* [1948] 4 Sud.Prak. SSSR 9.
[76] V. Ryasentsev, 'Questions Concerning the Nullity of Contracts in Court Practice' [1950] 9 Sots.Zak. 27 at p. 35.

the owner of the country cottage did not require the space. The college for civil cases of the Supreme Court of the R.S.F.S.R. ordered a new trial and declared that the cottage in the country was a place for summer rest and could not be considered as supplementary living space, or as a second flat.[77] The implication is that had it been such supplementary space, the owner might have been deprived of the right to oust the tenant. In this instance, as has been the case in some other countries of the west since the housing shortage has become acute, ownership is seen not to permit use of premises without regard to whether they are left vacant at times.

While property rights were recognised in still another case, it was indicated that in some instances a man who thinks he is an owner may not have the right to retain occupancy of a house to whose construction he has contributed. He may only obtain value for the services and property he has contributed. In this case[78] in the Georgian Republic a workman sought to establish his rights in a house which he had built with his own hands and with resources contributed by himself and obtained from a factory in which he was working. The evidence indicated that the houseowner had been living with his family in a barracks which had burned. He had then built the new house with the permission of the factory to whom the land's use had been assigned, although he had ceased to work at the given factory. Suit was brought by the factory, having the use of the land, to recover rent for the house. The college for civil cases of the Supreme Court of the U.S.S.R. held that rent was due, but that the workman should be credited with the value of the working time he had contributed and the resources he had put into the construction of the house.

The cases on houses indicate in much the same manner as the cases on cows that in moulding the New Soviet society the leadership has found it expedient to protect the ownership of private property, although the interests of the community in the property are not to be ignored. The weight to be given to the interests of the community in striking the desired balance with private rights is indicated also in articles of the civil code and an accompanying law having to do with confiscation and requisition.

77 *Golova* v. *Godunova* [1939] 8–9 Sots.Zak. 103.
78 *Factory* v. *Mikhin* [1948] 1 Sud.Prak. SSSR 8.

Confiscation is reserved for a limited type of case.[79] In this group are those cases in which a person is penalised for criminal activity of such seriousness that his property may be confiscated. Generally, a sentence includes this penalty only when there has been a conviction for counter-revolutionary or similarly serious activity threatening the foundations of the State. Confiscation is not a penalty for those who transgress less fundamental rules for the preservation of the community. Confiscation may also occur if property is possessed in violation of law, such as firearms, explosives, smuggled goods, and goods shipped in violation of postal or freight regulations.[80]

The interests of the community in privately owned property are thought to require preservation of the property in good condition. Thus it was established in 1921 that a house owner might be deprived of his home if it was not being maintained adequately.[81] A Supreme Court Order from the R.S.F.S.R. later declared that not every lack of good condition was cause for the application of the provision, but it must be established by the court that the lack of good condition was the result of uneconomic administration of the building and threatened the destruction of the building.[82] To this general rule the Supreme Court added a cautionary provision to the effect that it must be established also that the owner has the means to maintain the house, and no confiscation may occur of homes of workers who are unable because of inadequate funds or the absence of materials to make the repairs.

While the principle established in 1921 seems still to be in force, its early date of adoption suggests that it was related to the period of the New Economic Policy, and it is unlikely that it is being applied currently in any but the isolated case of the owner who leaves out of consideration the interests of the com-

79 Civil Code RSFSR, Art. 70 and law of March 28, 1927, [1927] 1 Sob.Uzak. RSFSR, No. 38, item 248, part 3.

80 For order of April 17, 1943, establishing the procedure to be followed in the event of confiscation, see 3 Spravochnik Po Zak. (1949) p. 252.

81 Decree of August 8, 1921, s. 11, note 1, [1921] 1 Sob.Uzak. RSFSR, No. 60, item 411. The determination of uneconomic care was reserved to the courts. See Circular No. 98 of the People's Commissariat of Justice, RSFSR, 1928, Sbornik Tsirk. NKYust. RSFSR (1934) p. 54. The principle was later adopted in general terms in Civil Code RSFSR, Art. 68.

82 Explanation of July 6, 1930, Sbornik Raz.Verkh. Suda RSFSR (4th ed. 1935) p. 51.

munity in the preservation of assets, even when they are privately owned. This conclusion is supported by the fact that annotations to post war editions of the civil code relate only to a declaration of nationalisation when there has been prolonged unexplained absence of the owner.[83]

During the period of the 1920's when some productive property was left in the hands of private owners, the court found it necessary to preserve the interests of the community in such property even though it was privately owned. It did so under the broad provisions of Article 1 of the Civil Code denying the protection of the code to persons who claimed rights under it but in violation of the social economic reasons for the establishment of those rights. Thus the Supreme Court thought that a factory owner should not have been permitted to retain the plant when she operated it at less than full capacity, sold some equipment and closed certain shops.[84] The time seems to have passed to apply Article 1 as a means of bringing the property owner to respect community considerations, for it is now argued that Article 1 is no longer required and should be stricken from a new draft currently in preparation to replace the existing civil code.[85]

Soviet law provides also for the requisition of private property required by the State but owned by citizens who have not been delinquent in their care of it or who have not committed serious offences against the State.[86] In such cases the property is taken by the State, and value, as computed by a special administrative commission, is paid by the agency into whose control the property passes.

PROPERTY AND POSTERITY

Enjoyment of property would seem incomplete to lawyers of the west if an owner were denied the right to transmit property by inheritance. The Soviet leadership was cautious in its first

83 See annotations to Art. 68 in editions of 1948 and 1950.

84 *Vladivostok District Department of Industry* v. *Voronkina*, Case No. 32,471 [1928] 24 Sud.Prak. RSFSR 3. This and numerous other cases applying Art. 1 are collected in V. E. Greaves, 'The Social Economic Purpose of Private Rights' (1934–1935) 12 *New York University Law Quarterly Review* 165 and 439.

85 M. M. Agarkov, 'The Problems of Misuse of Rights in Soviet Civil Law', [1946] 6 Izv.Ak.Nauk SSSR, otd.ek.i prava 424.

86 Civil Code RSFSR, Art. 69 and law of March 28, 1927, Part 2, *cit. supra*, note 79.

approach to the matter of inheritance because it associated the right with the preservation of economic and political power in the class it had ousted in the revolution.

A decree of April 27, 1918,[87] abolished the Tsarist inheritance law, but instituted a new system to be applied until the publication of a social insurance law. Under the new system an estate not exceeding 10,000 roubles in value and comprising house, household furnishings, and workmen's or peasants' tools passed directly to the heirs for administration and use. Any property in excess of the 10,000 rouble limit was to be taken by the local soviet, which was instructed to administer it for the benefit of the heirs not having a subsistence income. Heirs were defined as disabled relatives in a descending or ascending line, full and half brothers and sisters and the surviving spouse.

As early as 1919 the formal restrictions on inheritance began to be withdrawn, for the Ministry of Justice on May 21 declared in an interpretation that the 10,000 rouble limit on an estate which passed directly to the heirs was not to be applied to working families having a communal economy.[88] It was explained, however, that estates in fact rarely exceeded 10,000 roubles in value so that the general policy was not being changed. By this interpretation inheritance among the peasants became again formally subject to the customary peasant law in effect before the revolution.

With the adoption of the civil code to present the revised property concepts of the New Economic Policy, it was indicated that the attitude of the Soviet leaders had changed. Heirs, whether needy or not, were permitted to take directly the property of a deceased person up to the value of 10,000 gold roubles.[89] Any excess was to escheat to the State, if it could be separated

87 [1918] 1 Sob.Uzak. RSFSR, No. 34, item 456. The law of March 11, 1919, adopted in the Ukrainian Republic was similar, except that no provision was included to permit heirs to take immediately that part of the estate which did not exceed 10,000 roubles in value, [1919] Sob.Uzak. Uk.SSR, No. 24, item 268.

88 [1919] 1 Sob.Uzak. RSFSR, No. 20, item 242. To avoid confusing the reader by using varying terms for the same Soviet institutions, the title 'Ministry' is used throughout the text to designate an administrative department of government. These departments were actually entitled 'People's Commissariats' until changed to 'Ministries' in 1946.

89 Civil Code RSFSR, effective January 1, 1923, Art. 416. For original text, see [1922] 1 Sob.Uzak. RSFSR, No. 71, item 904. Property in the form of leaseholds or concessions granted by State agencies was not to be included within the 10,000 rouble limit.

without causing economic dislocation or inconvenience. If such were threatened, joint administration between the State agencies and the heirs was decreed, or the heirs were to be given the right to purchase from the estate the escheated portion.[90] The circle of heirs was redefined to exclude brothers and sisters, but to include any disabled and needy persons who had been in fact completely dependent upon the decedent for one year prior to his death.

By 1926 the limitations on the right to transmit property by inheritance were already accepted as undesirable, and the 10,000 rouble limit was removed.[91] The Minister of Justice indicated at the time that the reason for the change was not so much a change in doctrine as an appreciation of the fact that it was difficult to enforce the limitation. The agile property owner could transfer his property before death and make certain that none would escheat. Since 1926 there have been no limitations on the maximum size of an inheritance.[92] Soviet leaders seem to have found that once the property incentive is adopted to increase production, inheritance must be installed to obtain the desired effect.

Although the law has come to permit inheritance in unlimited amount, it has retained some restrictions on the absolute disposal of property by a decedent. While he may leave a will, he cannot distribute the property far beyond the circle of heirs who would be entitled to it if he had died intestate so long as any such heirs survive him, except to bequeath it to a State agency or a public corporation.[93] Nor can he disinherit a minor child.[94] The circle of heirs was enlarged in 1945 to add non-able-bodied parents even if they could not qualify as dependants of the decedent for a full year prior to his death.[95] Prior to 1945 such

[90] *Ibid.*, Art. 417.
[91] Law of February 15, 1926, [1926] 1 Sob.Uzak. RSFSR, No. 10, item 73.
[92] A graduated inheritance tax was applied to reduce large estates with rates set to discriminate against those who had acquired property as private entrepreneurs. Law of February 6, 1929, [1929] 1 Sob.Zak. SSSR, No. 8, item 78. In 1943 the inheritance tax was abolished. Law of January 9, 1943, 2 Sbornik Zak. SSSR, 1938–1944 (1945) p. 187. A filing fee is still charged of all but those inheriting the estates of persons perishing in the past war. It is graduated to 10 per cent and applies to the issuance of certificates of inheritance. Decree of April 10, 1942, *ibid.*, at p. 184.
[93] Civil Code RSFSR, Art. 418.
[94] *Ibid.*, Art. 422.
[95] Decree of March 14, 1945, 3 Sbornik Zak. SSSR, 1945–1946 (1947) p. 163.

relatives in the ascending line were permitted to inherit on equal terms with a surviving spouse and children of the decedent only if dependency were proved.

The great destruction of families during the war also led to the incorporation of a provision that if no immediate heirs were available to take an estate, it should be distributed to able-bodied parents, and in the absence of such, to brothers and sisters of the deceased. Further, if no such heirs survived, a testator might bequeath his estate to any one. Apparently, the State was by 1945 either so little interested in obtaining property by escheat or so desirous of ridding itself of the details of administration that it was willing to extend the right of inheritance beyond the limits previously thought desirable.

The conclusion that the State did not wish to be concerned with the management of property which it might obtain by escheat but preferred to have even heirs beyond the immediate circle inherit is supported by a 1949 case.[96] The property was a dwelling in Zhitomir, to which the parents of the deceased owner had renounced title as heirs of their son. The house had been transferred to the district housing administration in 1943 when the whereabouts of the son and his wife were unknown and the house required attention.

In 1945 the owners were declared dead on the basis of evidence then coming to light, and suit was brought by a brother to obtain the house. This was denied on the ground that the parents were alive and had first claim, and since they had renounced their right, the house had escheated. The Supreme Court of the U.S.S.R. declared that under the 1945 amendment to the code a brother and sister had the right to inherit property in the absence of heirs of higher priority, and the renunciation of the property by the parents had cleared the way for the brother to take the house.

While the circle of heirs was enlarged to permit less immediate members of a family to take an estate in the event that it would have escheated under the previously existing provisions, the circle was correspondingly narrowed as the result of other provisions in the 1945 amendment. This came about by virtue of the fact that the system of heirship was changed from a *per capita* system to a *per stirpes* system. Under the pre-1945

[96] *Case of Vakhter* [1950] 3 Sots.Zak. 63–64.

law grandchildren of a decedent shared equally with surviving children and spouse and dependants in the estate. After 1945 no grandchildren were permitted to receive any part of the estate under the intestacy law unless their parent, the child of the decedent, was also dead at the time of the distribution.[97]

Some courts are reported to have erred in thinking that the 1945 change was retroactive in effect. Thus, a court in the Karelo-Finnish Republic set aside the distribution of an estate made by the State notary among the following heirs: surviving spouse, her daughter and her three grandchildren, all receiving an equal share on the basis of *per capita* distribution. The distribution had occurred in 1938, but the surviving wife thought that the 1945 amendment to the law permitted her to eliminate the grandchildren and obtain half the property for herself rather than only a fifth of it. In consequence she brought the matter to the court and obtained judgment in her favour. This judgment was found to have been in error, and the distribution made under the old law was ordered to be left unchanged.[98]

Having made the decision to permit inheritance as part of the programme of stimulating production, Soviet leaders have found it necessary to provide a means of settling disputes among heirs. Litigation over estates suggests that the types of disputes which have required Court intervention are not yet those of an entirely new society.

Before the 1945 amendment of the inheritance law two nephews of a decedent who left no heirs within the circle permitted by the code sought to establish their status as dependants of the decedent for a year prior to his death. Both had spent most of their boyhoods with their uncle. They were denied any part of the estate because the facts showed that for a year prior to their uncle's death, they had been of age and completely able to work, so that dependency could not be permitted, even though it seems to have existed in fact.[99]

A seventy-two year old mother was permitted to share with a surviving spouse and child of her son in the ownership of a

[97] Decree of March 14, 1945, s. 1, *cit. supra*, note 95.

[98] *Case of Stepanova*, reported in A. Baryshev, 'Shortcomings in Court Practice in Cases Concerned with the Right of Inheritance', [1950] 7 Sots.Zak. 38 at p. 39.

[99] *Grigorii and Matrena Kvachadze* v. *Leso-Chinatskii Village Soviet* [1940] 8 Sots.Zak. 75.

house on the ground that she was of such an age that she qualified as a dependant.[1] It was not indicated in the report of the case that she had, in fact, been such a dependant at the time of her son's death.

A Church was denied property bequeathed to it in a will because it was not found to be a public organisation or State agency within the meaning of the statute permitting bequests to such organisations.[2]

Wills have given rise also to disputes requiring litigation. Courts seem not to have realised that they must be in writing and conform to the requirements of the statute, namely the certification of a State notary.[3] Thus, a court in the Lithuanian Republic gave improperly 500 roubles to a claimant on the basis of oral testimony of witnesses that the decedent had promised her daughter to leave to her a sewing machine.[4]

A will was ignored improperly by a court in the Quibyshev Province on suit of several brothers to set aside a mother's bequest of half a dwelling to their sister. The trial court took note of the fact that the brothers had helped their mother to build the house and held that under the circumstances all children should share equally in the house after the mother's death, even though she had selected her daughter in her valid will to receive half of it. Distribution under the will was ordered to be carried out.[5]

To the other extreme some wills have been improperly enforced against a minor child, who may not be disinherited under the law. Thus a court in the Stalin Province refused to set aside a will on the suit of a surviving wife when it disinherited two minor children of the deceased.[6] This was declared error.

PROPERTY REWARDS WITHOUT POWER POTENTIALITY

To judge by the law relating to property Soviet leadership is moulding a society in which no challenge to the leadership's position is to be expected from persons or groups deriving power from the ownership of productive resources. Yet, while the property owner of this type is being eliminated, there has been developing a property owner of a different sort. His wealth is

1 *Vorobeva* v. *Postnikova* [1948] 1 Sud.Prak. SSSR 25.
2 *Hamlet Soviet* v. *Kichatova*, Case No. 1068 [1948] 1 Sud.Prak. SSSR 5.
3 Civil Code RSFSR, Art. 425.
4 *Sabalyauskaite* v. *Sabalyauskas*, reported in A. Baryshev, *cit. supra*, note 98 at p. 40.
5 *Case of Makhrovis*, reported in *ibid.*, at p. 40.
6 *Case of Likhtarenko*, reported in *ibid.*, at p. 41.

derived from earnings computed in accordance with the leadership's evaluation of his contribution to the preservation of the system on the success of which their fate ultimately rests. To encourage this type of contribution, the leadership has shown itself willing to restore the property incentive and its concomitant, protection of property in law.

No thought that this new group of property owners will eventually rise up in protest successfully against the leadership seems to trouble the leadership. On the contrary, it appears evident that the leadership looks upon this new element as an element of strength in that it can be expected to support the system from which it has derived the comforts associated with property ownership. Yet, there is a difference in the way the new owners are treated and the way propertied elements of the past have been created to provide support for a regime. Like Napoleon, the Soviet leaders are aware, apparently, of the way in which inheritance law can be manipulated to obtain the political allegiance of a propertied élite, but they also seem to bear closely in mind the lesson they have found in their Marxist school books. They have not parcelled out to those who have served them well great estates or industrial empires. The faithful are rewarded, but not to the extent of acquiring what the Soviet leadership believes to be a potential threat to its power.

While the record presented by Soviet property law indicates that it is relied upon to supply the basis for continuing support of the Soviet leadership, it is equally clear that there are problems faced from other quarters by the leadership which seeks to retain power. State property must be utilised effectively if maximum production is to be achieved. Political leadership must be provided at all times and throughout all institutions. The recalcitrant must be taught to mend their ways. The working men and the peasants must be fitted into the production pattern so that they may toil effectively but may not interfere with the making of policy by the skilled few. The individualised character of many legal institutions must be replaced by the community emphasis, but without antagonising the individual or losing the advantages to be gained from enlightened individual initiative in the community. Potential sources of power other than property ownership must be controlled. Steps taken to utilise the formulæ of the law and the institutions of the lawyer to direct social change are the concern of the chapters which follow.

Chapter 2

ESTABLISHING A NEW ECONOMIC LEADERSHIP

Nationalisation of productive resources was but the beginning. Organisation of their use for maximum effect was imperative, yet Marxist doctrine provided no blueprint. Expropriation of private owners was not difficult, but it was another matter to utilise the expropriated machines and to establish an administrative structure which would facilitate the social change believed necessary to the ultimate achievement of communism.

With the advantage of hindsight one of the closest of Lenin's collaborators has said that the dream of the revolution has been lost through errors made in the administration of the national economy. Leon Trotsky rose to decry the steps being taken to form a centralised bureaucracy from which he feared the ultimate betrayal of the interests of the individual citizen.[1] Marshal Tito of Yugoslavia has more recently claimed that the Soviet pattern for the administration of nationalised resources creates only a form of State capitalism and not the socialism of Marx and Lenin.[2] In seeking to avoid the same social effects Tito has staked the future of his regime on a very different form of economic leadership.

Clearly, the pattern of property administration devised in the U.S.S.R. has become more than a matter of concern for the expert in administrative law. It has become the central point of argument among politicians engaged in attempting to introduce the social change espoused by Marx. Soviet authors defend their system as the only one capable of establishing the economic leadership required for the good society of their dreams.[3] Critics on the other hand, declare that in over-centralisation the Soviet leaders have wittingly or unwittingly established conditions under which the people have lost all possibility of influencing their destiny.[4]

[1] Trotsky, *The Revolution Betrayed* (1937) pp. 135–143.

[2] Tito, 'The Struggle of the Communists of Yugoslavia for Socialist Democracy', Report to the Sixth Congress of the Communist Party of Yugoslavia, November, 1952.

[3] Studenikin, Vlasov, Evtikhiev, *Sovetskoe Administrativnoe Pravo [Soviet Administrative Law]* (1950) p. 5.

[4] Dallin, *The Real Soviet Russia* (1944) pp. 129–133, and Utley, *The Dream We Lost* (1940) pp. 218–222.

Soviet administrative law is currently characterised by extensive centralisation tempered by measures designed to assure to the State the benefits of imaginative industrial managers. This relationship has been forged on the anvil of practice, sometimes at great cost in disappointment and even tragedy. When the commanding heights of the economy were nationalised in the series of steps described in the first chapter, government representatives entered the premises and took control. To avoid disruption in the production schedules, the administrative machinery of an enterprise was continued, whenever possible, as it had operated before the revolution. Old stationery was used, with an occasional stamping across the former letterhead to indicate that the enterprise had become a State enterprise. Co-ordination was provided by a Supreme Council of National Economy, organised on December 5, 1917.[5] It was given a seat on the Council of Ministers with the status of a Ministry.

The conditions of civil war caused everything to be subordinated to the winning of the war. The administrative process reflected this fact. The Ministry of Supplies was given authority to distribute raw materials as necessary to produce for war.[6] The Ministry of Labour planned the distribution of labour forces to meet the requirements of production, and the supreme Council of National Economy organised industry to utilise the materials and labour to best advantage. No centralised planning agency with the name existed to co-ordinate the whole effort. The Supreme Council of National Economy had to plan and operate at the same time.

Nationalised industries were subordinated to the Bureaux of the Supreme Council of National Economy.[7] There was immediate Ministerial responsibility for every detail of the operation of industry. Necessary funds and resources were made available to each factory as required to meet operating programmes, and receipts were returned to the financial department of the Supreme Council of National Economy without any attempt to balance expenses and income. To be sure the industrial plant was still relatively small, as Imperial Russia had been primarily an agricultural country. The direct responsibility

[5] [1917] 1 Sob.Uzak. RSFSR, No. 5, item 83.
[6] All Union Institute of Juridical Sciences, *Sovetskoe Administrativnoe Pravo* [*Soviet Administrative Law*] (1940) p. 116.
[7] Baykov, *The Development of the Soviet Economic System* (1947) p. 7.

of the members of the Supreme Council of National Economy for the operation of Soviet Russia's industrial machine was nowhere thought to be too extensive for a few individuals to shoulder, although, in fact, the Bureaux Chiefs are said to have been unable to cope with the many details of administration.[8]

The outsider will have difficulty in appreciating the reasons for the rather informal arrangements made to assume the burdens of industrial management unless he bears in mind the chaos of civil war conditions, the unpreparedness of the Soviet leadership for the assumption of power, the lack of any blueprint in the prerevolutionary literature on the socialist State, and last but not least, the expectation expressed in the Communist Party's Programme of 1919 that money would soon be abolished as a medium of exchange.[9] This ideal was expected to be realised first in the relationships between State enterprises. Here was to be an example of the 'administration of things' heralded by Engels as the rather vague goal of a Marxist society. Lenin expressed his hopes for the future of industrial administration when he reported that the Supreme Council of National Economy represented the type of organisation which would ultimately triumph throughout the governmental apparatus.[10] Presumably he thought that it would lead to the 'withering away of the State'.

STATE PLANNING BECOMES A CHARACTERISTIC

The simple administrative structure of the early years was not to last. Formal planning was begun in 1920 with the first experimental measures which were ultimately to place the entire Soviet industrial system within a highly centralised framework. A State Commission for the Electrification of Russia was created, and its plan was presented to the VIII Congress of Soviets in 1920 for approval.[11] Lenin explained that motive power was the central feature of all industry, and as power was developed in

[8] *Ibid.*

[9] Art. 15.

[10] 'The administrative apparatus in the proper, straight, narrow sense of the word, the apparatus of the old State is doomed to die, but the apparatus of the type of the Supreme Council of National Economy is fated to grow, to develop and to become strong, enveloping the entire principal activity of organised society'. Lenin, 23 *Sochineniya* [*Collected Works*] (3rd ed. 1928–1937) p. 36.

[11] Resolution of December 29, 1920, [1921] 1 Sob.Uzak. RSFSR, No. 1, item 11.

accordance with the new plan, control over its distribution would provide the means of directing the general course of the entire national economy. Lenin was so excited by the possibilities that he made his famous statement to the effect that Soviet rule plus electrification of the country equals communism.[12]

A State Planning Commission was created within the Council of Labour and Defence on February 22, 1921.[13] This Council was, in turn, an administrative agency[14] of the principal policy-making body for the country, called rather misleadingly the Central Executive Committee of the Congress of Soviets of the Russian Republic. The functions of the first Planning Commission were exceedingly limited in comparison with those of the Soviet planners of today. Its creation at the beginning of 1921 was dictated by the necessity of organising planning on some other basis than that offered during the civil war by the distribution of materials and the control of labour and industry. The new element requiring a different approach was the limited capitalist restoration being prepared by the Soviet leadership for the rehabilitation of the economy. Its restoration was to embody the reintroduction of private enterprise for the industry and trade of secondary importance, and this meant the development of a private sector of the economy beyond the reach of State administration. Control over the private entrepreneurs who were soon to be authorised to share in the development of the economy had to be established by other means than direct supervision, and their contribution to the economy had to be integrated with the socialised sector so as to assure its most effective utilisation.

The new State Planning Commission of 1921 seems to have been a rather weak ineffective body. Not until 1925–1926 did it begin to prepare annual statistics which could serve as control figures for the national economy, nor did it begin until that date the preparation of long range perspectives, later to become the foundation of the first of the five year plans.[15] The precise nature of its activities is hard to determine from this distance as Soviet

12 Report to Eighth All-Russian Congress of Soviets on the Work of the Council of People's Commissars, December 22, 1920, Lenin, 31 *Sochineniya* [*Collected Works*] (4th ed. 1950) p. 456 at p. 484.

13 [1921] 1 Sob.Uzak. RSFSR, No. 17, item 106.

14 Established by resolution of December 29, 1920, [1921] 1 Sob.Uzak. RSFSR, No. 1, item 2.

15 All-Union Institute of Juridical Sciences, *Sovetskoe Administrativnoe Pravo* [*Soviet Administrative Law*] (1940) p. 117.

authors refer to its early days only in passing as marking but a milestone at the beginning of planning. For this reason some students of the Soviet system have concluded that planning grew slowly in the minds of the leaders, who had not felt the need of it at an earlier time. It has been suggested even that Marxist prerevolutionary literature had not predicted its coming, much less prescribed it, but that it became part of Stalin's addition to Marxist doctrine.[16] Contrary-minded students find evidence of the intent to plan in the very first months of the existence of the Soviet government, but believe that conditions did not exist for its application.[17] Whether the origin of the five year plan lies in doctrine or in expediency, the planning concept has grown in the U.S.S.R. until, in Tito's opinion, it has engulfed the Soviet citizen. Tito argues that the Soviet citizen's freedom has been circumscribed to the point of slavery to the plan and to the administrators who command from headquarters. He would hold to little more than the type of skeletal planning introduced in the Soviet Russian Republic in 1921.[18]

With the introduction in 1921 of limited private enterprise the coexistence of the socialised and private sectors of the community received official recognition. The effect upon the administrative structure designed for State-owned industry at this juncture in Soviet development was soon to be felt in a manner later to become characteristic of all Soviet economic endeavour. The New Economic Policy was characterised by the introduction for State-owned industry of cost accounting and of the public corporation.

FEDERATION AFFECTS ADMINISTRATION

Before developing the steps taken to introduce the public corporation into the Soviet pattern of economy, attention must be focussed on another event which occurred almost at the same time and affected profoundly the administrative structure of the State. It was federation, brought into existence under the guidance of the Communist Party in the last days of December, 1922. Four Republics formed within what had been the

16 Berman, *Justice in Russia* (1950) p. 52.
17 Baykov, *The Development of the Soviet Economic System* (1947) p. 44.
18 J. Djordjevic, 'Local Government in Yugoslavia' (1953) 12 *The American Slavic and East European Review* 188.

boundaries of the Russian Empire signed a compact of federation on December 29, 1922.[19]

Even before federation the various Republics had taken steps to integrate their economic systems. In January, 1920, the Ukrainian government extended the laws of the Russian Republic to its own territory as they concerned transport, posts, telegraph, military organisation, production, labour and social insurance.[20] The Byelorussian Republic had combined its economic Ministries with those of the Russian Republic in 1920.[21] By a series of treaties in 1920 and 1921 between the Russian Republic and the other Republics the Russian Supreme Council of National Economy assumed responsibility for the conduct of all nationalised industry.[22] Federation brought to a formal climax the tendency toward union which had been nurtured by the necessity of survival and by the Communist leadership. The latter had acquiesced only for political reasons in the separatist movements which had arisen within the remains of the Russian Empire during the final days of World War I.[23] The Communists expected to quiet the fears of national minorities that the new Russia would be no better than the old in its policy of preferment for the Great Russians over the Ukrainians, the Byelorussians, the Georgians, the Armenians, the Azerbaijanians and the lesser peoples. As soon as the occasion offered, the Communist Party brought the various peoples together in a union called a federation, but a federation which bore little resemblance to the type which has become familiar as the United States of America.

Being the work of a Communist Party, which was not split organisationally along national minority lines but created as a unified whole centred upon an economic class rather than the nation, the compact of federation reflects little of the mutual suspicion evidenced by the States which drafted the Constitution of the United States. It gives to the federal government not a

19 The compact was incorporated in the first constitution of the USSR as Part 2.

20 *Istoriya Konstitutsii 1917–1936* [*The History of the Constitution 1917–1918*] (1936) p. 137.

21 The decision was incorporated in a treaty of January 16, 1921, *Izvestiya*, No. 74, April 6, 1921.

22 For text of treaties, see *Sbornik Deistvuyushchikh Dogovorov*, Vols. 2 and 3 (1921 and 1922).

23 Stalin, Interview with American Labour Delegation, 2 *Leninism* (English translation, 1933) p. 382.

limited number of designated powers as was the desire of the American founding fathers at Philadelphia, but very nearly complete power. Certainly this was the case in the economic sphere, which is of major concern in this chapter. The federal government obtained in the Constitution adopted provisionally on July 6, 1923,[24] not only the same minimum economic powers which had been granted to the federal government of the United States to assure economic survival and avoid chaos such as the right to coin money, to establish a postal service and a standard of weights and measures, but much more. It was authorised by the federating Republics to develop a general plan for the entire national economy; to establish general principles for the use of the soil, mineral deposits, forests and bodies of water; to direct transport and the telegraph services and to direct foreign trade.[25]

Ministries of Foreign Trade, of Posts and Telegraphs, of Railways, of Supplies, of Labour and of Finance were placed in the federal government together with a Supreme Council of National Economy to supervise nationalised industry. The only economic Ministries reserved to the Republics alone were those in each of them which were to be concerned with the supervision of the use of the land. These were called Ministries of Agriculture.

While the federal government obtained monopoly power over the national economy, it chose to delegate to the Republics some of its operating functions. This was done by creating two classes of Ministries. One was termed the 'All-Union' type and the other the 'Federated' type.[26] The difference between the two types was this. The All-Union type conducted its operations throughout the entire country, and therefore in the territories of the various Republics with its own employees responsible directly to the Ministry in Moscow. Governments in the various Republics had no immediate way of influencing operations under the control of this type of Ministry. While the Ministries were encouraged, and even commanded at times by

24 *Istoriya Konstitutsii 1917–1918* [*The History of the Constitution 1917–1918*] (1936) p. 353.
25 Art. 1.
26 In 1936 the 'federated' type was redesignated the 'union-republic' type. To avoid confusion to the reader the earlier term is used throughout this book.

the federal government to be considerate of the desires and susceptibilities of the local officials in the Republics, there was no formal channel through which the governments in the Republics could influence headquarters. This was not the case with the Ministries of the 'Federated' type.

The 'Federated' type of Ministry limited its activity at its office in the federal capital to planning of an overall character. In theory, at least, the headquarters Ministry was not to be concerned with the details of operations. These were the responsibility of Ministries of like name placed within the government of each of the constituent Republics. As such their Ministers sat as members of the Council of Ministers of the Republic concerned, and usually were selected from the national minority represented by the Republic. Thus, a Ukrainian and not a person of some other ethnic group would head the Ministry of the 'federated' type in the Ukrainian Republic. This Ukrainian Minister would be named by the Congress of Soviets of the Ukrainian Republic or by its interim body the Central Executive Committee of the Republic. To be sure the influence of Moscow might, and often did, play a part in the selection, but in theory the Minister was named and dismissed by the ethnic group from which he came. At the same time, he was responsible for the carrying out of any general programme forwarded to him by the Ministry in the federal government concerned with the same specific section of the national economy with which he was concerned.

In the division of the economic Ministries between the two types, the Ministries concerned with Foreign Trade, with Posts and Telegraphs, and with Railways were organised in accordance with the 'All-Union' pattern, while the Ministries of Supplies, Labour and Finance, and the Supreme Council of National Economy were organised in accordance with the pattern of the 'Federated' type. This meant that industry, subordinate to the Supreme Council of National Economy, was to be operated directly by the Supreme Councils of National Economy in the various constituent Republics, while co-ordination of effort was assured by the work of the Supreme Council of National Economy in the Federal government in Moscow.

By creating two types of Ministry the Soviet leadership seems to have been seeking to obtain the benefit of centralised planning and control while preserving the possibility of stimulating local initiative and originality in the operating process, at least in those fields of endeavour which might be thought to benefit from such an approach.

THE PUBLIC CORPORATION REPLACES MINISTERIAL OPERATION

Yet another step was taken to assure development of local initiative and originality within the limitations imposed by centralised planning. It was the step taken to establish the public corporation. The manner of direct ministerial operation of industry through the Bureaux of the Supreme Council of National Economy was abandoned with the reorganisation accompanying the development of the New Economic Policy and of the federal form of administration. A basic decree on the administrative mechanism to be utilised in operating State-owned industry was promulgated on April 10, 1923.[27] It has come to be known as the first decree on the 'trusts'. This was the word adopted by Soviet draftsmen to define a concept which has features in common with that known elsewhere as the public or government corporation.

The principle of competition with the private sector of the economy was enunciated in the decree. The 'socialised sector' was directed to compete with the private enterprises, newly authorised under the New Economic Policy, and to defeat them on their own playing field. Management of the State-owned system of means of production was to be developed in the crucible of intensive competition, subject always to the protective hand of the State if aid were needed to prevent disintegration of key industries.

The bell began to toll for the private entrepreneurs as early as the summer of 1927, although they were permitted legally to continue for some years longer as has been indicated in Chapter 1. The planning function was stressed in June, 1927, when a decree made the decisions of the State Planning Commission compulsory for all planning organs of the State.[28] A new basic law on the 'trusts' followed on June 29, 1927.[29] It no longer emphasised the points of similarity between the operation of

[27] [1923] 1 Sob.Uzak. RSFSR, No. 29, item 336.
[28] Decree of June 8, 1927, [1927] 1 Sob.Zak. SSSR, No. 33, item 373.
[29] [1927] 1 Sob.Zak. SSSR, No. 39, item 392.

private enterprise and State enterprise. The trust in the new law was ordered to function not on the basis of making profits in the open market, but to operate in accordance with the planned task set by the government. Three weeks later the principles made applicable by the new law to industrial enterprises were extended to State trading enterprises.[30] A movement was thus begun which was to spread the principles of the public corporation throughout all fields of State economic enterprise and to fix the system firmly upon the Soviet economy.

While the planners were coming to the fore, and centralisation was being espoused, the 1927 decree on the trusts caused to be extended to an even lower level the measure of independence allowed the managers of State-owned industrial enterprise. Under the provisions of the decree 'a State industrial trust is a State industrial enterprise, organised on the basis of a special charter as an independent economic unit with the right of a juridical person'. The large integrated industrial empires which had been operated as a single corporation were broken into their component parts and each part given the status of a public corporation. In some cases the component parts were made directly responsible to the Bureaux of the Supreme Council of National Economy. In others the old framework of the 'trust' was preserved as a 'holding company' or planning corporation between the Bureaux and a group of operating units which were now corporations in their own right.

From the point of view of social change the development of the public corporation introduced into society the beginnings of a new stratum of industrial managers with power, position and prestige.[31] This development of lasting importance to the Soviet social structure was made possible by the provisions of the second decree on 'trusts' of 1927, and the charters which were prepared in accordance with the provisions.

Under the decree the public corporation is assigned capital by the Ministry to which it reports and on whose decision it is created. It is responsible for the preservation of this capital, and is required to introduce a cost accounting system within the enterprise which will reflect upon a balance sheet and a profit

30 Decree of August 17, 1927, [1927] 1 Sob.Zak. SSSR, No. 49, item 502.

31 The increase in numbers of the managers and their progressively more important place in the social structure of the USSR is analysed in Towster, *Political Power in the USSR 1917–1947* (1948) pp. 326–327.

and loss statement the efficiency of management. The corporation alone is responsible for its obligations, and may be subjected to suit by its creditors. No agency of the State, whether it be the superior Ministry or the national treasury is responsible for the corporation's obligations and no suit may be brought against any entity other than the corporation. The corporation is authorised to bring suit in its own name against its debtors when the occasion requires.

THE CHARTER AND THE PLAN

Being established for the sole purpose of facilitating the performance of tasks set for it by the national economic plan, the powers of the corporation are set forth in its charter, and it may not exceed these powers. The powers are not stated broadly as is often the case in charters of corporations in private enterprise countries, but narrowly. The charter of the public corporation bearing the name of 'Eksportles' provides an example.[32]

The functions of 'Eksportles' are set forth in precise terms in seven paragraphs as follows: (1) it shall conduct operations for the export from the U.S.S.R. and sale in foreign markets and for the import into the U.S.S.R. of all types of timber, cellulose and paper commodities; (2) it shall participate in the preparation of drafts of long-range and operating plans concerning the export and import of the aforementioned commodities, and shall accomplish the plans in the prescribed manner; (3) it shall develop and put into effect measures designed to increase the export of resources relating to the subjects over which it has jurisdiction; (4) it shall participate in the development of standards and technical specifications for commodities which are exported and imported by the Combine; (5) it shall demonstrate the profitability of export and import operations with the commodities named, and shall develop and put into effect measures designed to increase the profitability; (6) it shall study the movements of foreign markets, and also the achievements of foreign technique in the field of the wood, paper and cellulose industry and commerce and shall take measures to utilize foreign experience; and (7) it shall compute ceilings for overhead and operating expenses concerned with the export of commodities.

The contrast presented by such limitation of powers is marked if comparison is made with a modern charter for an export-

[32] [1948] 9 Vneshnyaya Torgovlya 53.

import corporation created under the law of a private enterprise country. The latter is customarily broad in its provisions to leave open to management all possible ways of increasing the corporation's income. The Soviet manager is limited to the specific type of activity required to perform some element of the national economic plan. Within that restriction he has broad power to use his initiative and exhibit his originality in furthering the business of the corporation, but he may not exceed the limit.

The consequences of exceeding the limits set by a charter upon the powers of a corporation are indicated by a case involving an *ultra vires* clause in a contract between two public corporations.[33] Under the contract a baked goods corporation selling its product throughout the U.S.S.R. agreed to sell baked goods to the prison work camps operated by a corporation under the Ministry of Internal Affairs. In one provision of the contract the bakery agreed to serve as an agent for the camps in the presentation to the railways of claims for damage or loss in shipment. The camps receiving damaged shipments were to file their documents and claims with the local office of the bakery which would present them to the railway, receiving as agent a commission of 10 per cent of the amount claimed. The bakery also contracted to be responsible for any failure to recover on a claim if the failure was the result of its own delay in presenting the claim.

The manager of a camp delivered for presentation under the terms of the contract various claims against the railways totalling 68,120 roubles and 68 kopeks, being the amount of loss suffered by the camp as a result of the damage caused by the railways. The manager of the branch office of the bakery refused to accept the documents and to file the claims, and the camp manager complained to the bakery's head office. He was instructed by the head office to by-pass the local bakery manager and to forward the documents in support of the claim to the bakery's branch offices at the various shipping points. These were scattered throughout the country.

Hearing nothing for some time the purchaser brought suit against the bakery for the full amount of the loss, arguing that not a word had been received as to the progress of the claims,

[33] *Gulag* v. *Zagotzerno* [1935] 20 Arbitrazh 26.

and because of the large number of places to which the documents had been sent it was impractical to follow them up with queries. The bakery in its defence pleaded that it was not liable because of departure from the claims procedure set in the contract.

In reviewing the case the State Arbiter noted the departure from the terms of the contract on the instructions of the bakery, and the great inconvenience which had resulted to the purchaser in filing claims through the bakery agents at the many shipping points. The bakery was ordered to make an accounting within one month of the progress of the claims; to pay the court costs of the plaintiff; to strike from the contract the clause under which the bakery had assumed the function of claims agent, since this was *ultra vires*; and to fine the officials responsible for its inclusion in violation of the charter.

The case raises several questions as to the relationship of the State manager's authority under the charter and the national economic plan. As indicated in the 1927 law on the trusts, the corporation exists not to make a profit in the market but for the sole purpose of execution of the provisions of the national economic plan. Contrary to what is often believed outside of the U.S.S.R. the plan provides detail as to the government corporations which are to produce and consume commodities only for a very few key materials. For a very large part of the economy, the plan sets only overall goals, and it is for the State managers to seek out their opposite numbers as required to complete the task set by the Ministry to which they report.

When two corporations have found each other and reached agreement as to what products can be produced and on what time schedule and at what price, the terms of the agreement are incorporated in a formal contract executed by the parties. This contract then becomes the document governing the relationship between the parties. No unilateral variation from its terms is authorised on pain of suit by the aggrieved party. If there is an alteration during the life of the contract in the provisions of the plan in the furtherance of which it was negotiated and executed, the contract must be amended appropriately on the agreement of both parties.

Dispute arose among Soviet lawyers in the early days of the public corporation as to whether the agreements reached in furtherance of the plan could rightfully be called contracts.[34] It was argued that one of the elements of contract is that it be an agreement entered into freely by the parties, and this element is lacking in contracts between Soviet public corporations because they are entered into in furtherance of a national economic plan which is binding on all. The view which prevailed, however, discarded the criticism as unreal, seeing in the agreement an essential element in the utilisation of initiative on the part of State managers, and also in the provision of the detailed specifications and delivery dates which no master plan can prescribe.

CONTRACTS IN A PLANNED ECONOMY

The contract form has now been firmly rooted in the relationships between public corporations. In its favour Soviet authors are even prepared to argue that there is represented a new kind of freedom, in that it facilitates production. The fact that the individual's personal relationships are regulated by the plan in the interests of society is said not to reduce individual freedom. On the contrary, it is argued, the planned contract expands freedom by assisting in the achievement of abundance with which the horizons of the individual are expected to be pushed well beyond the possibilities open to the man who is required by poverty and economic compulsion to sell his labour force or his commodities at terms which are rarely advantageous.[35]

The Soviet argument presented in support of maintaining the contract relationship between public corporations is important at this point only to indicate how Soviet theorists present doctrinal reasons to support new legal institutions. Old terms are given new values for the purpose. For the pragmatically minded the important feature of the development of the contract in the planned relationship between public corporations is that it permits the State manager to exercise some initiative and show some originality within the limitations of the plan. A study of the contracts will indicate the extent to which managers have found it possible to exercise their ingenuity in establishing the relations necessary to permit them to complete the part of the plan for the execution of which they are responsible.

[34] All-Union Institute of Juridical Sciences, 2 *Grazhdanskoe Pravo* [*Civil Law*] (1938) pp. 35–36.
[35] *Ibid.*

The basic principles of the Civil Code apply to contracts between public corporations.[36] Thus, contracts must be in writing, and they must be executed by persons with authority.[37] If fraud or duress has entered into their conclusion, they are inoperative. If they are in violation of law or clearly against the interests of the State, they will be set aside. Contracts between a public corporation and an individual must be not only in writing but notarised if they concern 1,000 roubles or more, or unless they concern sales for cash, insurance, transfers of author's rights, storage, sales of articles on commission through government stores and in some additional cases.

In addition to the Civil Code an annual statute establishes the special provisions applicable to contracts between public corporations for the year concerned, setting, in particular, the date by which all such contracts must be concluded, and the matters which must be treated, such as the detailed description of the goods, the quantity, quality, price and period of performance.[38] In addition the contracts are to include provisions for the payment of fines, liquidated damages and penalties applicable in the event of delayed performance or failure of performance.

To facilitate negotiation of contracts between corporations whose requirements are co-ordinated by the supply department of a Ministry or by one of the few remaining 'trusts' supervising the conduct of affairs of a large number of small corporations engaged in similar activities, the law provides for the negotiation of 'general' contracts by the suppy department of the Ministry or by the trust with an equivalent supply department or trust.[39] When such contracts have been negotiated, the operating corporations within the jurisdiction of the two parties to the general contract negotiate 'local' contracts for what they wish to buy and sell. The general contract has set specifications and price. The local contracts set delivery dates and other pertinent matters of concern only to the operators.

[36] Arts. 26–51, 106–151, 180–205. For analysis of judicial decisions applying the rules of contract law to contracts between public corporations, see Berman, *Justice in Russia* (1950) pp. 66–78.

[37] Public corporations are denied the right granted private citizens to prove contracts for less than 500 roubles by parole evidence, see decree of February 18, 1931, [1931] 1 Sob.Zak. SSSR, No. 10, item 109.

[38] For an example, see decree of December 19, 1933, [1933] 1 Sob.Zak. SSSR, No. 73, item 445.

[39] *Ibid.*, at s. 4.

To enforce contracts between public corporations, there has existed since 1931 a specialised system of commercial courts entitled the State arbitration system.[40] Soviet authors have explained that the specialised tribunals were favoured over the regular courts for various reasons: the desirability of direct participation of the parties rather than lawyers representing the parties only for the purpose of the dispute, the resolution of the dispute to the advantage of the plan whenever possible, the desirability of bringing the disputants into agreement rather than of awarding damages to one at the expense of the other, and the utilisation of the information provided the authorities in the course of hearing many disputes from which procedural rules and policy directives might be devised for the assistance of all economic agencies of the State.[41]

In keeping with this reasoning the State arbitration system was organised as a system of three levels of tribunals. The senior tribunal is created by the Council of Ministers of the U.S.S.R. with jurisdiction over disputes of two types: where one of the parties ranks as an enterprise of federal importance, or where each of the parties has its place of business in a different one of the Republics which constitute the union. Even in these two types of cases the dispute must involve 50,000 roubles or more.[42]

The second level of tribunal is to be found in the capital city of each of the sixteen Republics forming the union. It is established by the Council of Ministers of the Republic concerned and hears disputes in which one of the parties is of republic importance or in which each of the parties has its place of business in a different province of the Republic. Even in these cases the dispute must involve 25,000 roubles or more.

Finally there is a level at the capital of each province of each Republic. This provincial tribunal is created by the Central Executive Committee of the Provincial Soviet to hear disputes under 25,000 roubles. Disputes excluded from any class of tribunal because of the insufficiency of the amount of money involved go before the tribunal having jurisdiction of the sum involved, regardless of the character of the parties.

[40] Decree of May 3, 1931, [1931] 1 Sob.Zak. SSSR, No. 26, item 203.
[41] Mozheiko and Shkundin, *Arbitrazh v Sovetskom Khozyaistve* [*Arbitration in the Soviet Economy*] (1938) pp. 5–6.
[42] The jurisdiction was altered to fall within these limits by decree of March 4, 1938, [1938] Sob.Post SSSR, No. 8, item 52.

The three levels are not to be compared with a three-stepped court system with the right of appeal from each level to the next highest level.[43] There is no absolute right of appeal, as emphasis is placed upon speed of decision, this being thought of greater importance to the effective implementation of the plan than the assurance that a decision is correct in all details with the inordinate delays accompanying the process of appealing. This does not mean that no case is ever considered at a level higher than that on which it starts, for there are reports in the official journal of review and also of directives by the Chief Arbiter of the highest level on rules of practice which he has found desirable to enunciate because of the experience of a lower level tribunal. Clearly, the Chief Arbiter finds it desirable and even necessary in the interest of uniformity to scrutinise on some sort of sampling basis the work of the lower level tribunals, and to take some appeals.

Some disputes between public corporations do not go before the State arbitration tribunals. All disputes involving a claim of less than 1,000 roubles go before the regular court system, as do disputes in which the State Bank is a party, in which the dispute concerns the collection of taxes, in which payment for communal services enjoyed under a lease is concerned, and in which the contract concerns railway or water transportation, unless the contract was made under the terms of a general contract calling for mass planned shipments.

A further exclusion of jurisdiction exists for disputes between two public corporations subject to the control of the same Ministry. Since such disputes have something of a family character, the Minister himself is responsible for their settlement, and he utilises for the purpose his own arbitration tribunal created by him and operating as a department of his Ministry.

FREEDOM TO NEGOTIATE A CONTRACT

Not only disputes arising after the conclusion of a contract but even disputes as to whether a contract shall be concluded come before the appropriate tribunal. In this jurisdiction there is evident a further restraint upon the freedom of the State manager of a public corporation to select the party with which he wishes to deal in meeting his obligations under the national

43 Decree of May 3, 1931, s. 10, [1931] 1 Sob.Zak. SSSR, No. 26, item 203.

economic plan. A case[44] will indicate the nature of this work of the tribunals.

Under the plan established by the Leningrad Provincial Soviet for the repair of agricultural machinery in the Province a nut and bolt corporation and a metal products distributing corporation were ordered to sell 83,000 nuts and bolts to the Agricultural Supply Corporation for distribution to the repair depots during the fourth quarter of 1935 and the first quarter of 1936. When the purchaser asked the sellers to negotiate and execute a contract to cover the transaction, the sellers refused, and the purchaser brought an action in the Provincial Arbitration Tribunal to compel conclusion of the contract. The Provincial Tribunal ordered the defendants to conclude the contract, and also set a fine to be paid in the event that one was not concluded within a fixed period of time.

The defendants appealed, and the Chief Arbiter of the U.S.S.R. Tribunal accepted the appeal under his supervisory authority. The defendants argued that they could not be compelled to manufacture nuts and bolts for the plaintiff, since the latter had no allocation of metal under the plan to be utilised in the manufacture, and metal was a critical item the distribution of which was wholly allocated by planning orders. At the hearing a representative of the State Planning Commission proved to the satisfaction of the tribunal that bolts, nuts and rivets were included within the list of commodities for which metal had to be allocated, and the State Planning Commission considered that the output of such items without an allocation of metal by an order of the Council of Ministers of the U.S.S.R. was prohibited. Further, an order of the Minister of Heavy Industry was introduced in evidence prohibiting the production of wholly allocated materials in excess of the quantities set forth in governmental orders issued in implementation of the plan, and it was proved that the defendants were under the control of the Ministry of Heavy Industry. The Chief Arbiter in the light of the evidence reversed the order of the Provincial Tribunal. No contract had to be concluded, for it would have been illegal to require one under the circumstances.

The opposite result was reached by the Chief Arbiter of the U.S.S.R. in a case involving the sale of vodka.[45] Suit was

[44] *Selkhozsnabzheniya* v. *Krasnaya Zvezda and Soyuzmetizbyt* [1936] I Arbitrazh 23.

brought by the Central League of Consumer's Co-operatives against the vodka bureau of the Ministry of the Food Industry to determine the form in which the relations between the two were to be stated for the year 1938. The Co-operatives argued that the parties should agree on the basic conditions of supply in accordance with which the Republic and Provincial Leagues of Co-operatives should conclude general contracts with the trusts supervising the corporations making vodka. Then the County Leagues of Consumer's Co-operatives and some large village consumer's co-operatives would make local contracts with the actual vodka distilleries.

The vodka bureau of the Ministry proposed a different set of arrangements. The bureau proposed that the parties to the dispute conclude a memorandum agreement incorporating a form of contract to be executed directly by the local distilleries on the one hand and the County Leagues of Consumer's Co-operatives and the large village consumer's co-operatives on the other. In short, the intermediate level of Republic or Provincial Leagues and the vodka trusts would be eliminated from the contractual relationship and perform their functions only in accordance with the necessities of the contracts negotiated at the operating level.

The Chief Arbiter finally persuaded the parties that the proper manner of handling the relationship was the following: the vodka bureau of the Ministry and the Central League of Consumer's Co-operatives would agree on the basic conditions of supply for the entire co-operative system, and this agreement would bind lower levels in each system in relationships which they had with each other. The agreement on the Ministerial level would incorporate provisions as to the total amount of vodka to be supplied to the entire co-operative system during the year 1938 and the form of the contracts to be negotiated by the lower levels. Then contracts should be concluded between the vodka trusts and the distilling corporations subject to their control, joined as sellers, and Republic and Provincial Co-operative Leagues together with the County Leagues of Consumer's Co-operatives and some of the large village consumer co-operatives, joined as purchasers.

45 *Tsentrosoyuz* v. *Glavlikervodka* [1938] 1 Arbitrazh 26.

Apparently the contracts would be concluded Republic by Republic, and in the large Republics such as the Russian, Province by Province with the producers so that the producers would always have as parties to each contract both the actual local sales outlet and the more responsible Republic or Province League to which the local consumer's co-operatives belonged.

A Soviet author in 1947 explained that there was no difficulty in deciding whether a contract could be required of a public corporation when the plan was sufficiently detailed to incorporate a system of distribution naming both of the parties, or if a means of bringing the obligation into existence other than the contractual form was provided for by special law.[46] In the first instance there would be a contract, but in the second there would not. In other situations, the State manager seems to be free to reach his own conclusions, and reports have been heard of managers who refused to make contracts with opposite numbers because their experience in previous years led them to expect that deliveries would be late or short or otherwise imperfect. The possibility of refusal to contract because of such experience has been hailed by Soviet teachers as a means of inducing excellence in management through pressures not unlike those operating in a free market system, thus adding an element of automatic rectification of poor management in situations of insufficient importance to require the intervention of the prosecutor.[47]

AMENDMENT OF CONTRACTS

Disputes over the necessity of amending contracts have also appeared in the reports of the work of the arbitration tribunals. They indicate another facet of the responsibility of management of public corporations under the plan and the extent to which there is room for originality in the conduct of the affairs of the corporation. One case[48] involved the quality of butter to be delivered by the Chelyabinsk Butter Enterprise to the Trading Enterprise for the Province. The matter came before the Provincial Arbitration Tribunal because of an order of the

46 Shkundin, 'The Influence of the Plan on an Obligation', [1947] 2 Sov. Gos i Pravo 37–38.

47 Such explanations were given in lectures attended by the author at the Moscow Juridical Institute in 1937.

48 *Chelyabinsk Provincial Trading Enterprise* v. *Chelyabinsk Butter Enterprise* [1937] 1 Arbitrazh 40.

Provincial Department of Internal Trade, attached to the Provincial Soviet and serving within the Province as the agent of the Ministry of Internal Trade. The order established the highest and lowest qualities to be sold within the Province and the pattern of variation between the two limits. This pattern of variation, if applied in the relations between the producer and purchaser in this case, would have reduced markedly the average quality of butter supplied under the terms of the contract between the two, for the contract provided for a pattern of variation which was focussed on a higher basing point. The question arose as to whether the Provincial Department's order required an amendment of the contract.

The Provincial Arbitration Tribunal reached the conclusion that although the highest and lowest qualities of butter were the same in the contract and the plan, the pattern of variation between them was different, and the contract should be amended to conform to the new pattern. The decision was appealed to the Chief Arbiter of the U.S.S.R. by the highest level on the producer's side, namely the Chief Administration for Butter Production within the Ministry of Heavy Industry, and the Vice-Minister of the Ministry of the Food Industry of the U.S.S.R.

The Chief Arbiter of the U.S.S.R. reversed the decision, saying that the contract should not have been ordered to be amended, since its terms did not conflict either with legislation or with the plan. Further the Chief Arbiter was of the opinion that the decision of the Provincial Arbiter in reducing the average quality of butter by applying the pattern of variation permitted by the Provincial Department of Internal Trade was discouraging the output of high quality butter, as was evident from the fact that in many stores butter of the highest quality was absent.

The case suggests that it is not always possible for a State manager to know which of the various orders from agencies purporting to have planning authority are binding upon him, unless he is skilled in the hierarchy of planning orders. The case suggests further, however, that he has a remedy when he is faced with a conflict and does not know what to do. He can take his problem to the State Arbitration System in the form of a dispute with a party with which he has a contract and obtain a decision which will protect him.

The possibility of varying the terms of a local contract from those established by a general contract by the headquarter agencies is indicated in the following case.[49] The headquarter agencies were in this case the Central Administration for Artificial Fibres of the Ministry of Light Industry, and the Rostov Textile Supply Enterprise, a public corporation. In the general contract they included, among other provisions, the procedure to be followed in filing claims for poor quality fibres.

A textile plant made a local contract with an artificial fibre plant, but it demanded that the procedure for filing claims relating to artificial silk be altered from that set forth in the general contract. The State Arbitration Tribunal of the U.S.S.R. agreed to the making of a contract with such a change in procedure, and to the amendment of the general contract to permit the variation, but the artificial fibre plant was not pleased with the decision, and submitted the matter to the Chief Arbiter of the U.S.S.R. who had not sat in person on the Tribunal which gave the decision. The Chief Arbiter set aside the decision of his Tribunal and held the parties to the procedure set out in the general contract as originally drawn, being of the opinion, apparently, that the experts in the headquarters agencies were better informed on the desirability of changing the procedure to meet conditions in the artificial silk industry than were the State managers of the producing and consuming plants or the State Arbitration Tribunal of the U.S.S.R.

The cases suggest that the amount of freedom left to managers of public corporations by their superiors in the Ministries to which they are responsible is much limited. Such a conclusion has recently been sharply thrown into question by a study of the materials relating to administrative supervision of managers by the Ministries.[50] It has been found that the managers have felt that they were free to make the operating decisions required to meet their assignment under the plan and have even violated directions sent down to them by the Ministries when they thought them incorrect.

THE INDEPENDENCE OF CORPORATION MANAGERS

Another study[51] of cases brought before the State Arbitration Tribunals for the recovery of damages suffered by a corporation

49 *Viskoza* v. *Moschulok* [1937] 12 Arbitrazh 24.

50 D. Granick, 'Initiative and Independence of Soviet Plant Management' (1951) 10 *The American Slavic and East European Review* 191.

51 G. I. Krynski, 'Management Problems in Soviet Public Enterprise as Indicated by Arbitration Awards' (1953) 12 *The American Slavic and East European Review* 175.

as the result of faulty performance by the opposite party on the contract indicates a wide variety of cases in which management made decisions which with the benefit of hindsight look unwise. The implication of these cases is that State managers have felt themselves sufficiently free to make a choice on their own account even if it be criticised later. They have not thought it necessary to ask the approval of headquarters. Two cases will illustrate the possibilities.

Suit was brought by the Leningrad City Construction Supply Enterprise, a public corporation, against Steel Supply Enterprise, a public corporation.[52] 700,000 roubles damages were claimed as having resulted from the delivery by the defendant of structural steel of specifications which departed from those fixed by the contract. The State Arbitration Tribunal in the City of Leningrad heard the case and found the following facts: under the contract the defendant was to supply 5,000 tons of I beams and girders with clearly defined specifications. Only 1,000 tons were delivered in accordance with the specifications set in the contract, and the balance was of different specifications, as the result of which the costs of construction were increased since the substituted sizes were heavier than the contract sizes, and there were higher transportation costs and handling costs than had been expected.

In defence the Steel Supply Enterprise argued that the substitution had been made with the consent of the purchaser, which had not only accepted the substitution but had urged speedy delivery. The defendant argued that the increased expenses should have been expected by the purchaser, and that, therefore, the seller was not responsible. The Arbitration Tribunal refused to accept the defence, saying that the substitution had been accepted by the purchaser only because it needed steel badly to meet its obligations, and the supplier had not been relieved thereby of its obligations to ship steel in accordance with the contract specifications. Damages were limited, however, to the increased transportation and handling costs, and not to the increased costs in the construction itself, resulting from the necessity of changing blueprints. 240,000 roubles were awarded.

52 *Gostroisnab* v. *Gump* [1937] 1 Arbitrazh 38.

The second suit[53] was brought by the Building Construction Corporation of the Ministry of Heavy Industry against the Central Office for Earthworking, a public corporation responsible to the Moscow City Soviet. Suit before the Moscow State Arbitration Tribunal resulted in the disclosure of the following facts: a contract had been executed to excavate 16,000 cubic metres of earth at a rate of 1 rouble 74 kopeks per cubic metre. Work began and after one month specialists representing both parties surveyed the excavation and reached the conclusion that a mistake had been made as to the quality of the soil, as the result of which the rate per cubic metre was too low. Yet, no amendment was made to the contract, and the work continued for another month. Then in the dead of night the excavating corporation moved its excavators from the spot and stopped work. The builders thereafter proceeded to complete the excavation by hiring manual labour, but no complaint was made until the work was complete, and then suit was brought. Damages to the amount of 83,271 roubles were claimed on the ground that this represented the excess cost of manual labour over mechanical excavation in completing the work.

The excavating corporation argued in its defence that it had been forced to stop work because the soil had become so wet that its excavators and lorries had sunk into ponds. Evidence was introduced by the builders that four days after the withdrawal of the excavating corporation they had put experts into the excavation who surveyed the soil and found that it was red heavy sandstone clay filled with medium sized boulders. This commission of experts had been put to work without any notice to the excavating corporation.

The tribunal's decision must have been a surprise to both parties. The arbitrator declared that the excavating corporation and the building corporation had both been at fault, and so seriously at fault that their action was criminal. The prosecutor was informed of the facts to determine whether prosecution should follow. The arbitrator was incensed that the excavating corporation had stopped work without notice to the other party, and that the building corporation had remained passive and spent 83,000 roubles of State funds on costly manual labour without trying to make the excavating corporation return to the

[53] *Zhilstroi v. Central Office for Earthworking, ibid.*, at p. 37.

job. No damages were awarded because the decision to employ manual labour had been taken by the building corporation on its own initiative and without trying to have the work completed by the other party.

The facts suggest that the managers of the two corporations felt remarkably free to make their own decisions in matters of great concern involving thousands of roubles of expense. While they were disciplined for their actions it may be presumed that they acted as they did because the general temper of the community at the time permitted such action.

SIMPLIFICATION OF THE ADMINISTRATIVE HIERARCHY

A tendency has been evidenced since the war to reduce the number of levels in the industrial administrative mechanism between the headquarters in Moscow and the producing corporations. This reduction in units has taken a form which was not, apparently, foreseen at the time of the creation of the 'federated' type of Ministry in 1923. At that time the concept was prevalent of a Ministry in the federal government which would plan but not supervise operations, and a Ministry of the same name in each of the Republics which would supervise all operations. In a few instances, however, some favoured projects in the hands of public corporations were subordinated to the Ministry in the federal government and not to the Ministry in the Republic. This by-passing of the Ministry in the Republic was, apparently, the result of the desire on the part of central administrators to assure the attention of the most highly qualified experts sitting in Moscow to the affairs and operating problems of the industries subordinated directly to the Ministry in the federal government.

By a series of administrative orders issued since the war, the number of such corporations subordinated directly to the Ministry in the federal government of the 'federated' type has been greatly increased. Transfers of corporations have occurred frequently from the Ministry in the Republic to the headquarters Ministry in Moscow. A few examples will illustrate the type of action taken.[54]

[54] Ved.Verk.Sov. SSSR, No. 2 (456), January 12, 1947; *ibid.*, No. 6 (460), February 12, 1947; *ibid.*, No. 17 (471), May 31, 1947; *ibid.*, No. 30 (484), September 10, 1947; *ibid.*, No. 31 (485), September 16, 1947; *ibid.*, No. 41 (495), November 30, 1947.

The Leningrad factory 'Promet' was transferred from the R.S.F.S.R.'s Ministry of Building Materials to the U.S.S.R.'s Ministry of Building and Highway Construction. Two brick factories of the Lithuanian Republic's Ministry for the Manufacture of Building Materials were transferred to the U.S.S.R.'s Ministry for Construction of Army and Navy Enterprises. The Leninakan Cotton-Paper Combine of the Armenian Republic's Ministry of the Textile Industry was transferred to the U.S.S.R.'s Ministry of the same name. The Minsk Pharmaceutical Factory of the Byelorussian Republic's Ministry of Public Health was transferred to the U.S.S.R.'s Ministry of the Medical Industy. Eleven flour mills of the Lithuanian Republic's Ministry of the Food Industry were transferred to the U.S.S.R.'s Ministry of Agricultural Stocks. Three shoe factories were transferred from the Armenian Republic's Ministry of Light Industry to the U.S.S.R.'s Ministry of the same name. Orders such as these are to be found in the official gazette for 1946, 1947 and 1948, ceasing to appear only with the issue of September 4, 1949. No one can be sure that the transfers ceased at that time, because it was a moment when the Soviet leadership ceased publication of much economic information, presumably to impede foreign estimates of Soviet economic strength.

The conclusion is suggested by the long series of transfers that harassed administrators at headquarters found local personnel inadequate to the task of reconstruction after the war, and took what seemed to be the easiest palliative measures. The corporations were subjected directly to the control of the headquarters Ministry with some immediate benefits, no doubt, but with the long-range danger of overburdening the experts at headquarters.

The problem of an overburdened headquarters had already arisen in serious form in 1932. At that time it caused the splitting up of the Supreme Council of National Economy between its heavy and light industry components.[55] The first were grouped together into a new Ministry of Heavy Industry of the 'all-Union' type. This meant that the operating corporations were subordinate only to the Ministry in Moscow and had no direct obligations to the governments of the Republics. The light industry components were distributed between the Republics

[55] Decree of January 5, 1932, [1932] 1 Sob.Zak. SSSR, No. 1, item 4.

under the supervision of a Ministry of Light Industry created in each Republic out of the staff of the former Republic Councils of the Supreme Council of National Economy, and a Ministry of Light Industry was created in the federal government to provide the over-all planning required of a headquarters Ministry of the 'federated' type.

From time to time since 1932 both the Ministry of Heavy Industry and the system of Ministries of Light Industry have been reorganised to split off component parts which have become of such size that administrative efficiency has been thought to require the organisation of a separate Ministry for their guidance. Some have been of an 'all-Union' type, and some of the 'federated' type. As a result of this process the burdens on headquarters have been spread over a large number of Ministries, in fact so many that in 1948 a reverse process developed. At that time some of the Ministries which had been created out of the parent Ministry were recombined with the explanation that the separate staffs had resulted in wasteful duplication of some of the services, and also the specialists available were not being used to their full capacity.[56] No doubt a Ministry with a specialist was reluctant to release him to advise the corporations within the framework of another Ministry. Such conclusions seem to be justified because the administrative problems of the Soviet Ministries are not unique but parallel the problems which have been disclosed by students of public administration in other States. The U.S.S.R. seems unique on this score only in magnifying its administrative problems with its very large number of State-owned industries for whose efficient operation the government is responsible.

A further reduction in the number of Ministries as the result of amalgamation occurred immediately following Stalin's death. By decree of March 6, 1953, fifteen of the Ministries were grouped in five clusters of Ministries. Eleven of the Ministries which lost their identity had specialised in industrial construction. These eleven were distributed between three new Ministries, designated as concerned with machine manufacture, electric power production and equipment for transportation media and

[56] Decree of July 29, 1948, combining Ministries of Ferrous and Non-Ferrous Metallurgy, Ved.Verkh.Sov. SSSR, No. 33 (532), August 12, 1948.

heavy machines. The other four Ministries which were merged into two new Ministries were of a different character. Two of them, the Ministries of State Security and Internal Affairs, were combined to form a single Ministry of Internal Affairs as had been done during the early crisis years of the past war. The other two concerned with foreign and domestic trade were combined into a single Ministry, as had been done during the crisis years of the New Economic Policy when the socialist sector of the economy was reported to be struggling for its life against the restored private merchant.

Again the placing of administrative authority in relatively few hands seems to have become the policy of the early post-Stalin era. No explanation of the reasons for merger was given at the time of the announcement, and the explanation may not be identical for all cases. It is possible that the occasion of reorganisation of government was seized to merge the industrial Ministries in continuation of a policy beginning with the mergers of 1948. Administrative efficiency may have dictated the change. A different explanation is suggested for the mergers in the fields of security and trade. It is suggested by the identity of the persons chosen to head the two new Ministries, namely Beriya and Mikoyan.

Beriya, who assumed charge of the combined security Ministries, has long been known in the U.S.S.R. for his skill in restoring orderly security procedures after the admitted excesses of the purges of the late 1930's. He has been severe but effective and has produced much less unrest than Ezhov who had preceded him during the purges. Mikoyan, who assumed charge of the trading mechanism, was well known before the war for his work in foreign trade, and during the war he combined in his person the distribution function of the hard-pressed Soviet economy.

With security declared by the leaders to be of paramount importance after Stalin's death, and with security depending in considerable measure upon the satisfaction of the people's desire for commodities, it is possible that the Soviet leadership thought it wise to indicate their intentions. This they did by appointing men known to every Soviet citizen for their proven abilities in these fields. Further the leadership reduced the number of administrators to be co-ordinated in the effort.

CENTRALIZATION BECOMES ENTRENCHED

Certainly there has been far reaching centralisation of industrial administration in the U.S.S.R. It has extended far beyond the steps taken following the revolution to administer the nationalised industries. State Planning has grown to the position of principal element of the Soviet system of economy. It pervades all economic life, although it does not dictate every detail.

In an effort to decentralise the decision-making process the public corporation has been developed. The managers of these corporations have become a new stratum in society, having a not insignificant measure of authority to make operating decisions and being encouraged with high salaries and many perquisites of their position.

Yet centralised control maintains a heavy hand over the managers and influences many of their decisions. Law has played its part in establishing this control through the structure of the Ministries and the proceedings of the State Arbitration Tribunals. While personal initiative may be exercised within limits, the all-pervading theme of Soviet society has become reference to headquarters in the national capital of an ever increasing number of problems. Soviet leadership has utilised the nationalisation of industry and its associated activities to establish highly centralised economic leadership with which it can mould the economic life of every community in the land.

Chapter 3

PUBLIC LAW AND POLITICAL LEADERSHIP

Preservation of a monopoly of political leadership has become the major task of Soviet constitutional law. The road through socialism to communism has been thought to be uninviting to those without the vision required to imagine the ultimate rewards. Reluctance to depart from established social patterns for the unexplored relationships preached by the politicians has been evidenced on every side. Gone are the days, in consequence, when many Soviet leaders seem to have believed that the way had only to be prepared by nationalisation and the gate thrown open to the road to salvation.

Marx and Engels seem to have felt that education would take time, especially when hampered by a bourgeoisie free to lure the proletariat away from what the historical materialists declared to be their destiny.[1] Political leadership seemed imperative although its character was not clearly defined. Lenin in the years that followed found the necessity for a strong political party in an analysis of the failure of the Paris commune of 1871.[2] The history of Soviet constitutional law is marked by the steps taken to create and preserve leadership. The measures adopted range through those designed to establish the one party State, and the one candidate election, to those concerned with establishing thorough control of public utterance. Through these measures the masses have been insulated from those who might guide them in other directions. The leadership has succeeded in freeing its hands to experiment without fear of opposition in the formation of a new society.

The development of the monopoly of political leadership has taken time. The communist party was not alone in making the

[1] Engels, *The Origin of the Family, Private Property and the State* (English translation, 1902) p. 211.

[2] Lenin, 'Lessons of the Commune', 12 *Sochineniya* [*Collected Works*] (3rd ed. 1928–1937) p. 162. Also, Lenin, *State and Revolution* (1917) c. 3. This view has now been stated in simplified terms in a Soviet school book, Shestakov, *A Short History of the USSR* (English translation, 1938) p. 128.

revolution. Three political groups, or parties were represented in the Second Congress of Soviets on the day in late 1917 when the Provisional Government, which had succeeded the Tsar, was surrounded in the Winter Palace and forced out of office. These parties reflected the interests of different revolutionary elements in the population. The largest was the Socialist Revolutionary Party which drew its strength largely from the peasantry and intellectuals who associated their interests with this historically revolutionary element.[3] While many of its right and centre members withdrew with the fall of the Winter Palace, the left wing carried on the name of the party and brought to bear for some months an agrarian influence on the further course of the revolution. The Russian Social Democratic Party had two wings, each of which had come to be a party in its own right. One of these, the Menshevik, drew its strength from the moderate intellectuals and the right wing trade unions. It withdrew from the Congress of Soviets after the fall of the Winter Palace, but some of its left elements, calling themselves the 'Internationalists', gave intermittent support to the new government for some time.[4] The other wing of the Social Democrats, the Bolshevik, drew its strength from the radical intellectuals and the left wing trade unions. This was the group which became dominant with the downfall of the Provisional Government. It was later to take the name of 'communist'.

From the outset the Bolsheviks indicated their desire to press forward with their programme and their impatience with the necessity for compromise with their collaborators. Yet, Lenin showed himself to be a realist and a skilful judge of the extent to which he could not afford to alienate the support of the collaborators in the early months of the revolution. As has been indicated in Chapter 1 he was frank to admit that the measures enacted in the first decree on the land, nationalising only the great estates and Church lands, were less than the Bolsheviks wanted and dictated by the necessity of placating the Socialist Revolutionaries who insisted on private ownership of land for the peasants.

3 The role of the Socialist Revolutionary Party has been set forth by one of its leaders, see Chernov, *The Great Russian Revolution* (1936).

4 The details of the seizure of power may be found in Chamberlin, 1 *The Russian Revolution* (1935) pp. 306–333. An interpretation of the steps taken by the Bolsheviks to win dominance may be found in Carr, 1 *The Bolshevik Revolution 1917–1923* (1950) pp. 70–101.

Astute leadership and the progress of events served the Bolsheviks well during the early months of 1918. The collaborators had been sufficiently undermined by January, 1918, to make it possible for the Bolsheviks to dismiss the constituent assembly composed of delegates chosen from all Russia to decide upon the permanent form of government to assume power from the instruments of the revolutionaries.[5] In consequence the soviets, which had been the instruments through which power had been established in the revolution, became the principal agencies of government. The Third Congress of Soviets, meeting at the end of January, 1918, faced no opposition to enactment of a series of decrees incorporating the existing system as the permanent government of Russia and establishing the principle that 'power must belong wholly and exclusively to the toiling masses and their plenipotentiary representatives, the Soviets'.[6] A constitutional drafting committee was named to prepare a formal document to incorporate the decisions.[7]

The first formal action taken by the Bolsheviks to announce to the citizens that there would be no subsequent co-operation with the collaborators of the period leading up to the revolution was taken on June 14, 1918.[8] By a decree the Bolsheviks expelled from the Central Executive Committee of the Congress of Soviets the right and centre groups of the Socialist Revolutionary Party, and the Menshevik wing of the Social Democrats. The decree recommended to all local soviets that they do likewise. Actually the right and centre groups of the Socialist Revolutionaries and of the Mensheviks, as has already been indicated, had long since ceased to support the revolution and had withdrawn from participation in governmental programmes. The decree seems, therefore, to have been but a declaration that there would be no turning back.

On July 6, 1918, the left wing of the Socialist Revolutionaries also broke finally with the Bolsheviks. Having differed over

5 For an account of how the delegates to the Constituent Assembly were chosen, see Radkey, *The Election to the Russian Constituent Assembly* (1950).

6 Declaration of the Rights of the Toilers and of the Exploited People, January 11, 1918, c. 4, [1918] 1 Sob.Uzak. RSFSR, No. 15, item 215.

7 For an account of the deliberations of the committee written by one of its members, see Gurvich, *Istoriya Sovetskoi Konstitutsii* [*A History of the Soviet Constitution*] (1923).

8 [1918] 1 Sob.Uzak. RSFSR, No. 44, item 536.

Brest-Litovsk, they now quarrelled over the Bolshevik victory in the new constitutional draft, which had allocated control over local government to central authorities.[9] From that time forward the Bolsheviks retained their monopoly of political power, although on two subsequent occasions a gesture was made in the direction of reconciliation. On the first of these a decree of October 30, 1918,[10] reversed the June decree for those Mensheviks who had broken with the bourgeoisie, but the Menshevik wing of the Social Democrats was never to resume its place as a party. Again on November 27, 1919,[11] a decree authorised the granting of consultative seats at the Seventh Congress of Soviets to all parties which had adopted a resolution to mobilise their members to defend the Soviet Republic in the civil war. Eleven splinter groups were named. Full voting rights were reserved, however, only for those elected with Bolshevik approval.

CONSTITUTIONAL SILENCE ON THE ONE PARTY SYSTEM

No provision in the first Soviet constitution, adopted by the Russian Socialist Federated Soviet Republic on July 10, 1918,[12] established a monopoly right to activity as a political party in the Bolsheviks, even though the latter had succeeded in establishing it in fact. The constitution incorporated the class concept of government, however, for it extended the right to vote and to be elected to office only to those who earned their livelihood by labour, or who cared for those who worked; to soldiers or sailors; and to disabled members of such groups.[13] The franchise was denied to persons hiring labour for profit, persons living on income not derived from their own labour, private traders and middlemen, monks and priests, policemen of the former regime and members of the former Royal Family, as well as to the insane and criminals deprived of rights by law or court sentence.[14] By these measures the leadership disclosed how its policy on the ownership of property, as discussed in the first chapter, was to be reflected in the electoral system.

[9] For an account of the dispute, see Gurvich, *Istoriya Sovetskoi Konstitutsii* [*A History of the Soviet Constitution*] (1923) p. 92.
[10] [1918] 1 Sob.Uzak. RSFSR, Nos. 91–92, item 926.
[11] [1919] 1 Sob.Uzak. RSFSR, No. 59, item 557.
[12] [1918] 1 Sob.Uzak. RSFSR, No. 51, item 582.
[13] Art. 64.
[14] Art. 65.

No monopoly position for the communist party was stated in the first federal constitution in 1923, yet it had become established completely by convention. By 1927 Stalin indicated that the convention had become an element of law, for he spoke of the communist party as 'the only legal party in the country'.[15] He was replying to questions raised by a labour delegation from the United States which doubted the desirability of the one party system on the ground that it seemed to offer the working class and the peasantry no way to express legally any opinions not acceptable to the communist party. Stalin replied that conflict of opinion could be expected to continue under the Soviet system, but it was not conflict over basic issues which divide economic classes, but conflict over means of improving the agencies of the Soviet State to achieve the objectives of socialism and communism. He repeated the Marxist formula that political parties exist only to represent economic classes, and since the Soviet system recognised only one economic class, there was need only for one political party to represent its basic objectives.

Stalin sought to strengthen the position he had stated by saying that it conformed not only to Marxist doctrine, but to conditions as they had developed since the revolution. He declared, 'The position of our Party as the only legal party in the country is not something artificial and deliberately invented. . . . Our Party's monopoly grew out of life, it developed historically as a result of the fact that the Socialist Revolutionary Party and the Menshevik Party became absolutely bankrupt and departed from the stage'.

History will hold this to be an over-simplification, for the early collaborating parties seem to have been pushed from the stage by legislative action and political manœuvring, yet the statement may have value for the chronicler of the development of Soviet constitutional law. It suggests that Stalin had reached the conclusion by 1927 that the communist party had a monopoly of political power supported by law, even though the constitution of the federal government and the constitutions of the various constituent republics were silent on the subject.

A CONSTITUTIONAL ONE PARTY SYSTEM IS ESTABLISHED

In 1936 the constitution of the U.S.S.R., promulgated to reflect the social changes which had occurred in the intervening years

15 Stalin, 1 *Leninism* (English translation, 1934) p. 373.

since the adoption of the first federal constitution in 1923, established the legal status of the communist party. It did so, however, without the clarity of wording which western lawyers might have expected. The matter was treated in a general article concerning the right of association. After listing the various types of public organisations to which citizens might belong, Article 126 read, 'and the most active and politically most conscious citizens in the ranks of the working class and other sections of the working people unite in the Communist Party of the Soviet Union (Bolsheviks), which is the vanguard of the working people in their struggle to strengthen and develop the socialist system, and is the leading core of all organisations of the working people, both public and State'.

While the constitutional formula contains no words granting monopoly rights to the communist party in unequivocal form, the monopoly position seems to be indicated by the structure of the Article. It purports to list all of the organisations to which citizens may belong. By listing only one political party the implication is made that there shall be no right to form any other political party. Further, by comparing the wording of the article with Soviet doctrine which acknowledges only the 'working people' as remaining in society there could be no other party because there are no other classes to be represented by a legal party. The monopoly position seems, therefore, to have been fully incorporated in Soviet constitutional law, even though there is no specific denial of a right to form a political party to compete with that of the communist.

In keeping with the doctrinal position that only working people remained in Soviet society by 1936, the new constitution removed from the franchise the restrictions which had previously excluded non-working class elements.[16] As indicated in the first chapter, statistics showed that the number of such excluded persons has been reduced to 2.5 per cent of the adult population in 1934. Stalin explained that while the priests and other previously excluded elements were still in the community, their number was too small to endanger the State.[17] It seemed to him

[16] Art. 134.

[17] Speech on the draft constitution of the USSR, November 25, 1936, Stalin, *Leninism* (English translation, 1942) p. 379 at p. 403.

to be time to include all the citizens in the electoral system, even though some might yet be hostile, because the plans for the society of the future called for universality of electoral privileges. He believed that the political work of the communist party was now sufficiently well organised to assure protection against enemies of the new social order.

There was reason for Stalin to exude confidence in the political instrument which had been refashioned in large measure after Lenin's death. Not only did the communist party have a legal monopoly of political activity throughout the entire country, but within its own ranks there had been established a monopoly position for those who supported Stalin's views on the conduct of affairs. Those who had argued for the preservation within the Party of factions had been silenced. The communist party rules, which have been called the party's constitution, had been revised in 1921 to exclude the right of members to form factions or voting blocks.[18] The principle has been retained in all subsequent revisions of the Rules.[19]

History has proved that some of the one party systems which have existed outside the U.S.S.R. have had sufficient elasticity to permit minority views to gain an effective platform for their expression through a referendum or 'primary' held prior to elections among the members of the party for the selection of the candidate on whom the mantle is sure to fall on election day. Some powerful parties have permitted minority groups to form factions through which they can state their views. Either of such procedures requires a majority to give heed to a minority's argument because the minority's voting block may attract sufficient strength to defeat the majority if it shows itself unwilling to compromise on issues where reason is not entirely on one side.

Trotsky has expressed the opinion that factions were essential to the democratic operation of the Soviet one party system,[20] but his views are deprived of some of their credibility because he argued the point as a disgruntled man. He had submitted loyally when the rule was adopted in 1921. Only later when the rule

[18] Resolution of Tenth Party Congress, March, 1921, 1 VKP (b) v Rez. i Resh. [*The All-Union Communist Party (bolsheviks) in Resolutions*] (5th ed. 1936) pp. 373–374.

[19] At the time Stalin spoke the principle was stated in Rule 58. Under the revision of 1952, the principle is stated in Rule 28.

[20] Trotsky, *The Revolution Betrayed* (1937) p. 94.

had been operated to his disadvantage did he conclude that vigorous leadership of the kind required to effect radical social change required preservation of the right to form factions.

For the student of public law, the battle over the issue of factions within the Communist party suggests that the Soviet leaders who have survived have become convinced that unity in the leadership group is essential to the execution of a programme of radical social change, and that permitting factions would be detrimental to preserving leadership in those with the knowledge and skill to remould society.

The party rules, as revised in 1952 repeat the formula as follows:

> 'The free and businesslike discussion of questions of party policy in individual organisations or in the party as a whole is the inalienable right of each party member . . . but extensive discussion, notably discussion on an all-union scale, of questions of party policy must be organised in such a way as not to lead to attempts by an insignificant minority to impose its will on the party majority or to an attempt to form factional groupings, to destroy the unity of the party, or to attempt at splitting which may shake the strength and stability of the socialist system'.

It is significant that the well-known 'purge trials' of 1936, 1937 and 1938,[21] were directed against individuals who had been noted, in many cases, for the espousal of the desirability of preserving factions within the party. While the crimes of which they were accused were found in action which was said to have been directed toward forceable overthrow of the regime, the fact that the defendants were the principal supporters of the faction principle was not lost on the junior members of the party. In the intervening years, it is to be noted that no one has risen in communist party circles within the U.S.S.R. to claim the right to form a faction or to urge a change in the party rules on the subject.

The no-faction rule seems to have extended even to the elections for officials within the soviets, although there is nothing in law to forbid the presentation of various candidates for the

21 The verbatim reports are published in English translation as *The Case of the Trotskyite-Zinovievite Terrorist Centre* (1936); *The Case of the Anti-Soviet Trotskyite Centre* (1937); and *The Case of the Anti-Soviet 'Bloc of Rights and Trotskyites'* (1938).

position of deputy to a soviet, each one standing for election on a platform embodying the views of a distinct group of persons who support ardently the goals of the leadership but have their own ideas on the means of achieving those goals. A review of the record of the year 1937 will provide material in support of such a conclusion.

THE ONE CANDIDATE ELECTIONS

The first elections following the introduction of the constitution of 1936 were called for December 12, 1937.[22] An extensive campaign was prepared to bring out the vote in the largest possible numbers. Under the new constitution, while the one-party system had been enshrined in Article 126, the chapter on the basic principles of the electoral law had opened the franchise to all.[23] Article 126 had itself provided that nominations for the positions within the various representative bodies of the State might be put forward by a large number of public organisations in addition to the communist party, such organisations being trade unions, co-operatives, youth organisations and cultural societies.

No Soviet citizen with any knowledge of politics could have expected that such organisations might support a candidate who stood on a platform of private ownership of the means of production, or a multi-party system, but there might well have been an expectation that with candidates brought forward by various public organisations the public would be given a choice between a man or woman who favoured or opposed co-education of boys and girls in the primary schools, or allocation of local resources to pave the streets rather than to build a cinema.

Stalin had even given support to such expectations, for on March 1, 1936,[24] he had given an interview to Roy Howard in which he had repeated his 1927 statement that a party represents a class and where there is but one class there can be but one political party. He had also told the American newspaper editor, however, that he expected candidates to be put forward by the various organisations permitted to do so by the constitution, and he had added 'You think that there will be no election contests. But there will be, and I foresee very lively election campaigns'.

22 Decree of October 11, 1937, [1937] 1 Sob.Zak. SSSR, No. 68, item 310.
23 Chap. 11.
24 *Roy Howard Interview with Stalin* (English translation, 1936).

The Electoral Regulations promulgated in accordance with the principles of the constitution had carried out this theme.[25] They had provided that the electoral committees in the various districts should publish the names of the candidates and the organisations nominating them, and further they had ordered, 'While in the room set aside for filling in ballots, the voter shall strike out of the ballot the names of the candidates except for the one for whom he casts his vote'.

The instruction to strike out all but one name was printed at the top of the model ballot,[26] and election posters illustrating the steps in voting carried the same legend under the sketch of a citizen sitting at a table in the voting booth.

The nominations proceeded in accordance with the pattern established in the constitution. Nominating groups in factories, educational institutions, large retail stores, railways, collective farms and army units put forward names, each group presenting one name for the post of deputy from the district in which the group met. The names were subsequently published by the electoral committees. In each district there were several names, some of well-known national figures and some of little known local production heroes. Then came the day set for the publication of the model ballot by each committee. In all cases which have been reported, but one name appeared on the ballot. In some fashion not disclosed to public view, the names of persons nominated within the district had been reduced to one. Voters could cross out the name but they had no other choice, and they could not write in a name.

Not a few people, both Soviet citizens and foreign observers, were surprised by the single candidate ballot which appeared. Under the Soviet procedure a candidate could stand from any district but he was required to select only one district in which to stand. Allowing for the elimination of names of national heroes who were widely nominated and whose withdrawal from all but one district would have resulted in the removal of their names from many lists, there was still no reason to suppose that all competition would be withdrawn.

25 Decree of July 9, 1937, [1937] 1 Sob.Zak. SSSR, No. 43, item 182.

26 This was done in accordance with the requirements of s. 80 of the Electoral Regulations.

The one candidate system has been continued to the present day. A recent study has indicated that it has been refined since 1937 so that the nominations now appear to be planned in advance to provide in each district a single name which can be placed on the ballot after the names of the other nominees are struck because they have been nominated elsewhere.[27] Only in one case when Stalin was nominated as the sole candidate by all public organisations in two districts, one in Moscow and one in Leningrad, was a district left without a candidate, when Stalin made known his choice. Another name was then substituted in the district which would otherwise have been without a candidate. The principle seems to be fixed that but one candidate will be offered to the electorate for each seat to be filled.

MEANS OF INFLUENCE

When Stalin was asked how the communist party was to exercise its leadership, he told the same American delegation who questioned him on the reason for the one party system that its first task was to secure the election of its own candidates to the principal posts in the government.[28] The procedure developed in 1937 and perfected since that time makes this possible while still adhering to the principle of secrecy, universality and directness adopted in 1936 to replace the previously more easily manipulated procedure of election by a show of hands, restriction of the franchise to those presumed to favour the programme of the communist party and election only of the lowest soviets by the citizens, leaving the places of deputies to the higher soviets to be filled by the vote of deputies in the soviet next below the soviet to which the deputies were being elected.

No statutory law or convention requires that only members of the communist party be nominated or elected to posts within the soviets. While all persons chosen to be deputies are presumed to support the programme of the communist party, for which reason the persons who are not members of the party are called 'non-party bolsheviks', there has been a varying practice. Reports of the credentials commissions for the various soviets

[27] Rigby, 'Soviet Electoral Procedures' (1953) 24 *The Political Quarterly.*
[28] Stalin, 1 *Leninism* (English translation, 1934) p. 365.

have shown that party members have always been in the majority at the highest governmental level, that of the Supreme Soviet of the U.S.S.R., or its pre-1936 form, called the Central Executive Committee of the Congress of Soviets. In the elections of 1950 the deputies who were members of the communist party in the two chambers of the Supreme Soviet constituted 83 per cent.[29] In the preceding election of 1946, the party members had constituted 81 per cent.[30] The 1937 elections had produced a roster of deputies, 76.2 per cent of which had been members of the party.[31] Thus, the non-party supporter of the regime can achieve the dignity of election to the Supreme Soviet, but his chances are becoming less on each occasion.

The increasing percentage of communist party members who hold seats in the Supreme Soviet may be due in part to the increase in total communist party membership over the years. In 1952 it was reported by Malenkov to be 6,882,145, including candidates of 868,886.[32] Five years earlier, in 1947, the figure stood at 6,300,000. In 1946 it had been 6,000,000[33] and in 1939 2,477,666.[34] Nevertheless, the total number of members has always been small in comparison to the population, and party members could not fill all places, even if it were desired. This fact is evident especially in the number of party members holding seats in the local soviets.

The village soviets had but 18.9 per cent communist party members among their deputies in 1937, while the city soviets had 42 per cent communist party members in their number. Nine years later the statistics were not issued in comparable categories, but the percentage of communists in Provincial, District, City and Village Soviets was reported.[35] It varied widely from Republic to Republic, the newly created Moldavian Soviet Socialist Republic having a percentage of communists in

[29] (1950) 2 *Current Digest of the Soviet Press,* No. 24, p. 25, translated from *Izvestiya,* June 15, 1950, p. 8.

[30] Report of the Credentials Commission, Stenographic Report, *Zasedaniya Verkhovnogo Soveta SSSR* (1946) p. 30 and p. 39.

[31] Report of the Credentials Commission, Stenographic Report, *Zasedaniya Verkhovnogo Soveta* (1938) p. 33 and p. 68.

[32] Malenkov, *Report to the Nineteenth Party Congress on the Work of the Central Committee of the CPSU (B)* (1952) p. 110. The Russian original is in *Pravda,* No. 280 (12,482), October 6, 1952.

[33] (1946) 6 *Embassy of the USSR in the USA,* Information Bulletin 115.

[34] Malenkov, *Report to the Nineteenth Party Congress on the Work of the Central Committee of the CPSU (B)* (1952) p. 110.

[35] (1948) 8 *Embassy of the USSR in the USA,* Information Bulletin 22.

its four lowest levels of soviets of only 13.41 per cent, while the long established Armenian Soviet Socialist Republic had the high percentage of 52.57 at the same levels.

Even the soviets in which the percentage of communist party members is small are greatly influenced by communist party policy, quite apart from the influence which may be exerted by the publicity given the notable 'purge trials' to which reference has been made. The reason for such influence lies in a requirement of the communist party rules that all members who find themselves in non-party organisations, such as soviets, trade unions, co-operatives and other mass organisations, where there are at least three party members, must organise a party caucus to intensify party influence.[36] As a result of the application of this rule there appears in each non-party organisation a group of persons who meet in advance to discuss the position they must take and who can be counted upon to argue and vote in accordance with the established position.

THE PROBLEM OF CIVIL RIGHTS

The custom of enshrining in constitutional law guarantees of various rights of the citizen has seemingly presented Soviet leadership with a problem. The revolution of 1905 in Russia had been fought partly on a wave of public enthusiasm for constitutional guarantees of freedom of expression. The Bolsheviks, through the Social Democratic Party, of which they were then formally but a faction, had shared in espousing the demands. During the intervening years, and especially after the abdication of the Tsar in March, 1917, they had pressed for the recognition of the right to assemble, to speak and to print. It was from the recognition of these rights that they had stood to benefit, for over the years they had found nearly crippling the Tsarist censorship of their periodicals and the arrest of their leaders. Further, the influence of the battle cries of the French revolution had been enormous among the workmen of Central and Western Europe, to whom the Bolsheviks looked for support in many forms including even revolution. This was especially the case in Germany, Austria and Hungary.

[36] Rule 67. The Russian original of the rules as adopted in 1952 is in *Pravda*, No. 288 (12,490), October 14, 1952.

In contrast to the political advantage to be gained both at home and abroad from continuing espousal of the principle of constitutional guarantees there was the stark reality of danger from forces who could use such rights to the disadvantage of the Bolsheviks once the revolution had been won. Believing as they did on the basis of Marxist doctrine that the bourgeoisie were especially clever in their use of the press and of education to gain support for bourgeois policies,[37] the early Soviet leaders seem to have felt the need for caution in approaching the matter of a constitutional bill of rights.

The chronicler of the proceedings of the constitutional drafting commission of 1918 has written that the bill of rights which appeared in the 1918 constitution of the Russian Socialist Federated Soviet Republic was added at the last minute in the drafting process.[38] The stir in the commission when the proposed bill of rights was introduced was apparently nil, for the chronicler reports that he is unable to recall with certitude who introduced the bill, although be believes it was Lenin, 'if I am not mistaken'. The reason for the introduction of the bill has a firmer place in his memory. It was because of its propaganda value, as indicating the special characteristics of the Soviet Republic 'as a State of the toilers and a democracy of the propertyless'.

The difficulty of choice between the dangers of losing support from the workers who thought still in terms of the demands of 1905, and the dangers of permitting to the opposition the media of mass persuasion is evidenced by the chronicler in his comments on two of the articles of the 1918 bill of rights. In explaining the inclusion within the article relating to freedom of conscience of the additional right of freedom of religious propaganda, the chronicler says that surely religious education was contrary to the aims of the Russian Social Democratic Labour Party, of which the Bolsheviks represented the dominant part. Nevertheless, the guarantee of religious propaganda was inserted because it was necessary to win adherents to the Bolshevik cause at a time of difficulty.

A similar explanation was given for the article inserted in the bill permitting association in any form and for any purpose. To the chronicler such a guarantee amounted to commission

37 Marx and Engels, *The Communist Manifesto*, Part 2 (1848).

38 Gurvich, *Istoriya Sovetskoi Konstitutsii* [*The History of the Soviet Constitution*] (1923) p. 79.

of a crime against one's self, 'since no State can make an unlimited promise'. Yet such a promise was made.

Other promises inserted in the bill included freedom of speech and of the press, but the draftsmen inserted some provisions which they must have thought protective of the interests of the revolution. The bill was introduced by an article, which read, 'The basic task placed during the present transitional moment on the constitution of the R.S.F.S.R. is the establishment of the dictatorship of the city and village proletariat and of the poorest peasantry in the form of a powerful all-Russian Soviet authority with the objective of complete suppression of the bourgeoisie, the exploitation of man by man and the installation of socialism, under which there will be neither division into classes nor a State authority'.[39]

The bill of rights was concluded with an article, reading as follows, 'Guiding itself by the interests of the working class as a whole, the R.S.F.S.R. deprives of political rights those individuals and specific groups who use these rights to the detriment of the interests of the communist revolution'.[40] All of the other Republics which emerged in what had been the Russian Empire adopted constitutions with similar explanations as to how they were to be understood. That of the new Ukrainian Republic was even more pointed in its phraseology than had been the opening article of the R.S.F.S.R.'s bill. It stated, 'By way of introducing on all sides the beginnings of the dictatorship of the proletariat and of the poorest peasantry, the Ukrainian Soviet Socialist Republic allows to the toiling masses the whole complex of rights and opportunities in the field of public and political rights'.[41] The communist leadership seems to have been providing itself a way of avoiding legally the application of the guarantees in cases in which elements believed hostile to their plans sought to use them to rally the citizens against the regime.

The first federal constitution of 1923 contained not a word about guarantees of rights. Apparently, the leadership thought the bills in the constitutions of the various republics forming the union adequate for the purposes they had in mind. When the republics which had formed the union revised their constitutions

39 Art. 9.
40 Art. 23.
41 Art. 22, [1919] Sob.Uzak. Ukrainian SSR, No. 19, item 204.

to bring them into accord with the fact of union, the provisions concerning civil rights remained substantially the same as they had been, with some exceptions not concerned, however, with freedom of expression.

THE FIRST FEDERAL BILL OF RIGHTS

With 1936 there came the second federal constitution, and for the first time a bill of rights appeared within it.[42] Outsiders have wondered why 1936 was chosen as the appropriate time to place a bill of rights in this conspicuous place. The answer generally given has drawn its inspiration from the very fact that the place was conspicuous. The new U.S.S.R. constitution was to be circulated widely both within the U.S.S.R. and abroad. Study groups were formed not only among the sheep herders of the Uzbek Republic, but also among students in New York. The world fairs in Paris and New York soon after its promulgation emblazoned the new federal bill of rights in gold letters upon the marble walls of the palaces erected by Soviet architects to attract the attention of the world. The late 30's were the days of the 'united front' policy of world communism and of collective security, designed to reduce the danger of the ominous Hitler regime in Germany. It required no imagination to suppose that Soviet leaders had realised that the various constitutions of the constituent republics of the U.S.S.R. had remained obscure, even for the citizens of the U.S.S.R. Certainly no one but the specialist on Soviet matters had read the republic constitutions outside of the U.S.S.R.

Drafting their new federal bill with what seems to have been an eye to its public appeal both at home and abroad, the constitutional drafting commission under Stalin's chairmanship incorporated somewhat broader guarantees than had been the case in 1918. The article relating to freedom of expression was rephrased to grant freedom of press, of speech and of assembly, but it included a short preamble reading as follows: 'In conformity with the interests of the working people, and in order to strengthen the socialist system, the citizens of the U.S.S.R. are guaranteed by law' the freedoms enumerated.[43]

[42] Chap. 10.
[43] Art. 125.

Foreign interpreters of the preamble have not been of one mind as to its meaning. Some have thought that it was surplussage, added only to emphasise that freedom of speech, press and assembly were thought by the draftsmen to be in the interest of the working class. Others have said that the words had no such meaning, but were words of limitation intended to restrict exercise of the rights enumerated to those cases in which they were exercised in the interests of the working class. Considering the limited area of conflict of opinion envisioned by Stalin in his 1927 interview with the American labour delegation, it seems likely that the wording was intended to permit only those views which concerned means rather than ends. Certainly no writer within the U.S.S.R. seems to have interpreted the constitutional guarantee as extending to him the right to agitate in favour of capitalism or of the two-party system.

Evidence of the interpretation to be given the guarantee of freedom of expression may be found in two places, the criminal code and the legislation concerning censorship and the licensing of meetings. The criminal code is invoked when those who speak are prosecuted under the article concerned with counter-revolutionary propaganda.[44] As such the matter is discussed in some detail in the chapter of this study concerned with the criminal law. The decisions of the courts interpreting the code suggest that the courts understand the criminal code to prohibit speech designed to overthrow or weaken the Soviet regime, and their concern is only to find whether such intent is really present.

Even though the courts search for criminal intent to overthrow the regime, they use language which suggests that the potential danger invoked by the speech is to be considered. For the untutored citizen of humble background they are not inclined to exact the penalties of the code, and they seem to be impressed by evidence that the speech caused no harm.

While the judicial decisions suggest that speech which is not in the interest of the working people will not result in conviction in every case, public policy is clear. The citizen is not to be permitted speech which seeks to overthrow the regime, and measures of education or compulsion will be used to discourage him. The constitutional guarantee seems to be limited to speech confined to the discussion of means and not of ends.

[44] Criminal Code RSFSR, Art. 58^{10}, available in English translation as *The Penal Code of the Russian Socialist Federal Soviet Republic* (1934).

CENSORSHIP AND LICENSING OF MEETINGS

Such a conclusion is supported by the legislation on censorship and the licensing of meetings. This legislation was promulgated during the period when the pre-1936 phraseology on civil rights was in force, but it has not been repealed since the 1936 constitution was made effective. It seems appropriate to consider the meaning of the constitutional draftsmen in terms of legislative policy expressed in the licensing laws.

The law currently in force in the R.S.F.S.R., accompanied by similar laws in the other Republics, provides for a Chief Administration for Matters of Literature and Publishing in the Ministry of Education of the R.S.F.S.R.[45] This Chief Administration is declared created 'for the purpose of putting into effect all types of political-ideological, military and economic control over items prepared for publication and distribution in the press, over manuscripts, pictures, drawings, etc., and also over wireless announcements, lectures and exhibitions'. The Chief Administration is empowered 'to forbid printing, publication and distribution of productions which: (1) contain agitation or propaganda against Soviet authority and the dictatorship of the proletariat, (2) reveal State secrets, (3) stir up ethnic and religious fanaticism, and (4) have a pornographic character.

It is this statute which explains the censorship number appearing at the end of all books printed in the U.S.S.R., together with the data concerning the size of the edition and the date of submission of the manuscript to the printers. Only the publications of the Moscow Patriarchate of the Russian Orthodox Church seem to be exempt from censorship by the Chief Administration, for they alone carry no censorship number. Possibly this may be to indicate that the separation of Church and State is as complete as the law declares it to be or simply because the Patriarchate has given evidence to the communist party leaders that it can be relied upon to perform its own censorship function adequately.

A suggestion that censorship is not limited solely to that provided formally by the Chief Administration is to be found in a case arising out of a suit for royalties.[46] An author sought

[45] Decree of June 6, 1931, [1931] 1 Sob.Uzak. RSFSR, No. 31, item 273.
[46] *Solonevich* v. *Publishing House 'Our Newspaper'* [1931] 15 Sud.Prak. RSFSR 4.

royalties for a pamphlet prepared under contract for a State publishing house. Judgment was given by the trial court, even though publication had never occurred. On review, judgment was set aside on the ground that the work had been found by the Cultural Sector of the Trade Union 'to lack ideological foundation'. The court added that the author knew the reason why the work was not publishable. It is implied that having been informed of its ideological shortcomings, he should not have pressed the matter of the royalty at all. Here was a case in which there was no suggestion that the work was criminal as seeking to instigate the overthrow of the regime. The criticism of the work was of a general character and related to what was probably unorthodox interpretation of doctrine.

Control is retained over the exercise of the right of assembly through the licensing of meetings. Under a statute of May 15, 1935,[47] no meeting may be called for representatives from all parts of the U.S.S.R. without the consent of the Council of Ministers of the U.S.S.R., while any meeting bringing together representatives of agencies within a single Republic requires the licence of the Council of Ministers of that Republic. If the meeting is to be attended only by representatives of departments within a single Ministry, the consent of the Minister concerned is alone required. Legislation in the Republics[48] concerns the procedure to be followed when a meeting is to gather representatives only of a single province in the Republic, leaving discretion in the Provincial Soviet's Executive Committee.

No association may be formed without a licence, the concept of the voluntary non-profit association without State authorisation being unknown in Soviet law. By a decree of January 6, 1930,[49] the federal government placed control in each Republic of those non-profit organisations of an all-union character which had their principal office in the Republic. Regulations were published in 1932 by the R.S.F.S.R.[50] By virtue of this series of decrees an association of bird watchers or Pushkin lovers would require a licence if it sought membership among persons living throughout the country. The implication seems to be that any association, no matter how cultural or scientific its concern,

[47] [1935] 1 Sob.Zak. SSSR, No. 26, item 209.
[48] Decree of June 20, 1935, [1936] 1 Sob.Uzak. RSFSR, No. 6, item 29.
[49] [1930] 1 Sob.Zak. SSSR. No. 7, item 76.
[50] Decree of July 10, 1932, [1932] 1 Sob.Uzak. RSFSR, No. 74, item 331.

requires State control if it seeks to attract a membership from an area which is sufficiently large to involve considerable numbers of persons. Perhaps the Soviet leaders recall their own revolutionary past when political groups sought disguise under all manner of cultural titles. Whether this be the case or not, the leaders of the U.S.S.R. have indicated their present intention to preserve their monopoly of leadership throughout the land.

PRESERVING THE ADVANTAGES OF CRITICISM

Complete control of all means of expression and elimination of the possibility of organising protest groups has its perils, and Soviet leadership seems to have realised that fact. If no one may seek election without endorsement of the party; if no one may form a faction within the communist party, much less a competing political party; if no one may lift his voice without careful consideration of the interpretation to be placed upon his motives, mistakenly conceived policies of the leaders or decisions of their subordinates could lead to difficulties and ultimately to disaster. It is a commonplace that democracies have an important element of strength in the freedom allowed the citizen to disclose a cancer before it destroys the State. Apparently, Soviet policies of control and the monopoly of political leadership have dulled in the citizen his desire to express himself critically even of means being used to achieve the ends set for Soviet society by its leaders. Cancers can grow to considerable proportions before being discovered. Local despots can emerge and rule their county, or province, with ruthless hands before someone dares to report the matter to the despot's superiors. Eventually the error of the despotic official's ways will be disclosed, but often not before enemies of the regime have been made among people who cannot distinguish between the aims of the Soviet State and those of its local representative. Legal measures to control the local despot are discussed in Chapter 5, but the means by which many of the despots are exposed may be discussed appropriately at this point because they concern the subject of freedom of expression.

The exposure of shortcomings in the work of an agency is deemed to be the task of 'self-criticism'. The term means more than the individual's evaluation of his own failures. It includes the evaluation by employees of a State agency of the failures of the agency for which they work. In 1952 it was re-emphasised in the Nineteenth Communist Party Congress that the word applied even to criticism within the party of the conduct of party officials. Khruschev as the rapporteur on the proposed changes in the communist party rules gave examples of the need for self-criticism within the party.[51] He disclosed that the Rostov Province Committee of the party had persecuted party members who exposed bribery within the party.

To emphasise the desirability of expanding self-criticism the Party Rules were amended to include not only the right 'to criticise any party functionary at party meetings',[52] but also the duty 'to report to leading party bodies, up to the Central Committee of the party, shortcomings in the work, irrespective of the persons involved'.[53] The section continues by saying 'A party member has no right to conceal an unsatisfactory state of affairs, or by-pass wrongdoing, thus damaging the interests of the party and the State. He who interferes with a party member carrying out such duties must be severely punished as violating the will of the party'.

Party members are also admonished 'to develop criticism and self-criticism from below to expose shortcomings in work and strive for their elimination, and to fight against a parading of well-being and the flush of success'.[54]

It seems possible to read into the renewed emphasis upon the importance of self-criticism a fear on the part of the highest Soviet leaders that the measures taken to establish monopoly of leadership have had undesirable consequences. They have tended to develop a Soviet man who is more docile in accepting leadership than the principal policy makers within the party desire. Even the local tyrant is not being exposed. The pendulum may have swung too far. Measures seem to have been taken to counteract the law's influence toward unconscious acquiescence in all orders coming from above. Yet, in spite of the evidence of disapproval among high Soviet leaders of what has occurred, no step has yet been taken to change the law which has made the undesirable development possible. Continuation of the monopoly legislation suggests that the leadership still fears serious difficulties in guiding the masses along the road it has charted.

[51] *Pravda*, No. 287 (12,489), October 13, 1952.
[52] Rule 4 (b). [53] Rule 3 (h). [54] Rule 3 (g).

Chapter 4

WHAT IS CRIMINAL?

Crime was associated with capitalism in the minds of the leaders of the Russian revolution. 'The hungry masses stole to survive'. 'The disgruntled workman protested his lot in murder and rape'. Socialism with its offering of adequate food, clothing and housing, and its promise of equality of opportunity for all was expected to spell the end of crime as a social phenomenon.[1]

It is small wonder that Soviet leaders holding such views paid much attention to the measures designed to maximise the productivity of property and less to the criminal law. The property law was laying the foundation for the future. The criminal law would fast become a relic of the past. Social change in the direction desired was expected to flow almost automatically from State ownership of the means of production. The criminal courts were not to become schools of citizenship. They were to function for but a short time while the transition was being made to socialism and while those who opposed the plans of the new regime on emotional grounds still required suppression. Ultimately the criminal law was to 'wither away'. Had not Engels predicted in his Origin of the Family, Private Property and the State, that eventually the apparatus of compulsion, the State, would become unnecessary and find its place in the museum alongside the bronze axe and the spinning wheel?

No criminal code was enacted for two years after the revolution. Occasional decrees defined acts deemed prejudicial to the State and named penalties to be applied, but there was no co-ordination of policy in the shape of a code from which a citizen could have obtained a general picture of what would and would not be tolerated in the new society.

Judges were instructed by the earliest decrees to administer justice in accordance with their revolutionary consciousness,[2]

[1] Programme of the Communist Party, adopted 1919, Arts. 2 and 11. English translation in Meisel and Kozera, *Materials for the Study of the Soviet System* (1950) p. 100.

[2] Decree of November 27, 1917, s. 5, [1917] 1 Sob.Uzak. RSFSR, No. 4, item 50; decree of February, 1918, s. 36 (undated), [1918] 1 Sob.Uzak. RSFSR, No. 26, item 347 (misnumbered as item 420 in some editions); and decree of November 30, 1918, s. 22, [1918] 1 Sob.Uzak. RSFSR, No. 85, item 889.

and by degrees there was developed a nearly autonomous police, called the *Cheka* to cope with mass threats against the very continuation of the regime.[3] The leadership seems to have been too busy with matters of higher priority to draft a criminal code. The few specific decrees brought particularly dangerous activities under criminal sanctions. For the rest the leadership seems to have left the preservation of order to men and women schooled in the political doctrines of the revolution and presumed to be able to act in recognition of activity that might threaten the life of the new society.

Not until December, 1919, was a general statute enacted as a guide to the courts in moulding the new society.[4] It defined no specific crimes, but informed the judges how they were to treat the insane, the minors, those guilty of unsuccessful attempts to commit crime and those who were accessories. It also listed the types of penalties permitted. Bearing the title 'Basic Principles for the Criminal Law of the U.S.S.R.', the decree set forth the reasons for its enactment. It found necessary the introduction of uniformity into the treatment of crime so that the proletariat might work out rules for curbing its class enemies and teach itself to rule.

For the non-Soviet student of the impact of law upon social change the secondary position given to criminal law by the Soviet

[3] Decree of October 28, 1918, [1918] 1 Sob.Uzak. RSFSR, No. 80, item 842. So many arrests were made that disruption of public administration followed. The *Cheka* was then ordered to give preliminary notice of arrest of subordinates to administrative supervisors, so as to permit appropriate arrangements. Decree of December 14, 1918, [1918] *ibid.*, No. 94, item 941. Discretionary power to impose penalties, including death against persons charged with armed activity, and in areas subject to martial law against persons charged with such offences as might be listed in the proclamation of martial law was preserved for the *Cheka* by decree of February 17, 1919, [1919] *ibid.*, No. 12, item 130. For other 'counter revolutionary' offences the right to sentence was transferred from the *Cheka* to a reorganised system of 'Revolutionary Tribunals'. A decree of June 20, 1919, [1919] *ibid.*, No. 27, item 301, established the offences which might be listed in the proclamation of martial law as within the jurisdiction of the *Cheka*. It included treason, espionage, concealment of firearms for counter-revolutionary purposes, counterfeiting, forgery of documents, arson, explosion, intentional injury to means of communication, banditry, armed robbery, burglary of State warehouses, and illegal narcotics traffic.

[4] Decree of December 12, 1919, [1919] 1 Sob.Uzak. RSFSR, No. 66, item 590. Judges were not entirely without guidance before publication of this decree. For example, a manual set forth in four pages some general principles of criminal law. See Commissariat for Military Affairs, *Sudebnoe Nastolnoe Rukovodstvo* [*Court Reference Aid*] (1919).

leadership seems startling. Many westerners, familiar as they are with the actions of dictators intent upon preserving their power, have thought that the key to control lies in criminal law. Some indication that Stalin did not see it this way is to be found in his comments to an American newspaper editor in 1935 on the life expectancy of Hitler's National Socialism.[5] No one can forget that the National Socialists made vigorous use of the criminal law and the institutions of the police in maintaining their control. Yet, Stalin thought the National Socialist regime could not last, and his reason for thinking so was that it had preserved capitalism. In short, a leadership which preserves private ownership of productive resources, which to Soviet theorists is the principal element of capitalism, cannot expect to survive, regardless of the measures of repression it controls. Stalin's statement some sixteen years after the revolution suggests that even with the apparent successes achieved by the well advertised Soviet agencies of repression, he was still prepared to consider that State ownership of productive property and not the criminal law held the key to long-term survival.

PUNISHMENT AND EDUCATION

In spite of this relegation of criminal law to a position behind that of property ownership Soviet leadership has given increasing attention to criminal law with the passage of the years. In 1922, at the time that Soviet law was generally being codified, the criminal law of the R.S.F.S.R. and the other Soviet republics took shape in codes drafted along lines familiar to students of criminal law in other lands.[6] In 1926 a revised code was adopted in the R.S.F.S.R. but with little basic change.[7] In June, 1930, Stalin indicated his intention of continuing to give important attention to criminal law when he argued before the Central Committee of the communist party that the State would not wither away by degrees but must remain strong right up to the time when it was no longer needed.[8]

[5] *Roy Howard Interview with Stalin* (English translation, 1936).

[6] Decree effective June 1, 1922 (no precise date given to the decree), [1922] 1 Sob.Uzak. RSFSR, No. 15, item 153.

[7] Decree of November 22, 1926, effective January 1, 1927, [1926] 1 Sob.Uzak. RSFSR, No. 80, item 600. For English translation, see *The Penal Code of the Russian Federal Soviet Republic* (1934).

[8] Stalin, 2 *Leninism* (English translation, 1933) p. 342.

Stalin's voice seems not to have been heard by the leading jurists immediately, for they continued to prepare for the gradual lessening in importance of the criminal law. They drafted and circulated widely a proposed code designed to return to the approach of the early years when judges were given broad discretion within a general framework.[9] But this derogatory approach to criminal law was but temporary, for Stalin's view prevailed, and the jurists who had thought otherwise were denounced as traitors, and some were tried for attempting to undermine the regime.[10] Criminal law was heralded with renewed emphasis as having both the qualities of a sword to eliminate enemies of the new social order and of a school to inculcate in the general public the principles by which they were expected to live in the new society.[11] Criminal law thus became an important string to the bow of a leadership bent upon bringing about social change. Punishment was seen to have value as a threat to incipient criminals.

While the criminal code is given the important task of eliminating enemies and educating the public, the leadership has not been prepared, apparently, to trust its fortunes to the protection afforded by it alone. There has been continued from the stormy early days of the revolution the arm of the special police having as its function the elimination of opposition when it takes mass form. As at present constituted under the auspices of the Ministry of Internal Affairs, this police and its system of prisons and work camps retains the authority originally granted to the well-known *Cheka,* and continued with the G.P.U., of dealing in its own way with those it believes to be dangerous to the regime.[12]

[9] On March 23, 1929, the Council of People's Commissars of the RSFSR adopted a resolution directing the Commissariat of Justice to work out not later than February, 1930, and to present to the Council a draft of a new Criminal Code. The draft was completed in May, 1930, and published soon after to inaugurate a long period of discussion. See Estrin, 1 *Sovetskoe Ugolovnoe Pravo, Chast Obshchaya* [*Soviet Criminal Law, General Part*] (1935) pp. 130–131.

[10] The nature of the errors they are charged with having committed was set forth by P. Yudin in 1937. For translation, see Lenin *et al., Soviet Legal Philosophy* (1951) p. 281 *et seq.*

[11] B. Mankovsky, 'Against Anti-Marxist Theories of Criminal Law', [1937] 7 Sots.Zak. 43 and 47.

[12] An exhaustive study of the record of the special police is in preparation at Columbia University by Ernest Hollis, junior. For a history of the activity of the early years, see Zelitch, *Soviet Administration of Criminal Law* (1931) pp. 34–48, and Gsovski, 1 *Soviet Civil Law* (1948) pp. 233–240.

By statute the Ministry of Internal Affairs maintains special boards, responsible only to the Prosecutor General of the U.S.S.R., with power to take repressive measures up to five years' imprisonment with hard labour against 'persons who are recognised as being socially dangerous'.[13] No published code or instructions indicates that any precise definition is provided to the Ministry as to what constitutes social danger within the meaning of the statute applied by the Ministry. The fact that such definitions exist in the criminal code,[14] and yet no reference to them is required by the Ministry suggests that the special boards are completely free to develop their own definitions. Further, the Ministry is specifically relieved of adherence to the provisions of the code of criminal procedure which bind the criminal courts.[15]

Discussion of the functions of the Ministry with those who have escaped to the west suggests that it is designed to cope primarily, but not entirely with mass dissension and unrest exceeding the capabilities of the criminal courts, which are necessarily limited in effectiveness in time of crisis because of their individualised approach and their relatively slow proceedings. The special boards and their arm, the special police, can be and are thrown into an area where the leadership is of the opinion that the psychological effect of tactics of terror will alone maintain control until the slower processes of pacification through individualised criminal trials and restoration of an economic base favourable to the Soviet regime can become effective.[16] As such they are the shock troops of social change influencing the course of events but contributing little, if anything, to the education of the public along positive lines.

While the special boards of the Ministry of Internal Affairs and its special police still function without a published definition of social danger, the whole trend of Soviet commentators has been to favour increasing definiteness in the criminal code.

13 Decree of July 10, 1934, [1934] 1 Sob.Zak. SSSR, No. 36, item 283, and decree of November 5, 1934, [1935] *ibid.*, No. 11, item 84.

14 Art. 6 provides a general definition. Arts. 58–204 define specific acts as socially dangerous.

15 Decree of October 16, 1924, [1924] 1 Sob.Uzak. RSFSR, No. 78, item 784. Introduced in Code of Criminal Procedure RSFSR. See Arts. 101, 104, 107 and 108.

16 Accounts of the practices of the Special Boards may be found in Beck and Godin, *Russian Purge and the Extraction of Confession* (1951).

It is argued that citizens can be expected to learn their new duties only if they are informed in clear terms what they must not do.[17] What then are the outlines of the desired social changes as evidenced by the definitions of the criminal code?

PROTECTING STATE-OWNED PROPERTY

Activities believed to impinge upon the successful development of an economy of abundance are receiving increasing attention in Soviet legal periodicals and the popular press. First and foremost of all the articles inspiring editorial writers are those having to do with offences against State-owned property: its destruction, its theft, and its misuse.[18] Only by degrees have these articles achieved their present importance. While articles of both of the R.S.F.S.R.'s criminal codes have concerned theft and embezzlement of State-owned property,[19] it was not until August 7, 1932, that a vigorous campaign was begun under the banner of a severe law [20] setting the death penalty for theft from transport and for theft of co-operatively owned property. For cases having extenuating circumstances the courts were authorised to sentence to ten years' imprisonment and confiscation of property.

By degrees the special statute of August 7, 1932, was extended beyond transport to all theft and embezzlement of a recurring or especially serious character so that it was made clear to all that State-owned property was, in the words of the statute, 'sacred'.[21] The political writers explained the reasons for such special attention to State property. Their text was Article 131 of the Constitution of 1936 which declared it to be 'the duty of every citizen of the U.S.S.R. to safeguard and fortify public, socialist property as the sacred and inviolable foundation of the socialist system, as the source of the wealth and might of the country, as the source of the prosperity and culture of all the working people'.

17 Gertsenzon, 'The Paths of Development of the Soviet Science of Criminal Law During the Past Thirty Years', [1947] 11 Sov. Gos. i Pravo 81.

18 Leading article, 'For Full Liquidation of the Theft of Socialist Property', [1950] 6 Sots.Zak. 1.

19 Code of 1922, Arts. 113, 180 and 186. Code of 1926, Arts. 116, 162 and 168.

20 [1932] 1 Sob.Zak. SSSR, No. 62, item 360.

21 Karnitsky and Roginsky, *Ugolovny Kodeks RSFSR Posobie* [*Criminal Code RSFSR—An Aid*] (1935), p. 67.

Further application of the death penalty provisions of the law of August 7, 1932, became impossible with the enactment of a decree abolishing the death penalty generally on May 26, 1947,[22] but within a few days the void was filled. A decree dated June 4, 1947,[23] treated the protection of State property comprehensively, placing together the various types of misappropriation, and providing a penalty of from seven to ten years in a labour camp for the first offender and a penalty of from ten to twenty-five years with confiscation of property for the second offender, or for those who commit the offence in an organised group or on a large scale. Even failure to inform State authorities of theft committed or in preparation by others was to incur a penalty of imprisonment for a period of from two to three years or banishment to remote regions for from five to seven years.

That the courts consider offences under the decree of June 4, 1947, exceptionally serious is evidenced by reports of various cases. One will indicate the attitude which has been assumed.[24] Three farmers: the president of a collective farm, the brigade leader and the director of the machine tractor station, were accused of stealing grain from a shipment made to the farm. Having been detected by the storekeeper of the farm, they were compelled to restore the grain. All were convicted under the decree, but the trial court had compassion on them and applied the article of the criminal code permitting a reduction below the minimum allowed by the article violated if exceptional circumstances existed in the opinion of the court. In consequence, instead of the minimum of eight years' internment prescribed by the 1947 decree, the court sentenced two of the defendants to two years' and one to three years' internment.

The Supreme Court of the U.S.S.R. remanded the case for new trial, saying that the fact that the defendants had restored the grain to the collective farm on apprehension was no reason to reduce their sentences below the minimum set by statute for the offence.

22 Ved.Verkh.Sov. SSSR, No. 17 (471), May 31, 1947.
23 *Ibid.*, No. 19 (473), June 11, 1947.
24 For a group of cases, see 'Court examination of cases concerned with the theft of State and public property', [1950] 6 Sots.Zak. 55.

The death penalty was restored on January 12, 1950, for 'traitors, spies and those seeking to undermine the State'.[25] No specific amendment to the June 4, 1947, decree has appeared, although the severe language used in referring to those who steal property could cause the outside observer to expect one. The possibility that the offence, if serious enough, might be interpreted as an effort to undermine the State, and hence subject to the death penalty, is suggested by the fact that in December, 1952, the Soviet press carried a report of the application of the death penalty to a band of thieves who had organised a system for regular large scale thefts. In spite of this case, the crime seems still to be rated as something less than treason, although because of its frequency it is attracting severe language from the editorial writers.

Criminal penalties await not only those who misappropriate State-owned property. They await also those who misuse that which has been committed to them for productive purposes. Thus, Article 128 of the Criminal Code penalises with imprisonment for periods up to two years persons who are directors of State or public offices or enterprises and who by virtue of negligent or unconscientious attention to duty cause waste or irretrievable harm to the property of the enterprise or office.

On the eve of the war a decree of July 10, 1940,[26] added to the code the offence of production of goods of a quality and completeness which were below standard. It provided that a director, chief engineer or chief of the technical inspection of an industrial plant in which such activity occurred should be penalised with imprisonment for periods from five to eight years. The decree was not, however, applied effectively against any managers except bakery heads or presidents of consumers' co-operatives until well after the war.[27] This laxness did not, apparently, stem from any failure to appreciate the important policy decision which had been made with the promulgation of the decree. It occurred because the notification procedure in use when poor quality was discovered was inadequate.

The practice during almost the entire first decade of operation was to rely upon the arbitration tribunals to inform the

[25] Ved.Verkh.Sov. SSSR, No. 3 (618), January 20, 1950.
[26] Introduced into the *Criminal Code RSFSR* as Art. 128A.
[27] G. Golst, 'The Struggle with the Issuance of Underquality, Incomplete and Below Standard Products', [1950] 6 Sots.Zak. 13 at 14–15.

prosecutors when a suit between public corporations disclosed poor quality. But this procedure is reported to have made it difficult to provide evidence for the prosecution since the suits in the arbitration tribunals occurred well after the event, and notice was usually sent to the prosecutor at the producer's place of business rather than at the place at which the goods had been received.

To remedy the situation, in 1950 there were established check points in supply depots. One such point was established in the central depot of the automobile and tractor supply combine through which spare parts from several factories flowed. Thus, the experts were able to determine immediately on receipt of a part whether it was of poor quality and to notify the prosecutor with the evidence in good time for prosecution.

Bench workmen who intentionally produce goods under the required quality from materials provided by the State are punished under a separate article, which reaches any intentional destruction or damage to property belonging to State or public offices or enterprises.[28] Such persons are not subjected to the same severe penalties as the director of their plant, but they are subjected to imprisonment for a period up to one year, or are sentenced to pay an instalment fine from their wages while remaining at their job. Likewise criminally negligent attitudes toward farm machinery and tractors belonging to State farms or tractor stations incurs a penalty of an instalment fine at the job for periods up to six months, or if repeated or causing great harm, to a penalty of imprisonment up to three years.[29] A separate section gives similar treatment to those who intentionally injure horses belonging to State and collective farms and service stables.[30]

DANGER TO THE REGIME

Social attitudes are also moulded by placing a considerable number of offences within a special chapter of the code following those having to do with intent to overthrow the regime.[31] As such they rank second only to treason in importance, even though the offender had no intent specifically to harm the regime when he engaged in the forbidden activity. In addition to such

28 Art. 79.
29 Art. 79 (2).
30 Art. 79 (3).
31 *Criminal Code RSFSR*, c. 1, Part 2.

obvious offences as avoiding military service,[32] disrupting rail traffic by damaging railway tracks,[33] theft of firearms,[34] counterfeiting,[35] and violation of currency regulations,[36] there are some offences on which special emphasis has been placed because they bear immediately upon the type of society which is declared to be the goal of the regime. One such offence is the spreading of propaganda or agitation directed toward the fomenting of religious or racial enmity for which a penalty of imprisonment for periods up to two years is provided, unless the offence is committed during periods of wartime or mass unrest in which event the penalty shall be not less than two years or even death.[37] A somewhat allied offence is that described as mass rioting accompanied by pogroms, destruction of railway lines or other communications, murders, arson or other such activity.[38] For these offences the penalties are not less than two years' imprisonment and extend to a maximum of death, if committed in wartime, and twenty-five years' imprisonment if committed in peacetime.

The severest penalties apply in every case to those who commit acts intended to harm, weaken or overthrow the regime. It is this group of offences which is termed 'counter-revolutionary' in that the acts included within it are directed against the regime which achieved power in the Russian revolution. It is here that one finds not only the offences of treason,[39] espionage,[40] assassination of officials of the State,[41] or intentional damaging of the machinery of a State enterprise,[42] but also giving aid of any character to the international bourgeoisie seeking to overthrow the communist system.[43]

32 Art. 59 (4).
33 Art. 59 (3B).
34 Art. 59 (3A).
35 Art. 59 (8).
36 Art. 59 (12).
37 Art. 59 (7). A group of peasants found to have hampered systematically, out of a feeling of racial prejudice, a group of Jews who had been resettled among them were convicted under this article in 1930. *Case of Parafalo, Lutsenko and Shapovalova* [1930] 2 Sud.Prak. RSFSR 13. Sufficient time has not yet elapsed to determine what effect the campaign against Zionism and the State of Israel will have currently upon the application of this article.
38 Art. 59 (2).
39 Art. 58 (1A). This article was introduced into the code in 1934.
40 Art. 58 (6).
41 Art. 58 (8).
42 Art. 58 (14).
43 Art. 58 (4).

There is also included among the serious offences against the State the communication of unpublished economic information to citizens of foreign States.[44] Since the war a series of decrees has reinforced this article of the code. On June 8, 1947, the Council of Ministers of the U.S.S.R. issued an instruction listing the matters which were considered State secrets.[45] In addition to information on the size and equipment of the armed services of the U.S.S.R., as a whole or in part, the reserves of manpower and supplies available to mobilisation, mobilisation plans, productive capacity for military supplies and the progress of research in weapons, the decree included among the items which might not be disclosed to foreigners the industrial production figures for the whole or a part of the U.S.S.R., the agricultural statistics, information on domestic trade, communications, finances, the place of storage of precious metals and banknotes, statistics on foreign trade, geological information, patents, technical improvements not yet released for publication, negotiations and agreements with foreign States not officially announced, and ciphers.

The revealing of such secrets by officials, military personnel and private persons, whether intentionally or as the result of negligent loss of documents was made the subject of a decree the following day.[46] The decree declared that it was applicable only when the offence did not fall under the more serious categories of treason or espionage. Penalties were set at from five to fifteen years' internment in a labour camp, and jurisdiction over the offence was placed in the military tribunals.

The manner in which State officials might communicate with representatives of foreign States was made the subject of a decree on December 16, 1947.[47] Direct communication with foreign consuls or business men such as regularly occurs in other countries was forbidden. Soviet officials were required to pass any communication to foreigners through the Ministries of Foreign Affairs and Foreign Trade.

Such provisions are obviously designed to reduce the effectiveness of any espionage efforts made by foreign States and to

[44] Art. 58 (6–Part 2).

[45] *Izvestiya*, No. 134, June 10, 1947. Printed as annotation to *Criminal Code RSFSR* (1952 ed.) p. 76.

[46] Decree of June 9, 1947, Ved.Verkh.Sov. SSSR, No. 20 (474), June 16, 1947. Printed as annotation to *Criminal Code RSFSR* (1952 ed.) p. 74.

[47] Ved.Verkh.Sov. SSSR, No. 5 (504), January 25, 1948.

mould a Soviet citizen who will have nothing to do with foreigners. They indicate that the new Soviet man is to be wary at all times lest the citizen of a State embracing the capitalist, or near-capitalist systems of economy, take advantage of him to the detriment of Soviet socialism.[48]

In these articles concerned with the dangers to be expected from the bourgeoisie one finds again the influence of doctrine upon the draftsmen of Soviet statutes. Soviet leaders have argued that the capitalist world cannot permit a new socialist economy to develop, for its unqualified success would cause eventually revolution in the capitalist States.[49] In consequence, it could be expected that the capitalist world would ultimately seek to overthrow in war the outstanding socialist State before unfavourable comparisons became generally apparent to all. For that reason war was believed to be inevitable and must be postponed at all cost until the Soviet Union had made itself invincible. Incredible as such thinking may seem to men of the west, it has been basic to Soviet attitudes and seems to govern the steps taken by Soviet leaders to form a new type of citizen who is impervious to wily attempts to subvert him.

While Soviet leaders are prepared to make some actions punishable regardless of the intent of those who commit them, the code and the courts have laid major emphasis upon intent, particularly since 1938.[50] The assumption is clear that in the socialist world man is not subject to an elemental force such as poverty driving him to crime. He is presumed to be able to reframe his social attitudes to co-operate in the building of socialism rather than to protest against the government, and the society it represents.

THE COURTS DETERMINE INTENT

Under Article 10 of the Criminal Code since its adoption in 1926 the penalties of the law have been applied to those who

48 Some of the same factors may have entered into the decision to forbid marriage with foreigners. Decree of February 15, 1947, Ved.Verkh.Sov. SSSR, No. 10 (464), March 18, 1947.

49 Lenin, 24 *Sochineniya* [*Collected Works*] (3rd ed. 1928–1937) p. 122 and 27 *ibid.*, at p. 117.

50 Vyshinsky in 1938 criticised sharply the then Minister of Justice, Krylenko, for saying that in criminal law there was no practical difference between negligence and wilfulness. Academy of Sciences USSR, Institute of Law, *Osnovnye Zadachi Nauki Sovetskogo Sotsialisticheskogo Prava* [*The Basic Tasks for the Science of Soviet Socialist Law*] (1938) pp. 62–63.

have acted wilfully. To clarify the meaning of wilfulness the code proceeds to define it as 'foreseeing the socially-dangerous character of the consequences of their acts, desiring these consequences or consciously permitting their occurrence'. Even before the current emphasis upon the increased danger of those who act wilfully, some judicial decisions indicated the importance given to wilfulness, especially in those cases in which the charge brought against the accused was that he wished to harm the Soviet regime. A court in 1931 had no difficulty in affirming a conviction for a counter-revolutionary act when it was indicated that the defendant had sought to burn down a commune by persuading a young girl whom he had previously seduced to set fire to a hay field.[51] The defendant's record showed that he was the son of a rich peasant who had been banished from the province, that he had been refused admission both to the collective farm and to the Young Communist Youth League because of his ancestry and that he had used threats on the girl to persuade her to set the fire.

Likewise, a man who murdered a State official who came to his village to improve the economic work of the village was sentenced to be shot as a counter-revolutionary when it was found that he had no profession, that he had a criminal record of conviction for arson, making illegal liquor and keeping firearms, and that when the official came to the village, he was followed to the house in which he was staying by the defendant and knifed early in the morning after having ordered the defendant to leave the house.[52]

Yet, intent to do harm to the Soviet regime has not always incurred severe penalties. It has been for the courts to determine in each instance whether the situation required such severity, and they appear to have taken into consideration the status of the defendant in the social structure and the extent of the injury actually caused. Thus, two young men who had broken a window in a clinic with the admitted intent of harming the Soviet State found their action reclassified by the Supreme Court of the R.S.F.S.R. from counter-revolutionary destruction of State property to the then relatively minor offence of wilful destruction of property belonging to State institutions.[53]

[51] *Case of Kholkin*, No. 2,843 [1931] 8 Sud.Prak. RSFSR 9.
[52] *Case of Savelev*, No. 24,142 [1931] 17–18 Sud.Prak. RSFSR 8.
[53] *Case of Shanev and Bezyaev*, No. 21,528 [1930] 11 Sud.Prak. RSFSR 9.

The court was of the opinion that the breaking of a window pane was not sufficiently serious to constitute a counter-revolutionary crime even when committed out of class hatred by two young men, one of whom was a sacristan and the other the son of a priest.

In similar fashion and at about the same time a group of elderly peasants, all of whom were poor or middle class, found the commutation of their sentence for mass disorder accompanied by pogrom affirmed by the Supreme Court of the R.S.F.S.R. over the protest of the Prosecutor even though they had participated in a riot in attempting to prevent the arrest of their village priest. The Supreme Court declared at the height of the anti-religious campaigns that the trial court had the correct approach in commuting the sentences which had been imposed because most of the defendants were old, all were working and came from the poor and middle groups, all were ignorant, and no serious consequences resulted from what they did.[54] The conditional sentence was thought an excellent means of handling the matter because, in the opinion of the Supreme Court, the right thing was to tell the peasants of their mistake and to warn them for the future.

In reaching its conclusions as to whether intent is or is not present when the evidence is conflicting, the Soviet courts have sometimes considered the parentage and economic circumstances of an accused person, reflecting again the influence of doctrine upon their thinking. The 'class enemy' who springs from a bourgeois family may possibly have a harder time proving his innocence of counter-revolutionary intent than the citizen whose ancestry was of working stock and whose activities have been clearly of a character beneficial to the State. This conclusion is suggested by the testimony of *émigrés* and also by a series of cases. In the most recent an Army officer accused of anti-Soviet speech on a drill field during the past war was acquitted in the absence of clear evidence of his intent because, in the opinion of the court, the comments could not have been evoked by any orientation against Soviet authority since the accused had served most of his life in exemplary fashion in the Army, had been a member of the communist party for twenty-three years, and had never in the past conducted himself in a negative manner which

[54] *Case of Yakunin et al.*, No. 2,634 [1929] 1 Sud.Prak. RSFSR 10.

would compromise him as an honest citizen devoted to his motherland.[55]

A man who spoke out years earlier in a village soviet meeting against the plans for the sowing season was successful in obtaining the quashing of his conviction because, as the court stated, 'from the record it is apparent that the accused was a workman, that he had been at the front in the civil war, that he was an invalid and that he was not a class enemy'.[56] Even a well-to-do peasant was successful at about the same time in having his case reclassified from counter-revolutionary speech to the lesser crime of insult to authority because no harm was caused by a speech in a village soviet against a plan for self-taxation.[57] The peasant had not limited himself to criticism but had cursed the village soviet in what the court described as 'unprintable words.'

Although no reported judicial decisions have been found to support the conclusion that a decision will go against a person with ancestry generally accepted as presumably opposed to the Soviet regime, a recent textbook opinion suggests that such might be the case. The author of the textbook states 'Counter-revolutionary crime can occur also when the person committing it has no direct counter-revolutionary intent. Such a case is one in which the counter-revolutionary crime is committed with so-called indirect or implied counter-revolutionary intent'.[58] The author then proceeds to caution his readers that negligent activity must not be interpreted as intentional. From the commentary a distinction arises between implying counter-revolutionary intent from one's background, in the absence of clear evidence on the matter, and implying it from the lighthearted manner in which a person performs some careless act. Evidence of motive is not to be confused with evidence of the commission of an act, without which there can be no crime. On this point, there seems to have been a variation in the acceptability of implications as to the fact from the circumstances of the case.

[55] *Case of K* [1944] 3 Sud.Prak. SSSR 8.
[56] *Case of Mikhailov,* No. 22,627 [1931] 14 Sud.Prak. RSFSR 9.
[57] *Case of Pankratov,* No. 21,070 [1930] 9 Sud.Prak. RSFSR 14.
[58] *Sovetskoe Ugolovnoe Pravo, Chast Osobennaya* [*Soviet Criminal Law, Special Part*] (1951) p. 61. The Russian word translated above as 'implied' is 'eventualny', a foreign word defined in the Soviet dictionary of foreign words in the Russian language as 'possible from the circumstances of the case'. The source for the textbook statement is given by the authors as being the minutes of the 1927 session of the Central Executive Committee of the USSR.

The problem was revealed by an order issued by the full bench of the Supreme Court of the U.S.S.R. in 1938.[59] At that time lower courts were informed that when there were indictments for counter-revolutionary activity in the form of undermining the work of State industry, transport, trade, the financial system or the co-operatives, or in the form of destruction of railways or means of communication, or in the form of sabotage, the crime must be proved by direct and not by circumstantial evidence.

The Supreme Court was speaking at the end of 1938 at a time when the economic life of the country had been seriously disrupted by the extension of the purges far beyond what had been anticipated when they were begun in the wake of the 'treason trials' in 1936. The order suggests that courts had been content to accept circumstantial evidence, and that a reversal of policy was necessary to restore order in a situation which appears to have degenerated into hysteria.

THE DANGER IN NEGLIGENCE

While counter-revolutionary intent is not to be ascribed to negligence, some of the lesser penalties are held in store for those who are negligent. The Criminal Code, after indicating that the first persons to be held liable are those who act wilfully, proceeds to indicate a second basis for liability, namely negligence. This is defined as 'failure to foresee the consequences of their conduct, although they should have foreseen them or lightheartedly hoped to avoid such consequences'.[60] A considerable number of judicial decisions clarify the types of negligence which must be eradicated from the social conduct of the new Soviet man.

A lorry driver for a State enterprise paid no attention to a flagman's signal at a railway crossing, but continued across the rails, knocking down the flagman and injuring him so seriously that he soon died. In the trial court the driver was convicted and sentenced to three years and six months' imprisonment, but the Supreme Court ordered a new trial on the ground that the penalty did not correspond to the seriousness of the crime, which had resulted from a serious violation of labour discipline.[61]

59 Order of December 31, 1938, [1939] 2 Sov.Yust. 19.
60 Art. 10 (B).
61 *Case of Sergienko* [1940] 23–24 Sov.Yust. 37.

Another lorry driver killed a six year old girl who appeared unexpectedly before his lorry at a distance of some five to six metres. The evidence disclosed that because of the faulty condition of the lorry's brakes the driver was unable to stop, and the street was so full of children that he could not drive to one side. The trial court convicted him of the offence of wilfully causing serious bodily injury and sentenced him to four years' imprisonment. The Supreme Court of the Turkmen Republic reduced the penalty to three years on the ground that the offence should have been classified under the Article of the code having to do with homicide because of negligence.[62]

Negligence is not always judged on the same basis as it is in western communities, as is indicated by a case in which an interested bystander killed his brother's assailant during a street fight by throwing a stone high into the air. The court convicted the accused of wilful killing, but the Supreme Court of the U.S.S.R. reclassified the offence as the wilful causing of serious bodily injury from which death results and reduced the penalty from the maximum penalty for murder, namely ten years' imprisonment, to five years' imprisonment. In doing so the Supreme Court declared that it is impossible to anticipate that death will result from a stone which is thrown, although the thrower should anticipate the possibility of causing serious bodily injury.[63]

Two bank auditors were absolved of responsibility in failing to identify a forgery on which money was paid out, partly because in the bank routine their audit occurred only after payments were made, but also because no evidence was presented to the effect that auditors had such special knowledge as would have permitted them to detect a forgery.[64] Clearly, negligence is not to be found if custom or bank regulations create no duty to act. In a similar situation a medical orderly was absolved of the charge that he had been negligent in failing to identify a stomach ailment as appendicitis, as the result of which a patient was sent to the hospital for an operation too late to survive. The College for Criminal Cases of the Supreme Court of the U.S.S.R. thought that there was clearly no duty placed upon an orderly

[62] *Case of Gukasov* [1937] 10–11 Sov.Yust. 110.
[63] *Case of Azhoichik* [1939] 1 Sov.Yust. 73.
[64] *Case of Hodareva and Gogiya* [1944] 6 Sud.Prak. SSSR 18.

by medical practice to identify appendicitis when the facts showed that the patient had appeared to react favourably to treatment for simple food poisoning.[65]

The problem of determining the extent to which the citizen is obligated to be his brother's keeper under the new pattern termed by the constitution 'the rules of socialist intercourse' to which all are required to adhere is not easy. A Chief Book-keeper in a State food industry processing station was indicted for negligent attention to his duties as the result of which the enterprise suffered a loss of food valued at 9,082 roubles. The defendant pleaded not guilty on the ground that he had done everything required by law as Chief Book-keeper, and he could do nothing more. He had written the regional office to which the enterprise was responsible, and he had notified the police of the illegal acts he saw. He had warned the clerks and had become so unpopular that all the clerks filed complaints against him as a squabbler and the Director removed him from his post, in which he was later reinstated only on orders from Moscow. He was convicted because he only made reports and did not demand that criminal action be taken against the clerks. The Supreme Court's College for Criminal Cases thought that the trial court had expected too much of the Chief Book-keeper, and that the prosecution should be terminated.[66] Reporting on the thefts was, apparently, all that was required under the circumstances, and the Book-keeper had no responsibility for the proper functioning of the law enforcement agencies.

A Chief Book-keeper who notified the police of illegal price raising, as the result of which the store manager and he himself had appropriated 27,000 roubles, found that his notification was too late to save him. The court found that the Chief Book-keeper had prepared false financial statements and had let the general book-keeping routine fall into such bad condition that the crime became possible. The court found that the report to the police had reduced the Chief Book-keeper's guilt but that it could not reduce his responsibility for executing obviously illegal orders, and the penalty was established at three years' imprisonment.[67]

65 *Case of Tochilov* [1942] 2 Sud.Prak. SSSR 19.
66 *Case of Eliseev* [1944] 6 Sud.Prak. SSSR 17.
67 *Case of Nikolaev* [1939] 5 Sots.Zak. 87.

ATTEMPTS, MISTAKES AND SELF-DEFENCE

Attempts are treated by the Criminal Code as being equivalent to completed crimes in danger, and full penalties are meted out.[68] At the same time the courts seem to appreciate that there is a problem of proof in an attempt. The Supreme Court of the R.S.F.S.R. has said that because of the problem of proof when action has not been completed, penalties should be applied only when preparatory acts have been manifested in a definite concrete form.[69]

The court had no difficulty in convicting a nineteen year old youth who set fire to a hay field, hoping to burn down a collective farm which occupied a farm formerly owned by his family.[70] The fire had been put out quickly by the members of the farm so that no harm resulted, but the act was classified as destruction with counter-revolutionary intent by fire of public property, and the lad was sentenced to five years of hard labour with loss of political and civil rights.

A more difficult problem arises for Soviet courts when a mistake occurs as the result of which a person other than the one against whom an attack is directed is injured. While no judicial decision has been found, a textbook suggests that the matter is complicated when the person against whom the crime was planned was not juridically equal with the one against whom it was committed.[71] Such juridical inequality arises in a case in which a person who is actually killed when assassination of a government official is planned is a simple citizen without official position. It is suggested by the text writer that if a political assassin actually mistakes his adversary and kills another man, the full penalty for counter-revolutionary action may be exacted since there was an attempt at such action, and it was accompanied by an intended killing.

A mistake in the other direction has been the subject of court action. A person having a contract under which he had purchased timber lying in a forest mistook the pile which belonged to a state school for the pile which he had purchased and removed

68 Art. 19.

69 Directive of 1926, published as annotation to Art. 19 in editions of *Criminal Code RSFSR* up to and including that of 1943. The annotation has been removed from the editions of 1950 and 1952.

70 *Case of Shmakov*, No. 2,982 [1931] 8 Sud.Prak. RSFSR 9.

71 *Ugolovnoe Pravo, Obshchaya Chast* [*Criminal Law, General Part*] (1938) p. 281.

it. He was indicted for theft of State property, and the trial court convicted. The College for Criminal Cases set aside the conviction on the ground that there was no intent to commit a crime at all, and, therefore, no basis for indictment for theft of the school's timber.[72]

Rules familiar to all systems of law apply to withhold from punishment those members of the community who are presumed to be incapable of comprehending the gravity of their acts. Thus the insane are subjected to medical measures, and minors are exempt from imprisonment.[73] Soviet conditions seem to have differed from those in many other States, however, for the age at which minors are expected to exercise discretion is now but twelve years. In the discussion of the role of the family, which follows later in this volume, consideration is given to the reasons for this unusually low age of discretion.

Also exempt from punishment are those who commit bodily injury in self-defence, but the rule of the Soviet code and judicial practice is qualified by the familiar requirement that the protective measures which are taken must not exceed what is necessary.[74] Thus, in a series of cases the court had to define the limits on the necessary measures. A man who was attempting to save his nephew from an attack by a rowdy group of boys drew a penknife after he and his nephew had been severely beaten. With the knife he slashed one of his assailants. The Supreme Court's College for Criminal Cases thought the measures of defence taken by the defendant to have been warranted under the circumstances.[75] Yet in a second case a person accused of striking another with a knife after the other one had been disarmed was found to have exceeded the requirements of self-defence. He was thought to have struck in a vengeful mood rather than to protect himself, and he was held responsible for the death which resulted.[76]

A woman's honour was found to require extreme measures of protection even in a case where the circumstances were rather doubtful that honour was in issue. The defendant had seized a poker in a struggle to prevent herself from being raped and had

[72] *Case of Kurtiashvili* [1942] 1 Sud.Prak. SSSR 12.
[73] *Criminal Code RSFSR,* Arts. 11 and 12.
[74] *Ibid.,* Art. 13.
[75] *Case of Larionov* [1929] 7 Sud.Prak. RSFSR 11.
[76] *Case of Selikhov et al.* [1929] 6 Sud.Prak. RSFSR 11.

struck her assailant three times from which he suffered serious injury. The Supreme Court's College for Criminal Cases found this permissible self-defence, although the facts indicated that the woman had been living in the same room with the man for some time, and had refused his invitation to share his bed for the reason that her eldest son was not yet asleep.[77]

Self-defence was not considered a proper plea in a case in which a defendant fired a shot from his window overlooking a court, thinking that the place was being entered by thieves. In fact, only a single man had entered the courtyard to relieve himself on the way home at night, and there was no threat of robbery. The shot struck the visitor, and he died subsequently as a result. The court found that it was not really self-defence at all, as there had been no attack, and that the shooting had been so reckless that the crime was murder of the second category. A retrial was ordered to fix the penalty.[78]

PUNISHMENT BY ANALOGY

Much debate has arisen in recent years over the educational features of the code in light of its preservation of the article permitting prosecution by way of analogy. The article in question[79] permits a judge who finds that an act has been dangerous to society to penalise the person who has been detained by analogising it to the most nearly similar act defined as a crime by the code. The article dates from the earliest Soviet code of 1922 and was said at the time to have been made necessary because it was then impossible to foresee all of the wily moves of the bourgeoisie to unseat the Soviet regime. With the passage of years and the strengthening of the regime the analogy article of the code came to be utilised less and less until a commentary directed that it be resorted to only in the unusual case, and never when the act was described already in the code as a crime.[80] In short it was not to be used to increase a penalty or change the seriousness of an offence from what the code declared it to be to what the court thought it ought to be.

A judicial decision indicating the manner in which the article was to be applied appeared during the war.[81] It involved the

77 *Case of Kosorukova*, No. 2,621 [1929] 1 Sud.Prak. RSFSR 10.
78 *Case of Totrov* [1940] 17–18 Sov.Yust. 32.
79 *Criminal Code RSFSR*, Art. 16.
80 A. Trainin, 'Practical Commentary', [1940] 7 Sov.Yust. 6.
81 *Case of Polezhaeva et al.* [1944] 6 Sud.Prak. SSSR 19.

indictment of some prisoners working upon a farm for falsifying records to conceal the death of lambs under their care. It was argued that the provisions of the criminal code relating to responsible officials could not be applied to prisoners, since they were not such responsible officials by virtue of the fact that they had the status of prisoners. While the court was doubtful of their guilt on the evidence submitted, it had no difficulty in saying that the prisoners might be punished by analogy to the provisions of the code relating to crimes by officials since the criminally negligent relationship to duties would not fall under any other article of the code.

A late wartime article [82] by a prosecutor suggested that under the pressure of war the analogy article was serving a useful purpose because it made it possible to raise the penalty on some acts, such as the manufacture of illegal liquor, when it was not desirable to amend the code. In this suggestion, there seems to have been a complete change in attitude from that prevailing just prior to the war.

After the war an author of prominence in Soviet legal circles revealed that discussions on the revision of the criminal code had led to the rejection of the analogy article for the proposed new code, but that there was no unanimity as to the desirability of such a move.[83] Since this comment there has been no further indication of a restriction upon use of the analogy principle, and it may be that with the mounting tension of recent years, the Soviet leadership again fears that it may not be able to anticipate all of the wiles of the forces ranged against it.

For the purposes of this study of social change, it is worth noting that the objection to the application of the analogy principle on the part of some of the Soviet authors was based on the conclusion that law could hardly serve its educational function in moulding the new Soviet man, if he were not to be informed of the rules he was expected to obey. These people looked upon law in quite the reverse fashion from those of the early 1930's who wished to reduce the criminal code in form to generalisations, leaving to each judge the determination of what acts were

[82] Shargorodsky, 'Questions Concerning the General Section of the Criminal Code under Wartime Conditions' (1945) 76 *Uch. Zap.* (Trudy Yurid. Fak.) p. 100 at p. 104.

[83] Gertsenzon, 'The Paths of Development of the Soviet Science of Criminal Law During the Past Thirty Years', [1947] 11 Sov. Gos. i Pravo 81.

criminal and what penalties would be appropriate. Society was thought to be subject to improvement by law only when its members can study a code of laws and inform themselves in advance of what is permitted and what forbidden. There was no suggestion that the citizen might familiarise himself with the judicial decisions and fill in the definitions omitted by the code.

The attitude that law had primarily a protective function rather than an educational function in the early years may also account for the attention given to the possibilities of reducing a penalty below that provided for by the code if a given defendant seemed to the judge to have lost his social danger. Such an attitude is a recurrent theme of many Supreme Court decisions, framed in accordance with the principles expressed in Article 51 of the Criminal Code. This article authorises a court to reduce a penalty below the minimum provided in the code for the offence if it believes that the more severe penalties are not required under the circumstances. The trial court is required, however, to set forth the reasons for reducing the penalty so that they may be reviewed by the appellate court, if need be.

Cases have indicated that the courts have availed themselves of the authority to reduce sentences below the minimum provided for in the code. A wartime acquittal of a workman who failed to report to work on the ground that it was a holiday was set aside by the Supreme Court because it felt it necessary to uphold the authority of the plant director to order work even on a holiday, but the defendant was released from penalty.[84] It was said that much time had elapsed since the crime was committed, and the circumstances of the case indicated that the defendant did not represent a social danger at the time of the review. The court, therefore, provided a rule for the future to guide other workmen who might be called upon to work on a holiday, but it released the person in whose case the rule had been made because it thought that no danger was to be faced in leaving him at large.

In one reported case[85] the Supreme Court of the U.S.S.R. refused to accept a reduction of penalty ordered by a trial court and affirmed by the Supreme Court of the Georgian Republic. The defendant was a book-keeper on a State farm, accused of

[84] *Case of Musienko* [1944] 3 Sud.Prak. SSSR 5.
[85] *Case of Gibradze* [1940] 21 Sov.Yust. 38.

forging a cheque which he took from the Chief Book-keeper's desk, with which he obtained 18,000 roubles. The trial court convicted and sentenced the accused to six years' imprisonment, with loss of electoral rights for two years, but then reduced the penalty to three years, leaving the provision relating to loss of electoral rights unchanged. The Supreme Court declared that the crime was so serious that it was out of keeping with the social danger involved to reduce the penalty. It felt that there was no reason to show clemency merely because the accused had already returned the 18,000 roubles.

Similar criticism of a sentence as being too mild issued from the Supreme Court of the U.S.S.R. when the Uzbek Republic's Supreme Court accepted a trial court's penalty of only six months instalment fine, amounting to 10 per cent of wages, for a cashier of a State farm who had embezzled 1,088 roubles by means of forging the cashier's records. The Supreme Court of the U.S.S.R. said that such a sentence did not assure continuation of a vigorous struggle with those who were stealing socialist property.[86]

SOCIALISM AND THE INCORRIGIBLE

Attention has been drawn in the west to a 1934 statute, incorporated in the Criminal Code as Article 58^{1c}, as having no relation to the effecting of social change, since it appears to punish persons who have committed no offence. Part of it penalises relatives who aid a member of the armed forces to flee abroad, or who knew of the preparations for flight and failed to notify the authorities. The second part penalises those who were adult members of the family or dependent upon the escaped service man by depriving them of electoral rights and exiling them to remote districts of Siberia for a term of five years even if they knew nothing of the planned flight. Certainly this statute represents a most severe form of threat to the potential deserter. It may cause a potential deserter to think twice before fleeing and in this way create a social attitude of loyalty to the regime, but it is not the kind of loyalty of which Soviet leaders wrote in the early years. It is not based upon appreciation of the value of loyalty and support to the regime for reasons of the success claimed in feeding, clothing, housing and ministering to the cultural wants of the population.

[86] *Case of Mileshkin* [1940] 21 Sov. Yust. 43.

As the years have passed and the Soviet leaders have felt that they have been able to demonstrate in a measure the potentialities of the system they have evolved to meet the needs of the people, there can be found a growing sense of exasperation with those who commit crime. The statute penalising the innocent members of a deserter's family is but the most extreme manifestation of the attitude Soviet writers have begun to take toward those who commit crime. Fourteen years ago Soviet authors began to argue that the thief, the bandit, the embezzler and the counterfeiter were beyond the reach of exhortation and demonstration.[87] Such offenders were no longer to be pitied for their poverty or for their ignorance, for the State had provided the opportunity to escape both.

The castigation of the criminal has gained momentum since the war. Those who are poor or ignorant today are being looked upon as bad citizens, if not enemies of the Soviet system. As such, they are said not to respond to rehabilitation, which was thought the proper approach in earlier years to a criminal population which had not yet shaken off the heritage of the past.[88] They are found to deserve only repressive measures to restrain them from interfering with the lives of those who have found the new way. In consequence, criminal law becomes an instrument with which the leadership may deal with its enemies. In a sense it is no longer an element with which social change may be effected. It has become an element to hold behind the barriers those who would prevent the social change for which the foundations have been laid in property law and in social organisation.

The new role of criminal law is disappointing, apparently, to many of the leaders who had hoped that order would flow from their social and economic system. They seek an explanation for the necessity of establishing the new role for criminal law. They declare that they have found the explanation. In his speech on the eve of the war in 1939 to the communist party congress Stalin expressed the reasons why he believed that the repressive power of the State must be continued even when the economic abundance for which his people had been striving had

[87] Denisov and Merkushev, 'The Draft of the Criminal Code of the RSFSR', [1939] 3 Sov.Yust. 4 and 4 Sov.Yust. 5.

[88] Chkhivadze, 'The Role of the Soviet Court in Overcoming the Relics of Capitalism in the Minds of Men', [1949] 2 Sov. Gos. i Pravo 17.

been achieved, as he seemed to believe would soon be the case. He laid the blame for the preservation of force at the door of capitalist foreign powers.[89] To be sure at that time, there was the threatening shadow of Hitler across his threshold, and few among his listeners could have doubted the need for caution. Yet the war was won, and Hitler defeated. The State remained repressive. Today the explanation is given that there are still foreign powers seeking to undermine the Soviet system by subverting its citizens.[90] Soviet leaders argue that, in consequence, the law must remain severe, and the criminal must be treated as the dupe or agent of the foreign enemy.

89 *Report to the Eighteenth Communist Party Congress,* 1939, Stalin, *Leninism* (English translation, 1942) p. 434 at p. 474.

90 Malenkov, *Report to the Nineteenth Party Congress on the Work of the Central Committee of the CPSU (B)* (1952) pp. 100–101.

On March 27, 1953, the new government which assumed power on Stalin's death decreed an amnesty for certain types of criminals and ordered a re-examination of the Criminal Code with a view to reducing penalties for the less dangerous crimes. Commentators outside the USSR have suggested that the step was taken to gain popular support at a time of threatened domestic unrest rather than to indicate a new attitude toward crime. Sufficient time has not passed to permit of a definite conculsion as to the reasons for the amnesty. For English translation from *Pravda* and *Izvestiya* of March 28, 1953, see 5 *Current Digest of the Soviet Press,* No. 10, p. 3, April 18, 1953.

CHAPTER 5

ASSURING ADHERENCE TO THE DEFINITION

The outline of the new Soviet social structure may be defined by the criminal code and by administrative regulations, but the ship of state may founder if the local official fails in the performance of his duties. Soviet leaders, like all leaders, must look to the performance of their representatives in the village and the city if they are to build firmly for the future. The centre can plan, but the local official executes. It is the policeman, the judge, the prosecutor, the railway conductor, the doctor in the State clinic, and even the store clerk who make friends or enemies for the regime. With nationalisation of the productive resources and of the principal distribution channels, the number of State representatives for whom the leadership bears responsibility in the eyes of the public is even greater in the U.S.S.R. than in countries of the west which still adhere in the main to the private enterprise system.

Soviet leaders do not expect their local officials always to be popular. Their very concept of leadership as disciples of Lenin has lead them to expect opposition. They are moving a population faster than it wishes to go in a direction which only the leadership believes itself competent fully to understand. As realists they know that they cannot antagonise in the introduction of new policies larger elements of the population than their police can control. They must strike a balance between their desire to move quickly and the natural conservatism of their peoples.

Once the balance has been struck, however, the local official must adhere to the decisions which have been taken, or the balance will be upset in the administrative process. The temper of the people, which has been carefully measured in the preparation of a new policy position, may be aroused beyond expectation if the local State officials exceed their authority or fail to exercise the authority which they have been given. This the criminal code recognises in two articles. One provides a penalty of imprisonment for from six months to ten years for the official who abuses the authority of his position, resulting in some definite interference with the proper working of an institution or with some right or interest of some individual citizen which is protected by law.[1] The other penalises with imprisonment not to exceed three years failure to use authority if injury results.[2] Failure to use authority is defined as non-performance by an official of an act which ought to be performed as part of his official duty.

Application of these key articles indicates the manner in which discipline among minor officials is enforced. Two judges in a Provincial Court in the Ukraine failed to notify a prison warden of a reduction in sentence of a prisoner. The Commissar of Justice of the U.S.S.R. ordered the judges to be prosecuted for their dereliction of duty.[3] A trial court judge in the Moscow Province was prosecuted and convicted for his delays and anti-social attitude. Witnesses testified that the local administrative authorities feared the judge and had not supervised his work for years. During a trial, he once snatched the minutes from the court secretary and called him a 'blockhead'. On another occasion he had cursed the woman janitor for failing to heat the court room. He had often asked the lay judges sitting with him on the bench to sign blank sheets of paper, promising to fill in the opinion at a later time. Fifty cases without written opinions were discovered in his office when he was arrested, and some of these were seven months old. The court found him guilty of maintaining a bureaucratic attitude towards his work and of impermissible delays. He was given a conditional sentence of six months' imprisonment and forbidden to hold a responsible position in the Ministries of Justice or Interior for three years.[4]

Delays even within a Supreme Court of a Republic have been the subject of penalties. The Byelorussian Supreme Court was accused of inadmissible delays after receiving from the College for Criminal Cases of the U.S.S.R.'s Supreme Court a petition by a convicted man for review. When no response was received for nine months, the Ministry of Justice of the U.S.S.R. was

[1] *Criminal Code RSFSR*, Art. 109.
[2] *Ibid.*, Art. 111.
[3] Instruction of June 2, 1937, *re Dolgov and Khalaim* [1937] 13 Sov.Yust. 53.
[4] *Case of Trofimov* [1929] 16 Sud.Prak. RSFSR 15.

asked by the U.S.S.R.'s Supreme Court to conduct an investigation and to take measures to speed action. The reply was received from the Ministry of Justice of the Republic, through whom the federal Ministry had sought information, that the Chief Justice of the Republic's Supreme Court had nothing to say. The federal Ministry was angered at this response and ordered a minute examination of the 'post audit' work of the Republic's Supreme Court and directed that those persons who were responsible for the delays be made to account.[5] This meant that prosecution would follow if it were merited by the circumstances. Likewise, the Supreme Court of the Estonian Republic has fallen foul of the disciplinarians. A defendant had been convicted in the city of Narva. Since the defendant filed no appeal, his sentence of three years' imprisonment became final. Through negligence, the trial court sent the file, however, to the Supreme Court of the Republic together with the appeal of another defendant in an entirely different case. The Supreme Court, after hearing the report by the member assigned to examine the case, decided to affirm the sentence. No one noticed that there had been no request for review. The Supreme Court of the U.S.S.R. was so incensed that it ordered the Ministry of Justice of the U.S.S.R. to take appropriate disciplinary action in view of what it termed a 'shocking fact'.[6]

PROSECUTION OF STATE OFFICIALS

Delays on the part of the office of the prosecutor to whom cases are referred for action have also been the subject of prosecution. In one case the Supreme Court of the Tadzhik Republic had reversed and remanded for retrial a decision of a trial court convicting the defendant of failure to complete the cotton sowing plan for a given area. After the reference had lain on the desk of the trial court for four months, the record was finally requested by the District Prosecutor. He held the record for an additional eight months without adequate reason and then returned it to the trial court where it lay for an additional eight months. Both the trial court judges and the District Prosecutor were indicted for the delays which had amounted to over twenty months.[7]

5 [1937] 18 Sov.Yust. 31.
6 *Case of Saratov*, reported in Baksheev, 'Improve the Review of Petitions for Post-Audit in the Supreme Courts of the Republics', [1950] 6 Sots.Zak. 6 at p. 8.
7 [1938] 9 Sov.Yust. 31.

Citizens are protected against loss of the documents on which so much of their welfare depends in the highly controlled and documented society being developed in the U.S.S.R. Thus, the criminal code penalises by confinement up to one year theft, damage, concealment, or destruction of public documents.[8] Those citizens whose future is hampered by wilful action of this character may rely upon this article, while those who find merely that their documents have been lost through the negligent conduct of the affairs of an office can rely upon the general article on dereliction of duty.

Bringing discredit upon authority because of personal misconduct on the part of an official is also made the subject of an article of the criminal code,[9] even when no individual has been injured because of it. In one case it was reported that a judge, a policeman and another law enforcement official had gone to a village to hold an assize. One evening they had a drinking party in the flat to which they had been assigned, and a quarrel occured, during which one threatened the other with a revolver. Later the judge succumbed to the hospitality and fell under the table in a drunken stupor. The hostess of the flat called in some local people who found the intoxicated judge rolling about on the floor. The judge was brought to trial and convicted of bringing discredit upon authority. He was sentenced to six months' forced labour and prohibited from holding a responsible position for two years. Both the Provincial and Supreme Courts of the Republic affirmed the conviction.[10]

Indignities brought upon a party in open court have also been punished. A Murmansk trial court was hearing a suit by a foreman to be reinstated in a job from which he had been dismissed because of a finding of ill health. In the course of the trial the judge called the plaintiff a 'grafter'. The record showed that the plaintiff had worked for six years for a mining enterprise; that he had received three awards for outstanding work, and that he had been issued a Certificate of Merit. When doctors advised the plaintiff that his health had deteriorated so that he could no longer work out of doors with safety, management offered him a job in a supply depot, but he refused it

[8] Art. 78.
[9] Art. 113.
[10] *Case of Doblinin* [1931] 4 Sud.Prak. RSFSR 15.

because he did not want to lose the privileges which attached to the rigorous outside job. During the course of the trial the plaintiff was re-examined and found unfit for outside duty. In dismissing the suit the judge insulted the plaintiff, as has been indicated. When the matter was brought to the attention of the Ministry of Justice of the R.S.F.S.R., it requested the Presiding Justice of the Murmansk Provincial Court to verify the details, and it asked the following rhetorical question: 'Is it necessary to demonstrate to what extent such acts of uncouthness are not permitted, acts which are one of the manifestations of lack of culture, bureaucracy and lack of respect for the dignity of a Soviet citizen in a Soviet court?'[11]

Judges have not, apparently, learned to the extent necessary the rules of behaviour expected of judicial officials, for in 1949 a law dealt with the subject in some detail.[12] In establishing a series of disciplinary penalties for judges who were negligent in their court work, or lacked the discipline required of a judge, or committed acts incompatible with the dignity of a judge, the new law stated the relationship between exemplary conduct and the interests of the regime. It declared 'Soviet judges, elected by the people, must value highly the confidence of the people and be models of honest service to the Motherland, of precise and unwavering execution of Soviet laws, of moral chastity and of irreproachable conduct so that they may have not only the formal right but a moral right as well to judge and to teach others'.

To determine the penalties boards for disciplinary cases were ordered to be organised in the Provincial Courts and in the colleges of the Supreme Court, before which the offending judges were ordered to be brought for a hearing, generally in public. The accused was to be permitted to make his explanation. Jurisdiction of the boards was limited to the issuing of warnings, reprimands and severe reprimands. If more was required because the action was so serious as to be considered a violation of the criminal code, the matter was to be turned over to a prosecutor.

Judicial decisions indicate that not only judges and prosecutors have found themselves prosecuted for improper conduct.

[11] *Case of Kuznetsov* [1937] 6 Sov.Yust. 41.

[12] Law of July 15, 1949, Ved.Verkh.Sov. SSSR, No. 31 (530), August 1, 1948.

A building inspector was convicted in a case at the end of the 1920's of the crime of insulting a dormitory manager. The record on appeal showed that the inspector had called at the factory school to examine a dormitory, and while doing so had entered into a dispute with the manager over the adequacy of some of the repairs which had been projected. As the discussion progressed, the inspector cursed the manager, struck him on the chest and tried to throw a small table at him. The penalty fixed by the court after convicting the inspector of criminal insult was a fine of thirteen roubles, a relatively small amount even before the inflation of later years. The prosecutor protested on the grounds that the offence was discredit upon authority and should have been penalised as such, but the College for Criminal Cases of the Supreme Court of the R.S.F.S.R. rejected the protest, and sustained the action of the trial court.[13]

The Chief of the Administrative Section of a District Executive Committee was prosecuted for bringing discredit upon authority. The evidence showed that he had arrived at a masked ball in an intoxicated condition. When asked to leave, he had raced through the theatre where the ball was being held, committing various indignities, striking the manager and shattering the janitor's office door. The man was a member of the communist party, and was expelled for his action. When the matter reached the court, it felt that his expulsion from the party and dismissal from his employment were sufficient punishment, and so no penalty was set after conviction. The College for Criminal Cases of the Supreme Court of the R.S.F.S.R. in its review of the case remanded it for retrial on the ground that the lower court had been too lenient.[14]

SOCIALISM INCREASES STATE OFFICIALS

Extension of State activity into areas formerly the province of the private entrepreneur has enlarged the area within which the leadership may be discredited by minor officials. As has already been indicated, the delays and inefficiency of a doctor become of concern to the State when he is functioning under the provisions of a national health plan as an employee of the State. Thus, two public health doctors were indicted for 'bureaucratic relation-

[13] *Case of Dortgolts*, No. 22,306 [1929] 6 Sud.Prak. RSFSR 13.
[14] *Case of Gusok*, No. 23,003 [1929] 8 Sud.Prak. RSFSR 12.

ships' in caring for their patients. The case which brought the issue to the fore involved the death of a woman who had applied for admission to a State hospital's maternity ward, but had been refused because the building was being repaired.

The woman had come many miles for medical aid, and when it was refused, she gave birth to her child in the streets and died. At the trial evidence indicated that patients had also been struck on other occasions in order to make them accept the hospital's regimen. On one occasion a 15 year old girl who appeared to have undergone an abortion had been denied aid because she had refused to name the person who had performed the operation. Another woman, whom the receptionist had admitted without the doctor's consent, had been turned out on the street. The trial court had refused even to docket the case for trial because it could not believe the report of the preliminary investigator, which included the evidence indicated. The College for Criminal Cases of the Supreme Court of the R.S.F.S.R., acting upon the protest of the Prosecutor, directed the court to proceed to trial, because a record such as the one prepared by the preliminary investigator required verification in open court.[15]

A suggestion as to the tolerance to be permitted in society at the present stage of development is offered by a case involving the receipt of gifts by a doctor. The doctor was charged in the indictment with the receipt of gifts of farm produce from relatives of patients in the hospital. Although the evidence supported a finding that the gifts had been accepted, there was no evidence supporting a claim that he had solicited the gifts. The trial court convicted the doctor and sentenced him to two years' solitary confinement with confiscation of his property, but the sentence was then reduced after an example had been made of his case. It was argued that the doctor's service in the army during the civil war, and the small value of the gifts, indicating little social danger, justified a reduction in the sentence in this particular case. The case was reviewed by the higher courts and finally reached the College for Criminal Cases of the Supreme Court of the R.S.F.S.R. It set aside the sentence on the ground that the acceptance of unsolicited gifts which had no effect upon the medical care rendered by the doctor did not constitute the offence of accepting bribes, even though the

[15] *Case of Shor,* No. 22,415 [1929] 6 Sud.Prak. RSFSR 12.

acceptance of gifts was not permissible. The penalty was reduced to a public censure.[16]

Bribery is a serious offence under the Criminal Code, both for the official who accepts the bribe[17] and the citizen who tenders it.[18] The code establishes grades of seriousness. Thus, the penalty is set at a period of up to two years' imprisonment for the receipt by an official personally or through an intermediary of a bribe in any form to perform or not to perform an official act in the interests of the person giving the bribe. The penalty is set at from two to ten years and may involve confiscation of property if the bribe was accepted by a 'high' official; by a person with a previous conviction for accepting bribes, or if there was any element of extortion in the transaction. The person giving the bribe, and the person serving as intermediary are subjected to a penalty of up to five years' imprisonment. A clause follows the article to exclude from punishment a person who gave a bribe only as the result of extortion, or who reported the bribe immediately to the prosecuting authorities.

During the period of the New Economic Policy the article was applied even against a government inspector who had demanded a bribe of 1,000 roubles on several occasions of a private business man to permit him to continue in business. The business man had reported the bribes to the G.P.U. The trial court had acquitted the official in somewhat summary fashion, perhaps because it was not sufficiently impressed with the determination of high government policy makers to stamp out bribery during the period of the N.E.P. The Prosecutor protested, but the Provincial Court affirmed the acquittal. Then the Prosecutor went before the College for Criminal Cases of the Supreme Court of the R.S.F.S.R. That court reversed and ordered a new trial.[19] The College found that only half of the witnesses had been heard on the first trial, and further evidence that the trial court had not acted in good faith was indicated by the fact that during the trial the judge had several times warned the accused to tell the truth.

Bribery seems to have dropped almost out of sight of the law enforcing agencies during the middle 1930's, but with the return

[16] *Case of Zvedris,* No. 23,245 [1929] 8 Sud.Prak. RSFSR 13.
[17] Art. 117.
[18] Art. 118.
[19] *Case of Nudelman,* No. 21,037 [1929] 5 Sud.Prak. RSFSR 11.

of serious shortages during the war and the general relaxation in discipline, the offence was reported in increasing numbers by the press. Finally, with the end of the war a campaign was begun to bring the matter under control. On two occasions, in 1946 and 1949, the Plenum of the Supreme Court of the U.S.S.R. issued long orders to the lower courts criticising some of the decisions that had been made and indicating what they should have been. These two instructions indicate the problem which had developed in the relationship between official and citizen, and the extent to which the high officials of the State had become concerned.

POST WAR JUDICIAL EXPERIENCE

The 1946 order[20] arose out of the following case which had been brought to the attention of the members of all of the colleges of the Supreme Court sitting as a Plenum. A railway engine fireman had permitted eleven passengers to ride on the coal tender of his engine from one town to another on February 22, 1946. He had required each of them to give him a bribe, the total of which was 220 roubles. For this action he was convicted and sentenced, but he appealed, claiming that he was not an 'official' within the meaning of the statute. The Military College of the Supreme Court of the U.S.S.R., before whom the appeal went because the railways were still at the time subject to war-time military discipline, held for the defendant and dismissed the charges against him. At this point the Prosecutor General of the U.S.S.R. protested the decision to the Plenum of all of the judges of the Supreme Court.

The Plenum agreed with the Military College that the fireman was not an 'official' within the statutory meaning of the word, and that the article of the criminal code concerning the receipt of bribes by an official was not applicable. Further, the article could not be applied to the fireman by way of analogy because it was specifically limited in its application to officials, and when such a limitation appears in the article itself, it cannot be extended by analogy to other situations.

While accepting the Military College's interpretation of the application of the article, the Plenum was not in agreement with its decision that no crime had been committed. To the

20 Order of November 29, 1946, 3 *Spravochnik po Zak* (1949) p. 419.

Plenum it was evident from the record that there had been a criminal violation of railway discipline, for such a large number of persons riding on the tender constituted a threat to the safety of the run. As such the act was punishable under Article 59^{3c}, as a criminal violation of discipline by a railway worker, in that it endangered the lives of people. Further, the Supreme Court thought that the record supported the conclusion that the engineer, who was a responsible 'official' within the meaning of the statute, could not have failed to know that eleven persons were riding on the tender. Also it was possible that the fireman had given him some of the money to keep quiet. A new trial was necessary to explore these facts, and also to determine whether the assistant engineer had not also been implicated. A general rule to be applied to all cases of this character was extracted from the decision and published as an annotation to the Criminal Code.[21]

The 1949 order[22] was inspired by several cases. One involved bribery of a District housing administration chief in the Smolensk Province who had accepted bribes to make available living space to certain citizens. He had been convicted and sentenced to five years' imprisonment. The Plenum of the Supreme Court thought that this was too short a period in view of the seriousness of the offence. The second case reached the Supreme Court from the Kazakh Republic. It was a conviction of a lawyer for giving 2,000 roubles as a bribe to the preliminary investigator to induce him to drop a prosecution begun against the lawyer's client. The Supreme Court criticised the penalty of only two years' imprisonment and pointed out that it did not take into account that the bribe had been given by a lawyer, who was one of the persons charged with the furtherance of Soviet justice.

The third case to arouse the ire of the Plenum was the conviction of a group of persons for giving bribes to housing administrators to obtain flats. The penalty had been limited to an instalment fine levied on their wages. This seemed too small a penalty to the Plenum. The Plenum also deplored particularly the fact that some officials had given bribes to other

21 *Criminal Code RSFSR* (1950 ed.) p. 201.

22 Order of June 24, 1949, [1949] 8 Sud.Prak. SSSR 1, also 3 *Spravochnik po Zak.* (1949) p. 417.

officials, thinking that this was in the interests of the enterprise to which they had been assigned in that it facilitated the completion of the plan for that enterprise. The Plenum found that some trial courts had considered these circumstances extenuating, and had failed to appreciate how socially dangerous such activity on the part of officials really was. The Plenum noted that it was difficult to determine which officials were sufficiently high in the hierarchy to fall under the second part of the article penalising with longer terms of imprisonment the receipt of bribes by high officials, since there was no indication of the point at which the line should be drawn between responsible officials and those of lesser status. In spite of the difficulty the Plenum thought that trial courts should attempt to distinguish between the levels of authority of various officials.

Return to the giver of the items which had been the subject of the bribe was decried by the Plenum, it being pointed out that the items should always be confiscated. A case in the Gomel Provincial Court was held up as a bad example, in that the court had ordered to be returned to the giver some gold watches which had been the subject of the bribe.

The increasing restlessness of the Supreme Court in the light of continuing crime was evidenced in its order, for it generalised upon what it had found in the individual cases and related it to the problem of effecting social change in the U.S.S.R. It said 'The struggle with capitalist relics in the minds of men is one of the most important tasks in bringing about communist education, since it is one of the necessary conditions for the gradual development from socialism to communism. Bribery is one of the specific survivals of capitalism, with which courts must conduct the most decisive struggle'.

PROTECTION AGAINST SERVICE OFFICIALS

Cheating of customers by clerks in State stores is also a cause of friction. The Criminal Code provides a penalty of imprisonment up to ten years for officials who cheat on weights or measures, or who violate the fixed prices for goods, or who sell low quality goods at the prices established for high quality goods or who conceal prices from the buyers.[23] The article was

[23] Art. 128c.

added to the code only in 1934,[24] after the free trade of the New Economic Policy had been suppressed, leaving the citizen without recourse to the private enterprise remedy of transfer of patronage if clerks in a store give unsuitable service.

Two Tiflis restaurant employees fell foul of the statute by charging customers more than the fixed prices for meals.[25] To conceal their activity, they maintained two sets of books, one showing the fixed prices and one showing the amount they actually charged. Through a misunderstanding of the situation, they were charged with embezzlement of State property and abuse of their official position. The trial court acquitted them of embezzlement since it found that the State had not been deprived of any of its property. The prosecutor protested the acquittal. The College for Criminal Cases of the Supreme Court of the U.S.S.R. agreed that there was no element of embezzlement of State property, but it remanded the case for new trial under the article of the code relating to the crime of fraud upon the customer.

The anger of disgruntled customers can, apparently, give rise to unfounded complaints. The court has had to step in to protect some clerks. Thus, a conviction of a restaurant employee in the Azerbaidjan Republic was set aside by the College for Criminal Cases of the Supreme Court of the U.S.S.R. in 1940 because the facts had not been explored sufficiently. The Supreme Court found that the record failed to show that the defendant had actually received cash from the patrons of the restaurant, or that prices had been raised illegally on the order of the defendant. Moreover, only two of the eighteen witnesses summoned to court had been examined, and these seemed to the court to have been the least credible since they prepared the dinner checks presented to the diners.[26]

An indication of further concern for the clerks appeared in the following year in the form of an order of the Plenum of the Supreme Court of the U.S.S.R. directing the attention of the lower courts to the fact that the article of the code relating to fraud upon the customer was applicable only when the offence had been committed intentionally and not when it was the result

24 Decree of September 10, 1934, [1934] 1 Sob.Uzak. RSFSR, No. 35, item 216.

25 *Case of Geguchadze and Dzhikiya* [1939] 3 Sov.Yust. 70.

26 *Case of Mollaev* [1940] 9 Sots.Zak. 74.

of negligence.[27] A clerk was also sympathetically treated by the College for Criminal Cases of the Supreme Court of the U.S.S.R. in 1950. A buffet manager for a co-operative association of employees of the woodworking industry had been convicted by a trial court in the Leningrad Province for serving short portions to three patrons. The appellate court had affirmed the conviction.

The Prosecutor General of the U.S.S.R. protested the conviction to the Supreme Court of the U.S.S.R., and the latter agreed that the conviction rested upon insufficient evidence. The record showed that the three customers on entry into the buffet had ordered five portions of wine, five portions of herring and some bread. Two glasses had been left on the counter while the customers took the other three and the herring and bread to a table. At that moment a local police inspector entered to check up on the honesty of the clerk. He went to the customers' table and measured out the wine, and weighed the herring and bread. Then he measured the glasses which had been left on the counter. To make the check he used a measuring glass and scales which he had brought with him. He found that the glasses at the table and the herring and bread were all short portions.

The Supreme Court noted that no effort had been made by the trial court to verify the police inspector's measuring glass or scales. Further it was a possibility that the wine in the glasses at the table had been spilled in measuring, or in carrying the glasses to the table, or some may have been consumed. As to the herrings, the shortage was only 3 grammes per portion, and the record showed that the portions had stood on the counter for a week before the purchase had been made. In this week they might have been dehydrated to the extent of 3 grammes. Finally the clerk claimed that only 450 grammes of bread had been ordered and not the 500 grammes which the inspector supposed.

The doubtful circumstances of the inspection coupled with the fact that the clerk had no criminal record led the Supreme Court to conclude that the guilt of the accused had not been proved.[28]

27 Order of May 8, 1941, printed as annotation to *Criminal Code RSFSR* (1950 ed.) p. 205.
28 *Case of Gracheva* [1950] 9 Sots.Zak. 87.

Over zealous performance of the duties of a conductor on the State railways was the subject of prosecution in 1929.[29] A junior conductor had been ordered to carry on a vigorous campaign to clear the cars of persons riding without tickets. In the performance of his duties he found a passenger without a ticket. To set an example which would dissuade others, he ordered the passenger to jump from the platform of the moving train. When the passenger refused, the conductor forcibly ejected him while the train was passing along an embankment. The conductor had taken similar measures with three other passengers.

The trial court convicted the conductor of abuse of authority, and sentenced him to solitary confinement for two years. He appealed on the ground that his active participation in the campaign against those who held no tickets justified the vigorous measures he had taken. His contention was rejected by the College for Criminal Cases of the Supreme Court of the R.S.F.S.R., and the conviction was affirmed. The Supreme Court's College noted that the regulations provided only a fine as the penalty for having no ticket, and the demand that the passenger jump from the moving train amounted to a penalty greatly in excess of that provided by the regulations. In consequence, it was socially dangerous, and justified conviction. Nevertheless, the penalty was reduced to one year's involuntary work subject to a deduction of a fine from wages during that period, but with the proviso that the defendant be denied the right to work on the railway during that one year.

SEX OFFENCES OF OFFICIALS

Sex offences on the part of State managers have also been the concern of the Court. Some cases may indicate the extent to which social unrest has been caused when officials have taken advantage of their positions to force women dependent upon them into sexual relations. An article of the Criminal Code,[30] while enacted in considerable measure to protect women from the private employer of the period of the New Economic Policy, has been applied specifically to the situation of the State official. It provides a penalty of up to five years' imprisonment for forcing a woman into sexual relations if that woman was dependent by virtue of her employment or financially upon the man compelling her submission.

[29] *Case of Dukov,* No. 2,783 [1929] 6 Sud.Prak. RSFSR 10.
[30] Art. 154.

A foreman in a State factory was prosecuted under the Criminal Code for compelling a woman dependent upon him for her job to enter into sexual relations.[31] The foreman, who was a member of the communist party, had promised to promote the woman, and on the day following their relationship the promise had been fulfilled. The woman testified at his trial that she had consented because she had feared that refusal would have led to assignment to inferior work. Substantial reason for such a fear was provided by evidence to the effect that a married employee who had refused to accede to the foreman's request had been dismissed when there had been a subsequent reduction in staff.

No 'coercion' within the meaning of the statute was found by the trial court, and the foreman was acquitted. The court felt that a promise to improve a position was not 'coercion'. The Prosecutor protested the acquittal, and the College for Criminal Cases of the Supreme Court of the R.S.F.S.R. agreed that the interpretation of the article had been erroneous. In its opinion, knowledge and exploitation of a woman's fear of being placed in an inferior position constituted 'coercion', even though no threats had been made explicitly. A retrial was ordered in accordance with the opinion.

A Director of a State theatre in the Crimea was accused of mismanagement and also of following what was called the 'old tradition' of theatre directors, in that he was 'master not only of the actresses' professional services, but also of them as women'. The Criminal College of the Supreme Court of the R.S.F.S.R. affirmed the sentence of one and a half years' confinement, and deprivation of the right to serve in a responsible directing position for two years.[32]

A bizarre case reached the College for Criminal Cases of the R.S.F.S.R. from the Tartar Republic.[33] The defendant was the Chief of the Administrative Department of the local police force. He was charged with breaking into the room of a minor police official during the latter's absence, and of making advances to the latter's wife. The testimony of the wife was to the effect that he had caressed her and had asked her to consent to sexual

31 *Case of Gribov* [1929] 6 Sud.Prak. RSFSR 12.
32 *Case of Chernobler* [1931] 3 Sud.Prak. RSFSR 17.
33 *Case of Listvin*, No. 21,475 [1929] 8 Sud.Prak. RSFSR 14.

relations, saying 'If you do not agree, I shall sack your husband' The woman resisted violently, and the Chief left.

Upon the husband's return the story was told, but he urged his wife to say nothing lest he lose his job. A second attempt was made by the Chief, and the woman then told the Chief's wife, who asked that nothing be said about the advances lest the Chief himself be dismissed. Later the minor official and his wife reported the events to a friend who worked at the G.P.U., and prosecution followed.

The trial court reasoned that the article of the Criminal Code was not applicable because the woman was not herself dependent upon the Chief either financially or for employment. It was thought that threat of dismissal of a husband did not constitute compulsion as to the wife, but was rather a form of psychological influence which made the defendant guilty under the article of the code concerned with rape. This article was applied and the defendant sentenced to two years' imprisonment.

The appellate court was prepared to leave the sentence at two years' imprisonment, but it believed it necessary to place the offence under the special article relating to coercion by a person on whom the woman was dependent rather than under the regular article relating to rape. In the appellate court's view, the approach to the woman through threats against her husband was in effect taking advantage of a woman materially dependent upon the accused, as indicated by the fact that both the woman and her husband were afraid to report the case lest the husband lose his job. The court held that both the husband and the wife were materially dependent upon the Chief. The fact that the defendant had not been successful in his advances did not reduce the offence since an attempt is punishable under Soviet law with the same severity as a completed crime.[34]

ALTERNATIVES TO CONTROL BY PROSECUTION

Examination of the law and practice of the U.S.S.R. indicates that the Soviet leadership relies in considerable measure upon the criminal law to police such of its local officials as feel no social responsibility in the performance of their functions. There is no civil procedure such as the common law writ of mandamus through which a citizen may compel an official to perform a

[34] *Criminal Code RSFSR*, Art. 19.

statutory function, with one exception. That is the exception provided by the code of civil procedure under which a citizen may take his complaint to a single judge and obtain an order requiring performance by the State notary of a statutory obligation.[35] In all other cases the recalcitrant official can be impelled to act only by means of a protest to the official's administrative superior or to the district prosecutor.

Perhaps it is for this reason that Soviet leaders have been at such pains to provide a representative of the central government ready to receive complaints in every district, namely the prosecutor. He has been given constitutional authority over all State officials,[36] and has been removed to the extent possible by statute from any fear of local political pressure. In the words of the constitution, 'The organs of the Prosecutor's Office perform their function independently of any local organs whatsoever, being subordinate solely to the Prosecutor General of the U.S.S.R.'.[37] In the words of the Prosecutor General of the U.S.S.R., spoken to his subordinates in 1948, a prosecutor must be a person of strong ideological and political vigour, high morals, completely honest, well able to appraise events of public life, thoroughly and correctly understanding party policy, relentless in pursuing anti-State and anti-party manifestations, an unselfish servant of the State and of the people, in principle and irreconcilably a defender of the law.[38]

Judging by this description, the men and women upon whom the functioning of the Soviet system rests its heaviest burdens must be the first product of social change if they are to approach the expressed expectations of their leaders.

Continuing complaints in the press from citizens who feel themselves outraged by the local bureaucracy indicate that the battle against the local official is far from being won. The local bureaucrat can be, and often is, a tyrant among those whom he is supposed to serve. Partly to provide an alternative to the complaint to the prosecutor or the administrative superior, Soviet leadership has been developing an approach through social pressure.

35 Arts. 231–234.
36 *Constitution of the USSR*, Art. 113.
37 *Ibid.*, Art. 117.
38 Boldyrev, 'The Political and Moral Character of Those Who Work in the Soviet Prosecutor's Office', [1950] 7 Sots.Zak. 1 at p. 4.

The system of public complaint called 'criticism and self-criticism' has been developed with increasing vigour since Andrei Zhdanov praised it in 1947 as the new dialectic, the new process of social change, which he believed to have replaced the class struggle as the motivating force of Soviet social development.[39] As has been disclosed earlier in this study, the campaigns of criticism and self-criticism have had a very practical value for the Soviet leaders at the top of the political and administrative hierarchy. They serve as the ears of the leadership among their subordinates. It is now apparent that the leadership relies upon such criticism from below to ferret out the bureaucrat who fails to perform his duties properly. It may even be that some of the leaders really believe, as some have said, that in such criticism the way is being prepared for a system of social controls to succeed the current legal restraints on malfeasance in office, so that the State may ultimately wither away. If that ever occurs, as often seems unlikely, social pressures will have replaced the repressive force of the prosecutor, the police and the Court.

It is, however, still the brave man who will arise in a public meeting or write a letter to the newspaper to criticise substantial shortcomings of those on whom he is dependent.[40] The secret complaint to the prosecutor or the administrative superior seems still to be preferred, if the cases which have been reviewed in this chapter may be accepted as representative. The aggrieved citizen still prefers to look to the complaint box and the call at the private office as his way of appealing against the slothfulness, the incivility, or even the tyranny of the local official rather than to public denunciation designed to arouse social pressures as an instrument of social change.

The path provided by the law seems likely to remain in Soviet society for a long time, as the route through which policy makers discover the shortcomings of their inferiors. Through the institutions of repression which they have created they can take the steps necessary to assure the correction of shortcomings before they imperil retention of power.

[39] Zhdanov, *Vystuplenie na Diskussii po Knige G. F. Aleksandrova 'Istoriya Zapadnoevropeiskoi Filosofii'* [*A Contribution to the Discussion of G. F. Alexandrov's 'History of Western European Philosophy'*] (1947) p. 40. Also published in [1947] 1 *Voprosy Filosofii* 5–501.

[40] See what happened to the school teacher who wrote a letter of complaint to *Pravda*, discussed below in Chap. 7, p. 182.

CHAPTER 6

STRIVING FOR COMMUNITY

THE communal organisation of society is the primary aim of those establishing the pattern of social change in the U.S.S.R. One hears often the Marxist scripture, taken from his *German Ideology,* 'Only in the collective can the individual find the means of giving him the opportunity to develop his inclinations in all directions; in consequence, personal freedom is possible only in the collective'.[1]

Stalin wrote in 1906 in his relatively unknown native Georgian on the importance of the mass in relation to the individual. In comparing the Marxist doctrines with those of the anarchists, Stalin said, 'In the opinion of the anarchists, the liberation of the mass is impossible until the individual has been freed. Hence, their slogan, "Everything for the individual". The keystone of Marxism is the *mass,* whose liberation, in its opinion, is the basic prerequisite for the liberation of the individual. . . . Hence, its slogan, "Everything for the mass"'.[2]

Some astute students of the Soviet regime have claimed that the Soviet leadership has fostered the community for reasons other than those given.[3] It is suggested that history has shown that it is easier to retain power in a society in which individuals are lost in the community and have no opportunity to strike out on their own in new directions than it is in a society where the tradition is one of rugged individualism in economic, political and social organisation generally. To these critics the answer the Soviet leadership seems to give is that the proof of the pudding will be in the eating, and literally so. They state that they cannot reduce controls until production has become ample to meet the needs of all, but that at such a time, which they feel to be not far off, the temporary character of present severity will be demonstrated by a relaxation of those controls which have forced individuals into communal patterns.[4] Meanwhile, the

[1] Karl Marx, 4 *Sochineniya* [*Collected Works*] (1933) p. 65.
[2] Stalin, 'Anarchism or Socialism', 1 *Sochineniya* [*Collected Works*] (1946) pp. 295–296.
[3] Chamberlin, *Collectivism a False Utopia* (1938).
[4] *Interview between J. Stalin and Roy Howard* (1936) pp. 12–13.

sole way of increasing production is said to be through State ownership, community organisation and communal effort.

Time will tell whether the critics or the Soviet spokesmen are right. Meanwhile the unquestionable emphasis is upon community, whether it be to facilitate governing to satisfy the selfish ambitions of the leadership, or to improve the lot of the citizen. Law reflects the communal emphasis, particularly as it relates to the use of the land and to the community to which the use of the land is assigned. Fostering of communal organisations has been manifested as a task which the Soviet leadership considers paramount in creating the social changes they desire.

The work of the Soviet legal draftsman in establishing the community desired in the agrarian field has been both aided and hampered by Russia's past. The Slavic elements of the population, *i.e.*, the Great Russians, the Ukrainians and the Byelorussians, as well as some of the non-Slavic minority peoples who lived in the Russian Empire, had lived for centuries as serfs before their liberation in 1861 by Alexander II. Even after the liberation, the peasants were bound together in village communities by virtue of the communal obligation created by the liberation laws to assure payment of the value of the land taken from the estates for peasant use.[5]

The tradition of the communal tilling of the soil is to be contrasted, however, with the individual resourcefulness to which eminent Russian historians, such as Kluchevsky, ascribe the survival of the Russian people against all invaders from the days of life in the great forests of the Eurasian plain.[6] It was an individuality fostered especially in the latter days of the Empire by a mounting desire for a plot of land to be held as one's very own, a desire which was encouraged by Stolypin shortly before the revolution in an effort to create a small class of prosperous independent peasants as a bulwark against revolution. Yet this desire to own one's own land was, in the main, thwarted, even by the well-meaning Provisional Government of Kerensky, which delayed to await proper organisation and ultimately fell, partly because of that delay.[7]

5 Pares, *A History of Russia* (1941) pp. 353–354.
6 Kluchevsky, 1 *A History of Russia* (English translation, 1911) p. 220.
7 Kerensky has spoken to this effect in lectures before the students of the Russian Institute of Columbia University.

Soviet policy makers have taken both the communal tradition and the desire for the private farm into consideration as they have directed the drafting of new legislation for the agricultural communities. They have attempted to strike a balance which will pacify the urge for a plot of land to develop as one wills, and yet mould the peasant masses into the community structure prized by the Soviet leaders.

THE USE OF THE LAND

The principal asset of the predominantly agricultural country of revolutionary Russia was the land. Under the doctrine of State ownership, already discussed, this land was made the property of the State, and its use was transferred to the whole toiling population, as represented by the local agencies of government, the local soviets. Although peasant resistance, exerted through the left elements of the Socialist Revolutionary Party, required the Bolsheviks to proceed gradually with the nationalisation process, it was completed within little more than three months after the seizure of power from the Provisional Government. The land decree of February 19, 1918,[8] set forth the major principles to govern the use of the land which was now the property of the people.

In setting up the pattern of use, the February decree followed the outlines of an administrative order of a few days earlier issuing from the Commissariat of Agriculture.[9] At the very start it was indicated that emphasis was to be placed upon the community, in accordance with the Bolshevik's plan for the future. Priority in the distribution of use was to be given to agricultural communes and collective groups. At the time three types of communal operation were envisaged, the commune, the agricultural *artel* built upon the structure of the co-operative associations of Tsarist Russia, and a less closely knit association for the pooling of work but not of property.

The commune was to be an experiment in the type of organisation envisaged for the future by those who dreamed of pure communism. Within it, the members were to own everything communally, the agricultural implements, the livestock, even their homes and barnyard animals and fowl. The agricul-

[8] [1918] 1 Sob.Uzak. RSFSR, No. 25, item 346.

[9] Izv. Sovetov Rab., Sold., i Krest. Deputatov g. Moskvy i Moskovskoi Obl'asti, January 30, 1918, No. 22.

tural *artel* was a continuation of an association which had been popular in the Empire because it made possible the purchase of mechanised agricultural equipment and production aids not available to the relatively poor individual. Within its structure the expensive implements were collectively owned, but the peasant families retained private ownership of their dwellings, their livestock and their barnyard animals and fowl. The third type of association, called the Toz, was designed to attract the most suspicious peasants who might be induced to work together but who seemed to fear any pooling of property. The two less communalised types were thought to provide the proper amount of community organisation to attract the peasants who were prepared to accept a measure of communal organisation, but who were not prepared in all instances to move immediately into complete community participation on the basis of the commune.

A fourth form of land operation was also organised to accept the use of land which had been farmed previously with specialised crops by the pre-revolutionary owners. This type of enterprise was the State farm, or sovkhoz. Under the February, 1918, decree orchards, nurseries, seed gardens, market gardens, experimental fields, agricultural experimental stations and state farms were to be transferred to such organisations to be operated as a business enterprise by a staff of experts employing labourers on a wage basis. This form of operation was in some measure like that of a factory, for the agrarian employees were in effect workmen in a farm factory, and the State enterprise operating the business took all the profits.

For those who were not prepared to accept employment in the State farms or to become members of one of the three types of co-operative associations, land was to be distributed by families, in accordance with the ancient Russian tradition that it was the family which was the responsible agrarian unit and not the individual. Distribution was to be by counties in accordance with norms established on the basis of the number of able-bodied persons in each family. No hired labour, past or anticipated, was to be taken into consideration. Sharp variations in the amount of land assigned to each household for use occurred from county to county because of the variation in population density, it being especially dense within the European parts of the country.

Orderly distribution in accordance with any plan seems to have been impossible, in spite of attempts made by a Statute on Socialist Land Status, published on February 14, 1919,[10] nearly a year after nationalisation. There was also an instruction to fill in details, published on March 11 of the same year.[11] These two documents sought to equalise allotments within each county, but the law is said to have been flouted. Finally a Land Code was adopted in 1922[12] at the time of general codification of all Soviet law with the introduction of the New Economic Policy. It accepted the state of things that existed and sanctioned any distribution which had taken place and guaranteed perpetual use of all land to those factually working it at the time of the new Code.

Since relatively few of the peasants had accepted the inducement to enter the communes or even the less closely knit types of co-operative associations, the Land Code of 1922 became the basic law for agricultural lands tilled by the peasantry. It did not relate to the use of land by State farms or by railroads or industries who were using the land. For these users there were negotiated contracts executed by the local State organs, the soviets, to which the rules of the Civil Code on contract law applied and not those of the Land Code.[13] A lessee under these contracts occupied from period to period and paid rent as stated in the contract, which could be terminated only if the land were used for a purpose other than that set in the contract or because of general misuse of privileges.

USE COMPARED WITH OWNERSHIP

The right to use land was clearly distinguished in law from outright ownership. It was certainly not the fee simple of the common law, or even an indeterminate estate of lesser character. Title to the land was reiterated by the Land Code to be in the State. The right to use this land, as conferred on a peasant household or a single peasant who had no household, could not be alienated. If any such transfer was attempted, it was forfeited.[14]

10 [1919] 1 Sob.Uzak. RSFSR, No. 4, item 43.
11 *Ibid.*, Nos. 39–40, item 384.
12 [1922] 1 Sob.Uzak. RSFSR, No. 68, item 901.
13 Decree of March 5, 1929, [1929] 1 Sob.Uzak. RSFSR, No. 21, item 248, superseded by decree of August 1, 1932, [1932] 1 Sob.Uzak. RSFSR, No. 66, item 295.
14 *Land Code RSFSR*, Art. 27.

A case indicates the operation of this principle.[15] One Zelensky sold one Soosar on April 1, 1924, a farm building for 1,100 poods of rye. The purchaser paid only 578 poods of rye within the time set, and the seller sued for the balance. The trial court reached the conclusion that the 578 poods already paid constituted value for the building, and that the balance claimed by the seller represented in fact a claim for the value of the land and the woods upon it. The trial court took into consideration Article 27 of the Land Code to the effect that the land and forests may not be the subject of a contract of sale, and held for the defendant. The College for Civil Cases of the Supreme Court of the R.S.F.S.R. reviewed the decision and the affirmation of the Provincial Court and decided that even the sale of the farm building should be set aside under the circumstances, because it had not been registered with the executive committee of the county soviet as required by the Civil Code. The case was remanded for new trial to arrange for the return to the State of the use of the land which Zelensky had attempted to alienate and also to determine the consequences of the failure to record the sale of the building.

If land which had been assigned to a family for use was not, in fact, used, it reverted to the State for reassignment while the value of the structures upon the land was to be paid to those who owned them.[16] There was to be no compensation for the loss of the use of the land. An exception was permitted to this rule, that land must be used to be retained, in those instances when failure to use was the result of temporary incapacity.[17] In this event the temporary alienation was to be effected under a contract executed by the principal user and his lessee.

Considerations involved in the assignment of use because of temporary incapacity to till the land were indicated in a case arising out of claim for services performed in managing a peasant farm by a grandson of a man and wife exiled for two years to the Irkutsk Province of Siberia.[18] When the couple returned from exile in 1927, the farm was restored to them, but their

15 *Zelensky* v. *Soosar,* No. 31,905, May 25, 1926, 2 Opr. GKK Verkh. Suda RSFSR za 1926 g. (1927) p. 36.

16 *Land Code RSFSR,* Art. 23, as interpreted, see Rozenblum, *Zemskoe Pravo RSFSR* [*Land Law of the RSFSR*] (2nd ed. 1928) p. 131.

17 *Land Code RSFSR,* Art. 28.

18 *Grigorii Timofeev* v. *Mikhail and Anastasiya Timofeev,* No. 362 [1929] 8 Sud.Prak. RSFSR 9.

grandson was apparently displeased at not having been recompensed for his time, and he sued for 648 roubles as the value of his services rendered in managing and protecting the farm. The trial court held for the grandson but not in the full amount claimed. It gave judgment for 240 roubles as the value of the plaintiff's time at 10 roubles a month. It also took into consideration that the care of the grandparents' farm had overloaded the young man with responsibilities to such an extent that he had been forced to let his own farm run down. When the case was appealed, the Provincial Court set aside the judgment, on the ground that it was a case of guardianship for which no payment was required.

On review, the College for Civil Cases of the Supreme Court of the R.S.F.S.R. held that it was not a case of guardianship but of simple transfer for protection and management during a period of exile, and the grandson had the right to demand compensation. The trial court's judgment was restored to force.

No problem of inheritance arises in connection with the use of land by peasant families, since the assignment runs to the entire peasant household rather than to any individual member. Thus, when the head of the family dies, the remaining members elect a new representative. The land remains, therefore, as a unit under the control of the family community, after the death of any individual member, even if that member has been the family patriarch. Division of the use is permitted if a son wishes to set up his own family, or if girls leave the family on marriage.[19] Such division has to be registered in the county soviet's office for land registry, and if a dispute arises as to the terms of the division, the county soviet's land registry is required to decide whether the division should be permitted.[20]

Servitudes were permitted by the code for the benefit of those who required them to enjoy the use of their own land.[21] Thus a right of way or the right to use well water might be registered as accompanying the right to use the land, but no easement could be acquired by prescription.[22] Only those were permitted which

[19] *Land Code RSFSR,* Art. 75.
[20] *Ibid.,* Art. 80.
[21] *Ibid.,* Art. 194.
[22] Explanation of June 29, 1925, of the Supreme Court RSFSR to Art. 59 of the *Civil Code RSFSR,* Sbornik Raz. Verkh. Suda RSFSR (1935) p. 45.

arose by virtue of necessity. Long uncontested use might serve as proof of necessity, however.[23]

To make a record of the right to use and any easements or servitudes which might attach to it, the law required the issuing by the local soviet's land department of a document bearing a solemn dclaration of the right to use in perpetuity.[24] It bore the title '*Zakon*', which meant simply 'a law'. The document constituted, in effect, a deed of use, subject to such laws controlling the use as the State might enact. If a member of a family to whom the use had been assigned found it necessary to leave his home temporarily, the right to use his portion was reserved for the group under the act for varying lengths of time, depending upon the reason for his departure.[25] Thus, if he left to enter military service, the plot of land representing his share of the family's allotment was reserved for the full period of service. If he left to enter industry, the share of the person departing was to be retained by the family for two rotations of crops, or in the event that no rotation of crops was observed, for a period of six years. If he left to enter an educational institution, the share was preserved for the family's use during the full period of attendance at the educational institution.

If an entire family died out or ceased entirely to carry on agriculture or moved permanently to another place, or if a court deprived a person of the right to use land because of some crime committed by him, the land reverted to the State for reassignment by the local soviet's land department.

The right to use conveyed the right to erect structures, and to plant such crops as were thought by the peasant household to be suitable.[26] The peasant household had to take into consideration the interests of the community and was, therefore, forbidden to use the land in a fashion which was deemed wasteful in the eyes of the State's representatives. Burden of proof before a court was upon the State's representatives, for there was a presumption that the household was operating within its rights. Use of the land might also be protested by neighbours who were of the opinion that it constituted a nuisance.[27] The neighbour's

23 *Land Code RSFSR*, Arts. 191, 194 and 207.
24 *Ibid.*, Arts. 143 and 204.
25 *Ibid.*, Arts. 17 and 18.
26 *Ibid.*, Arts. 24 and 58.
27 Ivanitsky, *Zemelnyi Kodeks RSFSR* [*Land Code RSFSR*] (2nd ed. 1926) p. 65.

remedy was to sue in court to abate the nuisance, and to remove the tenant if he failed to obey the court order.

If any assignee of the right to use found that his use was being interfered with or challenged by another, he could bring a 'possessor's suit' before the land department of the local soviet.[28] This latter was required without examining the motives of the person violating peaceful possession, to order return to the *status quo ante,* even though the trespasser might have entered into possession by force of arms, and it might order payment of any damages suffered by the person disturbed. The same form of action might be availed of to establish the right of peaceful use of buildings upon the land.

MOVING TOWARD COMPLETE COLLECTIVISATION

To judge by the record the legal arrangements for the benefit of the peasant households who desired to remain outside the communal groups such as the agricultural *artels* and the communes were sufficiently satisfactory to encourage them to ignore the continuing government propaganda campaign in favour of collectivisation. Although the peasant household found itself denied the right to enjoy the various rights normally associated with 'ownership' in the common law of England, in that they could not sell the use nor could they act with nearly complete lack of attention to the community, their right to perpetual use was sufficiently free to permit them to enjoy the fruits of their labour.

The statistics on grain production for the year 1927 were said by Stalin in a report upon the situation some years later to have shown that only 1.7 per cent of the total grain crop of the country was being harvested by the agricultural *artels* and the State farms.[29] The communes were so unsuccessful in attracting the peasantry that by 1929 there were only 3,500 in comparison with 19,200 *artels* and 34,300 of the TOZ.[30] The principal grain producer of the new Russia was not yet the community, as the leadership had hoped it would become, but the private family operating on a basis which was comparable to that to be

28 *Land Code RSFSR,* Art. 26.

29 Stalin, 'On the Grain Front', 2 *Leninism* (English translation, 1933) p. 14.

30 Schlesinger, 'Some Problems of Present Kolkhoz Organisation' (1951) 2 *Soviet Studies* 325 at p. 326.

found in a country such as Bulgaria. It was certainly not distinctive of socialism in any of the definitions of the term. The policy of the State had been successful in a measure in that it had persuaded the peasantry to begin producing again under the conditions of the New Economic Policy, but the form which had been popular was not the one on which the leaders wished to rely for the long term.

The leadership was still determined to introduce into the villages the communal forms of land cultivation, however. Stern measures were soon to be placed on the statute books to change the complexion of the country-side, and vigorous activity was soon to begin in the ranks of the communist party to impress upon all the desirability of a change.

The priority to be granted to communal use of the land was repeated in a statute entitled General Basis for Land Use, published on December 15, 1928.[31] While the right of every citizen without regard to sex, religion or nationality, as well as of foreigners living within the U.S.S.R to receive land for the purpose of agriculture was reaffirmed, it was stated, as it had been in the 1922 Land Code, that priority was to be given to agricultural collectives and to the poor and middle peasants who had no land or very little land to use. The preference was extended also to the quality and location of the land.

In 1930 two major steps were taken in the field of legislation. A decree[32] established a new model charter for the agricultural *artel*, now to be known everywhere as the 'collective farm', and another decree[33] ordered the liquidation of the wealthier elements of the peasantry, known as the '*kulaks*' as a class. The latter of the two decrees inspired immediate headlines in the press of the world. It meant that individuals, regardless of what their own personal conduct might have been, were to be removed forcibly from their farms and sent to remote regions in Siberia for periods of years to work in the forests, the mines and on other work projects operated by the State police, the G.P.U.[34] While local soviet authorities determined which persons were

[31] [1928] 1 Sob.Zak. SSSR, No. 69, item 642.
[32] Decree of March 1, 1930, [1930] 1 Sob.Zak. SSSR, No. 24, item 255.
[33] Decree of February 2, 1930, [1930] 1 Sob.Zak. SSSR, No. 9, item 105.
[34] The number of exiled *kulaks* together with their families is reported as having reached 5,859,000 persons by 1928. See Dallin, *The Real Soviet Russia* (1944) p. 170.

sufficiently wealthy to be classed as '*kulaks*' for the purpose of exile, the State police was given the task of conducting the transportation of these people and the creation of labour colonies in which they were to work. It was also later given the function of certifying them as good citizens and releasing them to become free labour.[35]

At the time that the *kulaks* were being exiled vigorous campaigns were inaugurated in all of the villages to persuade the remaining peasants to enter collective farms and to force them into the farms if they refused to enter. Within forty days before March 1, 1930, nearly 10,000,000 households joined collective farms.[36] Although the policy announced at headquarters in Moscow always declared that persuasion and not compulsion was to be the weapon of the organiser, there was frequent recognition in later years that many local officials had exceeded their authority and had not been withdrawn. Even Stalin declared just after the first rush of applications that many officials had forced peasants to apply for admission.[37] The reaction of the peasants to the pressure was to slaughter cattle in excess of those required for personal consumption and to destroy, hide or refuse to produce grain.[38] At this time severe famines occurred in some of the regions of the country, and the government took only inadequate measures to deal with them. Some foreign authors have charged the government not only with welcoming these famines but even with planning them so as to attempt to associate in the peasant mind hunger and refusal to join the co-operative movement.[39]

THE COLLECTIVE FARM CHARTER

The model charter of the collective farm superseded the old law on the agricultural *artel,* as it had existed from Tsarist times in the Civil Code of the Empire.[40] One who knows the structure of the co-operatives throughout Europe will find much that is familiar in the new charter. In principle, the co-operative is a free association of members combining for the purpose of con-

35 Decree of May 27, 1934, [1934] 1 Sob.Zak. SSSR, No. 33, item 257.
36 Baykov, *The Development of the Soviet Economic System* (1947) p. 196.
37 Stalin, 'Dizzy with Success', 2 *Leninism* (English translation, 1933) p. 215.
38 Baykov, *The Development of the Soviet Economic System* (1947) pp. 200–201.
39 Chamberlin, *Russia's Iron Age* (1935).
40 *Svod Zakonov Rossiiskoi Imperii,* Vol. 10, Art. 2198 *et seq.*

ducting agriculture and sharing its profits. In its details the charter showed the peculiar characteristics adopted to achieve the political aims of the Soviet leadership. Thus, membership was open to persons who had reached the age of 16, if elected by the organising committee, or by the general meeting of members after the co-operative came into existence. Certain groups of persons were excluded. These categories were *kulaks*; all persons deprived of electoral rights under the provisions of the constitutions of the various Republics (excepting children of *kulaks* who had been found to have worked well in activities deemed useful to society for a period of years, and former *kulaks* who had worked honestly at their period of exile for a period of three years in a manner indicating that they had been reformed—such persons could carry a certificate from the State police to this effect when they were released); and peasants who had slaughtered their cattle and disposed of their seed grain to thwart the efforts directed toward collectivisation. Some control was maintained over the general meeting, for nominations had to be made to it by the administration of the association. In this way, the general meeting could influence admissions only if it refused to re-elect the administration.

No detailed provisions for expulsion appeared in the charter until an amendment of 1935[41] which enlarged the charter considerably, while retaining the pattern of the 1930 charter. When the expulsion procedure was established, it provided that expulsion could be accomplished by the general meeting, but only if two-thirds of the members were present. Further the general meeting had to state in its minutes the number present and the number voting for exclusion. Appeal from the decision of the general meeting was made to lie to the Executive Committee of the District Soviet, which was empowered to reach a final decision but only in the presence of the appellant and the president of the collective farm.

An appeal against expulsion from a similar type of co-operative association reached the courts in 1940.[42] A woman belonging to one of the co-operative associations maintained for invalids so that they might work profitably at artisan's crafts was expelled in Kazan. She brought suit in court for reinstatement on the

41 Law of February 17, 1935, [1935] 1 Sob.Uzak. SSSR, No. 11, item 82.
42 *Antonova* v. *Kazintorg* [1940] 16 Sov.Yust. 45.

ground that her expulsion had been illegal. The trial court held for the co-operative association in that it found no illegality. On her appeal to the Supreme Court of the Tartar Autonomous Soviet Socialist Republic, the case was dismissed on the ground that a court had no jurisdiction over expulsion from the co-operatives.

The Supreme Court of the R.S.F.S.R. affirmed, and the matter was brought on the protest of the Prosecutor General to the Supreme Court of the U.S.S.R. It agreed with the Supreme Courts of the Tartar and Russian Republics and dismissed the suit, saying that under the model charter for the invalid co-operatives the expulsion of a member was the province of the general meeting. There was an appeal only to a grievance committee in the central agency of all of the invalid co-operatives, with a post-audit in the department of social insurance. The Supreme Court declared that when the charter established such a procedure, omitting the courts there was no jurisdiction in the courts to hear expulsion cases.

Administration of the affairs of the co-operative association was placed, as is always the case with co-operatives in any country, in the hands of a few persons. Under the Soviet model charter these are the President, the Board of Directors or 'administration' and an auditing commission, all of which are elected for two year terms by the general meeting. The auditing commission has to be approved by the Executive Committee of the District Soviet, but there is no statutory requirement of approval of the others.

Emphasis must be placed upon the fact that there is no *statutory* requirement of approval of the President, for there grew up a practice during the early 1930's of intervention in elections by central authorities, either by the communist party or by State officials of the Ministry of Agriculture (after it was given direct supervision over the collective farms in 1932).[43] In deciding in favour of this intervention the Soviet leadership took, apparently, a difficult decision. Stalin stated the problem in 1933.[44] On the

[43] Decree of October 1, 1932, [1932] 1 Sob.Zak. SSSR, No. 71, item 435, s. 2. While not mentioned specifically in the decree, the Central League of Collective Farms was also liquidated at the same time. See All-Union Institute of Juridical Sciences, *Kolkhoznoe Pravo* [*Collective Farm Law*] (1940) p. 95.

[44] Report to January Plenum of Central Committee of the Communist Party, Stalin, 13 *Sochineniya* [*Collected Works*] (1951) p. 161 at p. 195.

one hand he emphasised that it was the purpose of the co-operatives to shift the peasant on to the rails of a collective economy through a co-operative procedure by means of conviction as to the advantages of social, collective economy over the individual peasant economy. On the other hand Stalin made it clear that he felt it to be the government's duty to see to it that the co-operatives were organised and run on a profitable basis. The whole community had an interest in the proper functioning of such important sources of the food of the nation. Stalin thought it was not enough to demand that a co-operative be operated profitably; it was the duty of the government to insure that the co-operative had good leadership, and was aided in establishing itself on a firm economic foundation.

The election of persons from outside the membership of the co-operative farm to fill the position of President has been a very common development especially in the 1930's. General meetings of members took the suggestion of the State officials without complaint and went through the motions of voting the designated person into office. Evidence of such a practice is provided in a criminal prosecution of a president of a collective farm for negligent fulfilment of his duties.[45] When the Supreme Court of the U.S.S.R. reviewed the record of conviction of the President, it found that for ten years prior to his election as President of the collective farm he had been a workman in a factory and had had no practical experience in the agricultural work of a collective farm. The Supreme Court's College for Criminal Cases set aside the conviction because it felt that the man could not have been expected to guide the collective farm well, particularly since he had taken it over from his predecessor in a state of complete disorganisation and since he had been given no aid whatever in learning his new duties.

The case indicates that the local leadership must have been exasperated with the breakdown of the farm economy. They had introduced to the peasants a city man who had an excellent factory record for leadership but who had never worked on a collective farm in his life. The peasants accepted him as their President, and it is not hard to imagine that they would not have done so without some pressure. Events proved that the local leaders, whether party or Ministry of Agricultural officials, had

[45] *Case of Ermakov* [1939] 5 Sov.Yust. 75.

made a mistake in their choice, and prosecution had followed. Perhaps prosecution had been instigated to transfer the responsibility for the ill-advised choice from the shoulders of those who had made it on to the back of the unfortunate man who had been required to take over the post of President so that the angry peasants would not blame those who had really been at fault.

Perhaps in an effort to prevent misguidance by an unskilled President, or perhaps because the good-will of the peasants cannot be retained unless they have some veto over the administration, the model charter for the collective farm provides that the decisions on matters of the annual plan for sowing, as to the budget for the farm, as to the building of new structures, as to the evaluation of work within the farm and the rate of distribution of profits, as to the disciplinary rules and the contract between the farm and the depot operating the agricultural machines (the Machine Tractor Station) have no effect until confirmed by the general meeting.[46] In other words, the administration is not permitted under the law to put a decision into effect and then to seek the approval of the general meeting, perhaps after the decision is irrevocable in its effect because of what has been done under it. Such a practice is permitted in the governmental apparatus of the soviets, in which the executive takes the steps it believes necessary and seeks ratification of the steps later at one of the relatively infrequent meetings of the full soviet.

The President is required by the model charter to convene the general meeting not less often than twice a month. Voting is by a show of hands, which permits the President to determine those who are not with him in the decisions he is proposing, or in approving his election for a new term. A simple majority vote is required for approval of all matters except the election of the President and the Board of Directors, expulsion from membership, and the sum to be credited to the various accounts of the farm for capital construction and operating expenses. For these matters a two-thirds majority is required.

USE AND MISUSE OF LAND

The manner in which the collective farm is to obtain the use of land was defined in the model charter of 1930, followed by a

[46] 1935 Charter, Art. 20.

general law on the collective structure of agriculture, adopted in 1931.[47] The amended form of the model charter, adopted in 1935, incorporated the same principles and they remain the rule at the present time. Those entering the farm release their right to use the plots which had been assigned to them as individual households, and a new assignment is made to the association of the use of all of the plots contributed by the members. Boundaries between the former individual family plots are removed, and if it is found that there are important intervening plots of land still retained by peasant households who have not joined the association, these are acquired by State organs in exchange for other land on the periphera. The new communal land is then described in surveyor's terms and new boundary markers are set out. Finally a document is issued by the Executive Committee of the local soviet to the collective farm, describing the land to which the use is being assigned, and declaring that the use is to be in perpetuity. This document is called an 'Act', and it is prepared in formal manner and bound in folio size red gold-lettered covers over a foot and a half in height to give it an appearance inviting respect. A registry is maintained by each issuing authority in accordance with a form established by administrative order.[48]

No part of the land assigned to the collective farm may be alienated by it, nor may the use be transferred even for a brief period.[49] To this there was a war-time exception permitting a cattle co-operative associations to transfer the use to an agricultural collective farm of any land which because of the temporary absence of its members at the front it was unable to use, but the Council of Peoples' Commissars of the Republic had to grant a licence.[50] Judicial decisions indicate that some of the collective farms have not understood their obligation to retain use of the plot at all times.

The matter of illegal assignment of use came to the attention of the Supreme Court of the U.S.S.R. in 1941 on review of a judgment against a collective farm issued by a trial court in

[47] Decree of March 17, 1931, [1931] 1 Sob.Zak. SSSR, No. 17, item 161. A decree on the structure of State farms was issued on the same day. *Ibid.*, No. 17, item 160.

[48] Order of July 7, 1935, and appended instruction, [1935] 1 Sob.Zak. SSSR, No. 34, item 300.

[49] 1935 Charter, Art. 2.

[50] Decree of March 3, 1942, *Izvestiya*, No. 51 (7737), March 3, 1942.

Chkalov Province in favour of a handicraft producing co-operative association.[51] On investigation of the record it was discovered by the Supreme Court that the collective farm had leased to the handicraft co-operative the hay fields assigned to the collective farm for its use. Under the contract the handicraft co-operative obligated itself to deliver to the collective farm the hay which it mowed. This it did, but the collective farm did not pay the 6,334 roubles 30 kopeks demanded, and suit followed. The Supreme Court took note of the fact that the leasing of agricultural land was forbidden and declared the contract invalid, saying that the trial court should have applied the rules of the Civil Code relating to the disposition of assets in the event of a void transaction. Similar war-time contracts under which collective farms had attempted to lease the use of land to other organisations have been set aside.[52]

A District Prosecutor complained in 1939 that the President of a collective farm had rented to a private peasant eleven hectares of the land assigned to the collective farm for use and set aside by the collective farm's general meeting for clearing. The Prosecutor reported to the readers of his office's journal that the rental contract had been voided as illegal, and the President had been indicted on the ground that he had violated Article 87 (a) of the Criminal Code in breaking the law on nationalisation of land.[53] The lower courts have had difficulty, apparently, in appreciating that collective farm land may not be leased even to other State or co-operative agencies. As late as 1950 the President of the Supreme Court of the U.S.S.R. reported that the Moscow Provincial Court had sought to interpret and to enforce a lease by the Stalin collective farm of 100 hectares of pasture land to the supply depot of the medical clinic of the Ministry of Communications. The rental had been set at that provided by statute for the rental of pasture land in State forests. The Supreme Court's President declared that instead of seeking

[51] *Provincial Industrial Council* v. *Collective Farm Named in Honour of Uritsky* [1942] 1 Sud.Prak. SSSR 22.

[52] Cases of the same type were the following *Dmitrov Collective Farm* v. *District Repair Shop of the Army Quartermaster's Office*, in which the farm leased land to the quartermaster without obtaining the consent of the Council of Ministers of the Republic, and *Comintern Collective Farm* v. *Dzhigadzhur State Farm*, which involved an identical situation. See Sbornik Post. Pl. i Opr. Koll. Verkh. Suda SSSR, 1944, pp. 355 and 357.

[53] *Case of Smolkurov* [1939] 6 Sots.Zak. 90.

to establish the proper rent, the trial court should have set aside the contract as an illegal one, violating the principle of nationalisation of the land.[54]

Likewise, a trial court in the Vologod Province had given judgment to a public corporation which had mowed a hay field assigned to a collective farm and had sought to recover in kind for the hay which the farm had subsequently appropriated to its own use. The college for civil cases of the Supreme Court of the U.S.S.R. found it necessary in 1950 to set aside the trial court's decision. It declared that the corporation, having cut the hay without an order from the collective farm, had neither the right to receive a like amount of hay nor to receive the value of its mowing services.[55] The corporation could not be a lessee.

More than 3,000 hectares of land assigned to collective farms for use was reported to have been leased illegally in the Kirgiz Republic in 1949.[56]

The model charter for the collective farm provides that no land may be taken away from the use of a collective farm, once its use has been assigned, although land may be added.[57] It will be appreciated immediately that in a rapidly expanding industrial economy such as that of the U.S.S.R. the application of such a rule would prevent the construction of railways through agricultural areas and the construction of industrial development in any but urban areas. Obviously such development requires the use of land, sometimes from that previously assigned to a collective farm, in spite of the declaration in the model charter that the use of land may not be taken away from the farm.

To meet this situation the Ministry of Agriculture of the U.S.S.R. issued an instruction on November 4, 1936,[58] stating that land may be withdrawn from collective farms for State and public requirements but only with the permission of the Council of Ministers of the U.S.S.R. to be obtained, after a request for such permission has been filed with it by the Provincial Soviet's

[54] *Stalin Collective Farm* v. *Supply Depot of the Medical Clinic of the Ministry of Communications* [1949] 4 Sud.Prak. SSSR 20. For comments upon this case, see A. Volin, 'Preserve Strictly Legality in the Work of the Courts', [1950] 1 Sots.Zak. 4 at pp. 9–10 and Leading Article, [1950] 9 Sots.Zak. 1 at 4.

[55] [1950] 2 Sud.Prak. SSSR 39. For comment, see Leading Article, [1950] 9 Sots.Zak. 1 at 4.

[56] Leading Article, *Pravda*, May 17, 1950, and Leading Article, [1950] 9 Sots.Zak. 1 at 3.

[57] 1935 Charter, Arts. 2 and 3.

[58] [1937] 10 Fin. i Khoz. Zak. 21.

executive committee and the Republic's Council of Ministers. The Ministry added that withdrawal of such land is to occur only in exceptional cases when there is no land not being used by a collective farm which could be used to meet the requirements for the given State or public structure. Further, the Ministry required the land department of the Provincial Soviet's executive committee to verify the need on the spot, and even the Republic's Ministry of Agriculture was required to determine that no other land was available before recommending that the transfer be permitted by the federal government's chief administrative agency. To those familiar with the criticism levelled by Soviet authors at capitalist conditions to the effect that they retard and even prevent planning because of the necessity of respecting property rights, the Ministry's instruction suggests that the Soviet leadership has found it necessary to make some real concessions to retain the good-will of the peasantry in the collective farms.

PRIVATE GARDEN PLOTS FOR CO-OPERATIVE MEMBERS

Not all of the land assigned to the collective farm in the official 'Act' is worked in a co-operative manner. A plot of land is set aside around each house in accordance with the provisions of the model charter for the private use of the peasant household concerned.[59] The size of this privately used plot varies from one-quarter to one-half and even one hectare, in accordance with the region within which the farm lies. Not only is this provision incorporated in the model charter, but it was enshrined in the new Constitution of the U.S.S.R. promulgated in 1936 to mark the advent of socialism. By Article 7, paragraph 2, it is declared, 'Every household in a collective farm, in addition to its basic income from the common, collective farm enterprise, has for its personal use a small plot of land and, as its personal property, a subsidiary husbandry on the plot, a dwelling-house, livestock, poultry and minor agricultural implements—in accordance with the rules of the agricultural *artel*'.

A collective farmer who had been deprived of the use of this private plot of land sought relief in a court in 1943, in the form of damages resulting from what he claimed to be the illegal withdrawal of the use of the plot.[60] The trial court refused

[59] 1935 Charter, Art. 5.
[60] *Dogadin* v. *Collective Farm 'Krasny Pakhar'*, No. 155 [1944] 6 Sud.Prak. SSSR 28.

relief, and the Provincial Court of the Moscow Province affirmed. The matter was taken to the Supreme Court of the U.S.S.R. which said that 'the right to use garden plots attached to a peasant home is decided by land agencies and not by a court'. The Supreme Court held, however, that once the local soviet's land department had decided that the withdrawal had been illegal, a court should determine the value of materials and labour expended on the plot and lost when its use had been taken away. In the case at bar, since it appeared that the administrative authority had concluded already that the use of the plot had been taken away illegally by the collective farm, the case was remanded for trial of the question of the value of the materials and services lost.

No rent is paid by the collective farm to the State for the use of the land assigned to it, but all collective farms are required by law to sell to the State from each harvest a portion which varies from year to year.[61] The sale price of this State portion is considerably less than the price which might be realised by sale on the open market, and to this extent the differences between what is realised and what might have been realised has been called by some western students of the Soviet system a tax covering the cost of use. Soviet lawyers would deny that it has any of the aspects of rent. Collective farms are also required to comply with the State plan for agriculture, so that they are not free to plant what they wish.

During World War II collective farm households seized the opportunity to expand their private garden plots beyond the permitted boundaries.[62] After the war Soviet newspapers were full of reports of the widespread nature of this practice, and it was universally condemned. Local officials were ordered to survey the plots and to take action to restore their original boundaries and to prosecute those that had permitted such encroachments upon the land. It was apparent that the peasant households were alert to the opportunity caused by the confusion of the war and a certain laxness in the enforcement of law to return

[61] Decree of September 21, 1935, [1935] 1 Sob.Zak. SSSR, No. 51, item 422. In addition, a tax is levied on the collective farmer's income, Decree of August 11, 1948, Ved.Verkh.Sov. SSSR, No. 34 (533), August 18, 1948.

[62] There is a dispute among non-Soviet authors as to how much land could have been involved, see R. Schlesinger, 'The Kolkhoz System. A Reply' (1952) 3 *Soviet Studies* 288 at p. 292.

to their private enterprise activities. Recognition of this was found also in a new tax statute raising the rate of tax on profits derived from the sale of produce grown on the private garden plot and discriminating against those who were below retirement age (60 for men and 55 for women).[63] Two years later the rate was again increased for those with private incomes of over 4,000 roubles a year.[64]

What now appears to have been too drastic action to reduce activity on the private garden plots of collective farm households occurred soon after the war. A campaign was begun to encourage collective farmers in their general meetings to vote to combine two or more collective farms[65] and also to move their homes to what was called an '*agrogorod*' or agricultural city.[66] When such a city was established the private garden plots remained in their original locations, and this meant that they were often miles from the new homes of those to whom they had been assigned. It became impossible for the members of the household to reach them and return within the short period of daylight remaining after the daily communal work had been performed on the farm.

The effort at amalgamation of farms was said to be based upon the need for amalgamation of plots of land to obtain the benefits of large-scale mechanisation of agriculture and, no doubt, this was the decisive factor in the decision. There was also probably a further matter of doctrinal concern which has been present constantly in the literature of Marxism, and was restated in October, 1952, by Stalin in his article on theory presented to the XIX Congress of the Communist Party.[67] It is the problem proclaimed by Marx of bringing into some sort of equality the work of the peasant and the industrial workman, the village and the city. In the opinion of Soviet leaders this problem has not yet been solved.

The *agrogorods* may have been an attempt at solution, but they were declared a failure by the party after an experiment of

63 Decree of July 13, 1948, Ved.Verkh.Sov. SSSR, No. 30 (529), July 17, 1948.
64 Decree of August 7, 1950, Ved.Verkh.Sov. SSSR, No. 22 (637), August 16, 1950.
65 Rumyantsev, 'Collective Farm Amalgamates for Greater Progress' (1950) 10 *USSR Information Bulletin*, Washington, D.C. 590–591.
66 'Construction of Agro-Town' (1951) 11 *USSR Information Bulletin*, Washington, D.C. 224.
67 Stalin, *Economic Problems of Socialism in the USSR* (1952) pp. 29–30.

relatively brief duration. The collective farmers simply would not agree to live in the new cities, and certainly not in blocks of flats which differed so radically from their peasant cottages. While all of the farms which had been amalgamated remained combined for purposes of joint agricultural operation,[68] the peasant households have been permitted up to the present to retain their old home sites. The difficulty met by high Soviet leadership in introducing the amalgamation programme while retaining the principle of decision making by the general meeting of members of a farm was evidenced particularly in 1950. *Pravda* in its leading article of June 25, 1950, ordered the officials in communist party agencies and in the soviets to take a hand personally in explaining the new programme to the collective farms and in helping the farmers to take the organisational steps. Yet, at the same time it was indicated that the decision to unite a farm with its neighbouring farms must be made by the general meeting of members, attended by not less than two-thirds of the total membership of the association. The executive committee of the County Soviet was ordered to verify compliance with designated procedures before a decision to combine with other farms could be put into effect. Once again, the leadership indicated its desire to achieve its ends without antagonising the peasants to the extent that production would be disrupted and disorder caused.

In its order the leadership indicated not that it was interested in determining the will of the parties as to the direction in which society was to move, but rather to obtain their consent to the direction chosen for them by the leadership. The reason for seeking consent of the general meeting was probably to make certain that the education given by the local party leadership had been adequate to effect the change without resistance with its costly accompaniment of lost production and social disorder. That the farmers were not adequately prepared for the change was indicated by the resistance which developed in the part of the programme having to do with the *agrogorods*.[69]

68 The 250,000 farms of January 1, 1950, are said to have been reduced to 97,000 farms by amalgamation by October, 1952. See Malenkov, *Report to the Nineteenth Party Congress on the Work of the Central Committee of the CPSU (B)* (1952) p. 65.

69 Leading Article, [1950] 9 Sots.Zak. 1 at p. 6.

THE FUTURE OF CO-OPERATIVES

The collective farm programme has obviously met with difficulties and is not yet accepted willingly by the peasants in all places, yet statistics show that the major aim of the Soviet leadership has been achieved. Agricultural produce is coming from farms operated by communities and not from those operated by individual peasant households. As early as 1937 the number of peasant households which had become collectivised was 18,500,000 or 93 per cent of all of the peasant households in the U.S.S.R.[70] By 1940 the portion of tillable agricultural land being farmed by the collective farm process had reached 99.8 per cent of the tillable land in the entire country, and 96 per cent of the peasant households were in the farms. The individual farmer and his family are to be found today only on the periphera notably along the rivers of Siberia in the pioneer clearings fronting on the rivers. The collective farm has become established as a major step in the social change desired by Soviet leadership.

The question remains as to whether the co-operative organisation of productive activity within the U.S.S.R. is a goal in itself or a means to achievement of a more remote goal. A clue to the answer to such a question may be found in the experience of other forms of co-operative organisation which have existed in the U.S.S.R. In addition to the form to be found in the agricultural *artel* other forms of co-operative activity were inherited from Tsarist Russia by the new Soviet regime. There were the credit co-operatives, the consumers' co-operatives and the producers' or peasant handicraft co-operatives. All had experienced vigorous growth in the years following liberation of the serfs and especially after the turn of the century.[71]

The credit co-operatives had become a strongly supported system of banks financed by the thousands of persons who were their members. They were used as depositories even by the Imperial Government and its agencies. Their principal business was to grant loans to peasants to permit them to purchase agricultural machinery. This they did either through the agricultural *artels* or through the chain of consumers' co-operatives. The

70 20 *Let Sovetskoi Vlasti* (1937) p. 34.

71 For a history of the Russian co-operatives, see Blanc, *The Co-operative Movement in Soviet Russia* (1924).

Tsarist Government had been suspicious of the co-operatives as possible sources of revolutionary fervour, and in 1897 there had been published a model charter for the consumers' co-operatives which required the approval of the local provincial governor in each individual case before the co-operative might be chartered. The credit co-operatives were also subject to review by the State Bank's examination department, established in 1904.

When the Bolsheviks began to introduce their programme leading toward the socialism of their dreams, they approached the co-operative movement with caution. While they nationalised private banks within little more than a month after the revolution, they did not include the credit co-operatives headed by the Moscow Peoples Bank. Yet they thought the credit co-operatives a potential threat to their plans, apparently, for they withdrew the deposits of the State and pressed those agencies which they controlled to withdraw likewise, hoping apparently to bankrupt the credit co-operatives without formally abolishing them. It is testimony to the strength of these co-operatives that they were able to call sufficient of their loans to meet the demands of depositors and finally on December 2, 1918,[72] a year after the decree nationalising the other private banks, the government issued a decree nationalising the credit co-operatives also. They have never been permitted to reappear. Financing of the collective farms is currently the province of a special State bank created for the purpose.[73]

A split of opinion appeared shortly after the revolution in the ranks of the communist party as to the proper approach to the consumers' and producers' co-operatives. Some members argued that they fostered a capitalist mentality and were potential sources of danger to the Soviet regime. Others said that they performed an essential purpose in meeting the needs for consumers' goods which the State could not supply at the time. Lenin who was the spokesman for this view, drafted a decree requiring every citizen to join a consumers' co-operative,[74] but

[72] Decree of December 2, 1918, [1918] 1 Sob.Uzak. RSFSR, No. 90, item 912.

[73] Arnold, *Banks Credit and Money in Soviet Russia* (1937) p. 481.

[74] Lenin, 6 *Selected Works* (English translation, 1935) p. 445. An editorial note states that the draft was adopted as law in January, 1918, *ibid.*, p. 641. Yet no such decree is found in the official gazette. The first decree on consumers' co-operatives is that of April 10, 1918, [1918] 1 Sob.Uzak. RSFSR, No. 32, item 498. Although no provision requiring

the criticism within the party continued. Finally, to silence it, Lenin made a speech at the IX Communist Party Congress in 1920,[75] in which he argued against those who thought it already time to fuse the consumers' co-operatives with the local administrative agencies of government, namely the county soviets. His reasons were practical, namely that nothing was more important to the success of the regime than the increase in production of goods, and so long as the consumers' co-operatives met this need, they should be continued. He warned that if they failed in this task they should be punished. He pointed out that the consumers' co-operatives obtained much of their goods from the producers' co-operatives, so that the two were subject to the same considerations.

The issue was settled for a time. A model statute was enacted to incorporate the voluntary principle in a new charter for the consumers' co-operatives on May 20, 1924.[76] The producers' co-operatives were put under a new model statute on May 11, 1927.[77] A Central Society for the co-operatives of the U.S.S.R. was created out of the old central society existing under the Tsarist law. It was given its new charter to act as a co-ordinating agency in 1928.[78] In so doing, it was technically the creature of the consumers' co-operatives in that it was financed by dues paid by each co-operative society, and governed by a general meeting composed of delegates from the consumers' co-operative association leagues in each Republic. Actually, it was thought of by the Soviet leadership as a type of quasi-Ministry, and its plans were co-ordinated with the national economic plans.

STALIN ANTICIPATED NEW FORMS

Stalin explained the reason for continuing interest in the co-operatives in an article dedicated to the Leningrad organisation of the communist party in 1926.[79] He said, 'Co-operative societies assume special significance after the consolidation of the

all citizens to join appears in the decree, compulsory membership was, apparently the law, for a decree of December 28, 1923, [1924] 1 Sob.Uzak. RSFSR, No. 17, item 173, declared that thereafter membership should be voluntary.

75 Lenin, 8 *Selected Works* (English translation, 1935) p. 226.

76 [1924] 1 Sob.Uzak. RSFSR, No. 64, item 645.

77 [1927] 1 Sob.Zak. SSSR, No. 26, item 280, amended July 5, 1933, [1933] 1 Sob.Zak. SSSR, No. 42, item 248.

78 Order of May 24, 1928, [1928] 2 Sob.Zak. SSSR, No. 27, item 122.

79 Stalin, 1 *Leninism* (English translation, 1934) p. 261 at p. 276.

dictatorship of the proletariat, during the period of widespread construction. They facilitate the contact between the proletarian vanguard and the peasant masses, and create the possibility of drawing the latter into the channel of socialist construction'.

Stalin's reference to the co-operatives as having importance during the period of widespread construction suggests that he thought of them even in 1926 as transitional and not as agencies of permanent value to the Soviet leadership. One may wonder whether he expected them to be absorbed or abolished as production by State agencies and distribution by State agencies reached the levels associated in his mind with abundance.

There was a suggestion nine years later that the position of the co-operatives was to be only temporary. It was in the form of a decree of September 29, 1935,[80] ordering the consumers' co-operatives in the cities to be liquidated and the transfer of their assets and staffs to the Ministry of Internal Trade. Yet at the same time the decree ordered the consumers' co-operatives to enlarge their work in the villages and criticised the past work of these societies as having been inadequate. The conclusion seems justified that the State agencies had reached such a level of production and efficient distribution that the leadership thought it possible to transfer from the co-operatives their work to the level of the whole community represented by the State. The co-operatives had served their function in the striving for community. In the future they would serve only in the villages, where the process was still not complete.

The 1936 Constitution of the U.S.S.R. which followed the next year restated the emphasis placed upon co-operatives by listing them as constituting one of the forms in which 'socialist property' existed.[81] Soon after there came the second world war with its destruction of producing and distributing facilities. At its end a new decree was issued on the consumers' and producers' co-operatives.[82] They were ordered to redouble their efforts and were reinstated in some of the cities. But there was now a new development. It appeared in the form of the creation of agencies to bring the co-operative movement into closer

80 [1935] 1 Sob.Zak. SSSR, No. 52, item 427.

81 Art. 5.

82 Decree of November 9, 1946. While its text was not printed in the official gazette, a summary appeared in the leading article of *Izvestiya*, No. 265 (9181), November 12, 1946, p. 1.

relation with the State. The decree established a new Chief Administration on Affairs of the Producers' and Consumers' Co-operatives and attached this to the Council of Ministers of the U.S.S.R. In effect, the Chief Administration was a type of Ministry, having less administrative duties but serving as a central source of information and planning for the co-operative movement. A Council for Collective Farm Affairs was created on September 19, 1946,[83] to provide direction to the agricultural producing co-operatives, and to propose the policy to be adopted by the Council of Ministers in handling their affairs.

The communist party congress of October, 1952, provided Stalin with a fresh opportunity to express his view that the co-operatives are only transitional. In his article written for the occasion[84] he found the collective farms beginning to be a retarding influence in the further development of production within the U.S.S.R. This retarding influence was seen in their position as a semi-private unit within the economy, which because of its semi-private character created obstacles in the way of the complete planning of the Soviet economy. He expressed his conviction that the further the U.S.S.R. developed its economy, the more the collective form of agricultural production would retard the growth of the nation's productive forces.

The solution to this contradiction between full development of the economy under all-embracing State planning and the semi-private form of collective farm agriculture, under which only a part of the crop is dictated by the plan, lay, in Stalin's opinion, in the gradual transformation of collective farm property into the 'commonwealth of the people'. In other words, the community which is the co-operative association is to be enlarged into the community which is the entire nation. The farm in all of its activities is to be absorbed into the national economic scene. This does not mean necessarily that it will lose its identity as a unit of planning, for the industrial plant has not lost its identity as a unit of planning, but the decisions affecting the farm would be those of a State manager and not of a general meeting of members.

[83] [1946] Sob.Post. SSSR, No. 13, item 254, s. 10. The members of the Council were named in an order of October 8, 1946. *Ibid.*, item 255.

[84] Stalin, *Economic Problems of Socialism in the USSR* (1952).

Stalin saw no speedy move in the direction of transformation. On the contrary, he stated that he expected it to take a long time. He thought that it would begin with the elimination of the authority now granted the collective farms to sell on the open market, produce in excess of that obligated to the State under the plan. He remarked that this step had already been taken with the collective farms which had become specialised in the growing of cotton, sugar beets and flax. In these farms the entire production of the farm is delivered to the State, and the collective farm receives in return consumers' goods and tools under a form of barter which Stalin calls 'product exchange'.

When 'product exchange' became the universal rule Stalin foresaw the possibility of including the entire product of the collective farm in the system of economic planning. He believed that this system would be advantageous to the farmers themselves, as well as to the urban dwellers. Universal planning would, under his hypothesis, increase the amount of the total product and thus result in greater farm deliveries with which the urban dwellers could produce more of the goods of industry. From greater industrial production the farmers would benefit again by hypothesis. Proof was offered in the increase of consumers' goods, which were said already to be flowing to the farms raising cotton, sugar beets and flax.

While the co-operatives of the U.S.S.R. continue to appear to be private associations of individuals combined in nearly classical form for the purpose of their own economic welfare, they have a distinctly public character. Their production is already fitted in large measure into the economic plan, and Stalin indicated that for the agricultural co-operatives the entire production will in the foreseeable future be fitted into the plan. Even now the co-operatives are required to serve the productive purpose for which they are permitted to exist or to accept management which is capable of serving the purpose.

The position of the agricultural, consumers' and producers' co-operatives seems to be transitional on the Soviet scene. They appear to be tolerated, as Lenin had explained in the early days of the revolution because they help to meet productive needs and to win over peasants to the communal form of organisation espoused by the leadership of the State. It would not be surprising to those who have followed Soviet developments to find the co-operatives pushed from the national scene if the State's own industries and distribution media prove entirely adequate to the requirements of the people.

It is the community of the whole and not some intervening association, which is heralded as desirable when the citizenry has become prepared for the transition.

Chapter 7

LABOUR AND ITS PLACE

The Russian revolution was fought in the name of the proletariat, and the bench workman claimed a preferred place in society after the victory. The leadership had reached the conclusion from its studies and from its experience in the battles of the revolution that the workmen would be the most reliable element in establishing the kind of society desired for the future. It was the workmen who were thought to have been convinced of the necessity of communal effort. No factory hand could dream of producing industrial goods upon his own lathe without the co-operation of others in the same factory. The individualism which remained a possibility among the peasants, who needed no help to wring food from the land, had become impossible of achievement at the factory bench.

Workmen were to be the core of the new regime's plans for the future. The most politically-minded of them were Lenin's choice for the leadership group he had formed in the communist party. The rest of them were indispensable to the increased production believed necessary to the achievement of communism, and to the maintenance of mass political support without which the new regime could not retain power for long enough to develop its programme.

Indulgence of the whims of the workmen was as much a cause for the relaxation of labour discipline after the victory as the desire to give them a sense of participation, from which they might be expected to increase their efforts at the bench. Workers' committees were established in the factories to watch such of the distrusted managers as were held over from the past and to manage the factories from which the professional managers had fled or been removed.[1] Foremen consulted with members of the shop to obtain agreement before initiating work. Workmen came to feel that the revolution had been fought to give them a share in management. The result was chaos in many a fac-

[1] Decree of November 14, 1917, [1917] 1 Sob.Uzak. RSFSR, No. 3, item 35. As to the popular pressures for workers' control, see Carr, 2 *The Bolshevik Revolution 1917–1923* (1952) pp. 66–73.

tory, with consequent loss of production. Yet production was required by the new social order for its success.

Lenin saw the problem presented by a working-class population who looked upon the revolution primarily as its liberation from authority. He found it necessary to warn that nationalisation of industry was not enough to assure success. A new attitude toward work had to be established, one which would be characterised by an understanding of the social necessity for work and by recognition of the responsibilities required of every member of the team which works together on the complex industrial mechanism of the present century. He wrote, 'Not having fallen into Utopia, we cannot think that when capitalism has been destroyed, people will begin to work immediately for society without rules of law, and also the abolition of capitalism will not provide immediately the prerequisites for such a transformation'.[2]

Trade unions also faced a problem of reorientating their thinking. They had developed with difficulty under the legal prohibitions which existed up to 1905 and continued thereafter in police practice when serious strikes occurred. They had been agencies of protest, first to obtain economic improvements, and then to press for political change.[3] The large pre-revolutionary strikes against industry had sometimes turned into mass demonstrations against the government, from which bloodshed had aroused the people to demand the complete overthrow of the Tsarist system and the economy which it was thought to typify.

With the victory over the Provisional Government, the trade unions acquired some political functions. There had been since 1906 in the factories electoral committees named to supervise the choice by the workmen of their deputies to the State Duma created at that time. The revolution merged the trade unions with these electoral committees, so that the trade unions shared in the organisation of the election of delegates to the new agencies of government, the local soviets.[4]

[2] Lenin, 21 *Sochineniya* [*Collected Works*] (3rd ed. 1928–1937) p. 435.
[3] For historical materials, see Grinevich, *Professionalnoe Dvizhenie Rabochikh v Rossii* [*The Trade Union Movement in Russia*] (1908). For a summary of the events, see Harper, *Civic Training in Soviet Russia* (1929) pp. 138–141 and Deutscher, *Soviet Trade Unions* (1950) pp. 1–12.
[4] Harper, *Civic Training in Soviet Russia* (1929) p. 140.

When resistance to the new Soviet government spread to the country as a whole and took on the form of civil war, the trade unions recruited workmen for the armies called to oppose the troops of the 'white' opposition.[5]

Although some elements within the trade union movement, notably the printers' union, wished at the outset to keep the movement outside the structure of the new Soviet State, they were submerged in the common effort to save the State during the civil war. The Webbs have concluded that the unions became in substance, if not in form, agencies of the State.[6]

RESTRAINTS ON PRIVATE EMPLOYERS

Labour legislation began with a decree establishing the eight hour day immediately after the revolution.[7] A year later the decree was incorporated in a Code of Labour Laws[8] concerned primarily with the protection of workmen against exploitation by such private owners as remained in the economy to employ labour. Its emphasis was upon setting maximum hours and minimum wages and standards to govern private employment. An amendment in 1920[9] added a restriction on overtime.

Most jurists considered the new Code, with all law, only a transitional measure necessary until the new social pattern should be established, when employment would be by enlightened State managers representing the workmen's own State, and work would be carried on by men and women, who performed it as their social contribution rather than merely to survive.

With the inauguration of the New Economic Policy, bringing as it did a restoration of private enterprise on an expanding scale, it became necessary to rethink the position to be assigned the trade union and labour law in the new controlled capitalist economy.[10] Some argued that the trade unions should be developed further along the lines of the civil war, namely as armies of industrial workmen performing their labour duty for

[5] Deutscher, *Soviet Trade Unions* (1950) pp. 25–26.
[6] S. and B. Webb, 1 *Soviet Communism: A New Civilisation?* (1936) p. 167.
[7] Decree of October 29, 1917, [1917] 1 Sob.Uzak. RSFSR, No. 1, item 7.
[8] Decree undated, but printed in official gazette of December 10, 1918. [1918] 1 Sob.Uzak. RSFSR, Nos. 87–88, item 905.
[9] Decree of June 17, 1920, [1920] 1 Sob.Uzak. RSFSR, No. 56, item 242.
[10] S. and B. Webb, 1 *Soviet Communism: A New Civilisation?* (1936) p. 168. Also Carr, 2 *The Bolshevik Revolution 1917–1923* (1952) pp. 221–227, 317–321, and Deutscher, *Soviet Trade Unions* (1950) pp. 33–42.

the State just as the men in the military forces performed their military duty. Others argued that with the restoration of private enterprise, even though in limited form, the trade unions would resume some of the functions which had been theirs traditionally. Labour law, under this approach, would require development to define the powers and duties of the private entrepreneurs, and a strong trade union movement would be needed to police the Code and to take appropriate action to oppose the employers when the occasion required.

The debate was indicated as having been settled when the IX Congress of Soviets resolved in December, 1921, that the trade unions should be cut free of the machinery of the State. Their task was to be primarily the representation of the interests of their members against private employers.[11] In those plants which had been nationalised and were to remain so, their task would be orientated toward co-operation with management in a common effort, but they were to watch management and oppose any bureaucratic attitudes on the part of the managers in performing their duties.

A new and greatly expanded Code of Labour Laws became effective on November 15, 1922,[12] to put the policy decisions into effect. Although in force only in the R.S.F.S.R., the new Code had almost identical counterparts in each of the other republics. It adopted formulæ quite familiar to those versed in the contents of the codes of other industrial countries. Some of the definitions will indicate the tone of the new Code. The employment contract was defined as, 'an agreement between two or more persons, in which one party (the employee) offers his working power to the other (the employer) for wages'.[13] The function of collective agreements was stated to be the establishment of 'conditions of work and employment for a given enter-

[11] Resolution on the NEP and Industry, December 28, 1921, par. 10. *Sezdy Sovetov RSFSR v Post. i Rez.* (1939) p. 224. This followed the decision taken at the Tenth Communist Party Congress in March, 1921, to which there was vigorous continuing opposition. The December 28 resolution was expanded upon by a further resolution of the Politburo of the Party on January 12, 1922, emphasising the role of the trade unions in protecting members against private employers. See Carr, 2 *The Bolshevik Revolution 1917–1923* (1952) pp. 326–327. Also Deutscher, *Soviet Trade Unions* (1950) pp. 42–52.

[12] Decree of October 30, 1922, [1922] 1 Sob.Uzak. RSFSR, No. 70, item 903.

[13] Art. 27.

price, office or economic unit or for a group of such, and to specify the substantive terms of personal (employment) contracts to be concluded in the future'.[14]

The terminology chosen to describe the employment contract was far from that expected by some of the advanced thinkers of the time, and it does not conform even to the definition urged today in some of the capitalist countries where it is said that the employment contract is no longer a sale of labour power but an expression of an agreement to co-operate in the interests of the good of the community. In spite of the new type of thinking among Soviet policy-makers the old formula of a sale of labour power was adopted, but a considerable number of provisions were inserted in the Code to protect the workmen against what was expected to be the inevitable desire of the private entrepreneur to increase profits by exploiting labour.

Provisions appeared in the Code concerning the terms under which working men held their jobs, and the conditions under which they might be dismissed, the minimum wage payments permitted, the maximum working hours, and minimum vacations, safety measures, protection of women and children, social insurance and a procedure for settling disputes. Although drafted for the control of private employers and to reflect the aspirations of the working men as expressed in their struggle against employers before the revolution, the Code served as a set of rules for the State employers as well. Viewed from the perspective of over thirty years of experience with the Code, it now seems remarkable that it has been possible to continue it in force long after the last private employer has been eliminated. Although the amendments have been numerous, the Code adopted in 1922 remains even today the basic set of rules governing the relationship between State managers and workmen throughout State industry, transport and distribution, and also throughout what would be called the civil service in other lands.

The 'civil service', or to be more precise, those employees of the State who worked in the administrative offices of the Ministries (then called Commissariats) was given no special status. As with all other employees, their employment was subject to the provisions of the Code of Labour Laws, but it was governed additionally by a special statute. This supplementary

[14] Art. 15.

law may have been thought necessary because of the special problem believed to be faced by State agencies. Be that as it may, there was enacted on December 21, 1922,[15] almost immediately after the promulgation of the Code of Labour Laws, a statute entitled 'Temporary Rules of Service in State Offices and Enterprises'. It forbade employment of a person under a court sentence prohibiting it, as well as the employment in the same agency of two persons of close family relationship, if one would be under the control of the other (excepting for employees of the post office and telegraph agency, teachers, artists, musicians, medical doctors, agronomists, meteorologists, and laboratory workers). While designated as 'temporary', the rules have remained in effect to the present day. That they still require separation of relatives is evidenced by a 1950 order of the Prosecutor General of the U.S.S.R. directing the head of the Chief Administration for the cellulose industry to revoke the appointment of a woman as head of the department of technical inspection in a factory in which her husband was employed as chief engineer.[16]

PLANNING INTRODUCES PROBLEMS

The features of Soviet labour law which have come to be associated with the requirements of a planned economy began to appear in the special enactments governing the 'civil service'. It is here that one first finds an order standardising employment nomenclature and wages.[17] By degrees[18] this principle spread to State-owned industry until in 1938 an order required every Ministry and central agency of the U.S.S.R. to pay wages not only within the Ministry but throughout the enterprises responsible to the Ministry, in accordance with a fixed tariff which could not be violated without submitting oneself to prosecution.[19]

The introduction of the first five-year plan in 1927 began the tapering-off of private enterprise as it had developed under

15 [1923] 1 Sob.Uzak. RSFSR, No. 1, item 8.
16 [1950] 6 Sots.Zak. 87.
17 Order of June 9, 1925, [1925] 1 Sob.Zak. SSSR, No. 42, item 321.
18 To clerks in credit agencies, social and State insurance and the administrative personnel of trusts, Order of December 7, 1929, [1929] 1 Sob.Zak. SSSR, No. 76, item 737; to coal miners in the Donbasin, Order of May 21, 1933, [1933] 1 Sob.Zak. SSSR, No. 31, item 183; and then to railway employees, Order of July 8, 1933, *ibid.*, No. 41, item 242.
19 Order of June 4, 1938, [1938] Sob.Post SSSR, No. 27, item 178.

the New Economic Policy. It caused the beginning of a considerable discussion as to the place of the trade union in an economy of the type being established by the plans. To the trade union leadership of the time there seemed no reason to change their approach to management and to their duties of protection of their members.[20] They seemed to have looked upon management as being composed of over-zealous individuals who had a task to perform for the State which caused them to lose sight of the interests of the workmen in their employ. In consequence the trade union leadership anticipated that it would continue to oppose management on issues in which the rights of the workmen to good working conditions, appropriate hours and wages were threatened. The right to strike which had been preserved during the New Economic Policy as the ultimate weapon of the trade union movement was still espoused as essential to preservation of its usefulness. While this was the view of the trade union leadership, the communist party's leadership thought otherwise.

The matter came to a head at the VIII All-Union Congress of Trade Unions in December, 1928.[21] The President of the All-Union Central Council of Trade Unions, M. P. Tomsky, argued that the trade unions should not lose their freedom to press for improvements in the material conditions of members, and that they should not be enlisted in the campaign to increase production. He believed that it was the task of the State manager to concern himself with such matters.

In opposition to this view there were speakers from the communist party who argued that with the abolition of the New Economic Policy and the introduction of the five-year plan a new approach was necessary. The trade unions, in this view, had to bear in mind that the plan took into consideration all workmen, not only those who had the strongest unions. Wages would represent a planned part of the gross national product, and no increase would be possible unless the product was increased. To permit the increase of wages for workmen represented by a union having the strength to strike effectively would be to permit the upsetting of a systematic distribution of wages in accordance with a plan based upon reasoned factors such as

[20] Deutscher, *Soviet Trade Unions* (1950) pp. 75–76.
[21] *Ibid.*, pp. 76–81.

contribution of each industry to the national good and strategic necessity. There would have been a substitution of pressures having no relation to these reasoned factors for the work of the economists and policy-makers of the land.

Having lost the confidence of his party, the trade union leader Tomsky was retired to work at lesser things for a span of years before committing suicide in 1937 at the moment of his arrest on a charge of treason. From the 1928 date onward the central committee of the trade unions required all members of the trade unions to give attention to production. This principle was reinforced by the XVI Congress of the Communist Party in 1930,[22] for it was here that the decision was taken to require the trade unions to press for greater production on the part of their members through means such as the sponsoring of competition between the workmen in various plants to achieve maximum production. To indicate the relation the party saw in this type of competition to the goals of social change set before the citizens of the U.S.S.R., it was called 'socialist competition'.

Such a change in policy from emphasis upon protection of members in their struggle with management to emphasis upon labour's duty to share with management in pressing for greater production, and sometimes even to force management to take measures of work rationalisation which management was reluctant to take, could not but be reflected in the labour law. It was but a step to make of the trade unions an arm of the government. Some have seen the preparation for this on the eve of the revolution when Lenin equated the workers and the State in his *State and Revolution*.[23]

With the conception of the State as the instrumentality of the workers, the argument ran that these workers were only helping themselves when they directed their unions to press for greater production. They faced no elements in society with any interests contrary to their own. Management was but their agent in organising the mechanism to make production possible, and they utilised their trade unions as their enlightened and tutored leadership to show them how to make the best possible use of that which management had prepared for their benefit.

22 Resolution on the Five Year Plan of National Economy, 2 *VKP (b) v Rez. i Resh.* (6th ed. 1940) p. 325 at p. 328.

23 Carr, 2 *The Bolshevik Revolution 1917–1923* (1952) p. 66.

The time had not been ripe for such a relationship during the earlier period because there had been retained in the social structure a large number of private entrepreneurs who had to be combatted, as they had been combatted by trade union activity in capitalist economies; but this time had passed with the liquidation of the New Economic Policy and the inauguration of the five-year plans.

To symbolise the change in function of the trade unions, the Ministry of Labour was merged with the Central Council of Trade Unions in 1933.[24] The administration of social insurance and the labour inspection system were later made the responsibility of the trade unions.[25] Some have seen in this transfer a necessary step in keeping the trade unions alive, since they had lost their traditional functions of opposing management in seeking to better the worker's conditions. While this may have played a part in the decision, since Soviet leadership has usually been acutely aware of the possibility of gaining psychological advantage from strategic allocation of administrative functions, it may have been a decision inspired by the doctrine to which reference has been given.

One can imagine that a trade union movement which had only the function of pressing for production would have had few members on a voluntary basis, for workmen have nowhere demonstrated their preparedness to adopt new views for those rooted in the experience of several generations of combatting management. To keep the membership necessary to make the production campaigns a success there had to be new attractions, and perhaps the leadership thought this could be provided only by some dramatic function from which all could see the benefits, namely such helpful work as the labour inspection to check on the preservation of safety measures by management and the distribution of social insurance benefits to those who were temporarily ill or absent because of injury.

COLLECTIVE BARGAINING AND PLANNING

The change in function of the trade unions seems to have had influence upon the law of collective bargaining. Once the close relationship of management and labour in the production pro-

[24] Decree of June 23, 1933, [1933] 1 Sob.Zak. SSSR, No. 40, item 238.
[25] Order of September 10, 1933, [1933] 1 Sob.Zak. SSSR, No. 57, item 333.

cess had been established and the trade union system had been made a branch of government, it seemed to the leadership, apparently, that there was little to be achieved by continuing the collective bargaining process. In 1933 the collective bargaining agreements were negotiated for the last time in most industries, although they were extended for the subsequent year when they expired.[26] In the remaining industries the year 1935 marked the last negotiation of contracts, although the textbooks and even the trade union orders continued to refer to them as an aspect of trade union activity. The practice was not to be revived until after the war in 1947.

Some students of the subject have found in the cessation of collective bargaining a manifestation of a lack of confidence in the political reliability of existing union leadership.[27] To be sure there followed soon after the cessation of collective bargaining the first of the well-publicised 'treason trials' which inaugurated a series of purges which ran throughout the administrative apparatus and, undoubtedly, had to do with Tomsky's suicide. Soviet authors have not suggested this as the reason, however, but they have ascribed the dropping of the practice of collective bargaining to the fact that the increasingly detailed regulation of all aspects of labour relations by decree had left no room for bargaining between unions and management over labour conditions, hours of work and wages.[28]

There is evidence in support of both explanations, and there may have been an element of causation in each of them. It was certainly true that the Soviet leadership in the late 1930's seemed to fear all but the most intimately associated with Stalin, for even the Minister of Internal Affairs, the Minister of Foreign Trade and the Vice-Minister of Heavy Industry fell in the purges together with many high army officers. But it was equally true that the plan had fixed wages to an increasing degree as industry had been expanded, and nomenclatures and wage scales had been standardised.

Although management and labour were combined in the 1930's in a common effort to increase production, the unions

26 'Collective Bargaining in the Soviet Union', A Note (1949) 62 *Harvard Law Review* 1191 *et seq.*
27 *Ibid.*, at p. 1195.
28 Aleksandrov, Astrakhan, Karinsky and Moskalenko, *Zakonodatelstvo o Trude* [*Legislation on Labour*] (1947) p. 15.

were not made a part of management. There were no union representatives seated upon a Board of Directors or its equivalent, as has been the case in some other countries where industry has been partly nationalised, as in France.[29] The Soviet experience has indicated that Soviet leadership has found it desirable to keep the two forces of the production process separate. In 1937 Stalin declared that even the limited consultative function which trade unions had enjoyed with regard to management prior to that time would be discontinued. Management had its special tasks, for which it, and it alone, was to be held responsible, and the unions were not to interfere in the performance of these tasks. They could only serve as a check upon the fulfilment of the law, and as a channel of complaint to higher echelons if management took measures which seemed illegal or ill-conceived.

The practice of executing collective agreements was renewed under an order of the Council of Ministers of February 4, 1947,[30] and the Central Council of Trade Unions issued the requisite regulations on the matter. In 1947 over 25,000 agreements, relating to 14,000,000 workmen were reported as having been negotiated. In 1948 the number was raised to 40,000 concerning 17,000,000 workmen.[31] What had happened to make this about-face in policy desirable?

Since the plan continued to fix wage scales and production requirements, and the labour laws continued in force to set the terms of employment, the renewal of the practice of concluding collective agreements in 1947 seems to have had no relation to any new need for collective bargaining on such matters. One reaches the conclusion that the renewed interest in collective agreements stemmed from an appreciation of the psychological value they might have for the workmen themselves, a psychological value which no one was sufficiently imaginative to foresee at the time they were discontinued in 1935.

Such a conclusion follows both from the statements which emanated from trade union headquarters at the time and from the practice of the years since the restoration of the practice.

29 Robson, 'Nationalised Industries in Britain and France' (1950) 44 *American Political Science Review* 299.
30 *Izvestiya*, No. 42 (9264), February 19, 1947, p. 1.
31 'Collective Bargaining in the Soviet Union', A Note (1949) 62 *Harvard Law Review* 1191 at p. 1198.

The chairman of the Central Council of Trade Unions, Kuznetsov, declared that the purpose of renewing the practice was to improve the use of resources allocated by the plan.[32] In practice the unions have taken upon themselves the task of exploring with management the possibilities of rationalising production in accordance with suggestions made by the union members. If the management is reluctant to introduce such measures the union officials conduct campaigns in their papers. The contracts have also set the responsibility for increased production upon the workmen themselves, and they promise to exceed the norms assigned to them.

The agreements restored to vigour in 1947 have incorporated another feature, which suggests that they have another function. They have included specific and detailed obligations assumed by management to improve the welfare of the employees by utilising resources available from the increase in production beyond the plan for the purpose of improving the plant restaurants, reading rooms, children's crèches, and even living quarters. It may be that in this way a more popular distribution of the profits is achieved for the benefit of the workers than would have been possible by issuing orders at headquarters to which management would have had to adhere. It may also be that this feature was added to catch the enthusiasm of the workers, called together as they are in mammoth plant meetings to hear reports on what is being done. In spite of all that has been said by Soviet leaders it is apparent to outsiders that unadorned pressure for increased production has not yet caught the imagination of the great mass of workmen. Law can provide that increased production will result in payments to a 'Director's Fund' to be used to the benefit of the workman, but such laws require dramatisation for complete effectiveness psychologically. The collective agreements with their promise on the part of labour to increase its contribution of work seem to be thought to provide a good occasion to restate the inducement. The onerous obligation to work harder can be juxtaposed in the agreement to the 'consideration'.

The collective agreements seem to be looked upon in some measure as an indication of the social relations to be anticipated

[32] Report of speech of February 18, 1947, at meeting of the Presidium of All-Union Central Council of Trade Unions, *Izvestiya*, No. 42 (9264), February 19, 1947, p. 1.

under communism, when its achievement is finally possible. Soviet authors say that the principal means of enforcing them is moral suasion.[33] To be sure this moral suasion is buttressed in some degree by the administrative and court penalties provided for those who violate the agreements. If the quarterly check by management and trade union officials of performance of the agreement shows that there has been violation, management may be prosecuted under Article 134 of the Criminal Code for any wilful violation. Diligent reading by a careful student of the subject is reported as having produced no reports of such prosecution, although it did produce evidence that the agreements were often violated.[34] The chief safety inspector, who is the nominee of the labour union, is also empowered to fine management up to 500 roubles if he discovers any violation of the safety rules enshrined in the agreement. No penalty seems to apply to the union officials for failure to obtain increases in production from their membership, and the Code of Labour Laws provides specifically that the union shall not be held responsible in a civil action for any liability arising out of a collective agreement.

One case indicates that a union thought it might recover in a civil suit from management for failure to perform under an agreement.[35] In this case, reported in 1938, a Provincial Committee of the union of workers in the wood and floatage industry sued the management of the wood industry for the payment of 30,000 roubles for the construction of a rest home. Under a collective agreement executed in 1935 management was obligated to pay 40,000 roubles towards the construction of a rest home. It paid only 10,000 roubles, and then refused to pay more, arguing that the unpaid balance reverted when it was not used in 1935, and there was no budget allocation for the project in 1936. The trial court gave judgment for the union, but the defendant appealed, and was successful in having the judgment set aside. The College for Civil Cases of the Supreme Court of the R.S.F.S.R. referred to an order of the Council of People's

33 Aleksandrov, *Trudovoe Pravootnoshenie* [*Labour Relationships in Law*] (1948) p. 70.

34 'Collective Bargaining in the Soviet Union', A Note (1949) 62 *Harvard Law Review* 1191 at p. 1206.

35 *Trade Union of Workers in the Wood and Floatage Industry* v. *The Wood Industry Management* [1938] 7 Sov.Yust. 52.

Commissars, dated April 16, 1936, which seems to have annulled any provisions in collective agreements to pay for the construction of rest homes, although its text is not set out.

The case suggests that there might be a civil action for the recovery of damages arising out of the failure of management to perform an obligation which was not illegally assumed. Other decisions based upon such a principle have not, however, been found in the published reports, and one can assume only that either there have been no suits, or the Supreme Court has not found the matter sufficiently important in the conduct of the work of the lower courts to require publication of such decisions as there may have been.

While the development of a large body of statutory law relating to the details of the employment relationship, which are usually incorporated in collective agreements, has not resulted in the disappearance of the collective agreements, the reverse seems to have been the case with the personal employment contract. A Soviet author says that, except for unusual cases, the personal contract between the individual workman and management has ceased to exist in written form.[36] It is now only implied in the employment relationship, and may be proved, if need be, by any evidence whatever. To this practice there is now only the exception of contracts by which collective farmers who leave their farms are employed in industry.

One such written contract was adopted in model form by the Council of People's Commissars in 1944 to govern the relationship between collective farmers and the mining industry in the Don Basin.[37] It provides in great detail for the obligations to be assumed by management, including a precise statement of wages, travel expenses to be paid, the bonus to be paid for leaving the farm, the living quarters to be provided on arrival at the pit, the food to be sold at ration rates in the dining hall and any supplementary rations to be issued for extra heavy work, rights to cultural facilities such as those offered by the health and social agencies, rights to education to improve his skills, and the honorary titles for which the employee may compete. The contract also provides that the employee may return

[36] Aleksandrov, Astrakhan, Karinsky and Moskalenko, *Zakonodatelstvo o Trude* [*Legislation on Labour*] (1947) p. 20.
[37] *Ibid.*

to his farm without hindrance at the end of the term, with his full pay computed and paid within two days after the termination, and, if he does not wish to return he may extend the contract, receiving a vacation at home at the management's expense, and a loan to build a dwelling, as well as the expenses of bringing to join him those members of his family able to work.

Examination of this model contract in the light of the reports of a member of the United Nations Relief and Rehabilitation Administration who happened to be in the Ukraine during the campaign to persuade collective farmers to go to the mines, suggests that the farmers were reluctant to leave their farms. It was, apparently, necessary to win their confidence by providing in written form exactly what the terms of employment would be. The fact that such a procedure was adopted suggests, further, that there must exist among Soviet peasants confidence in legal procedure and forms beyond that often surmised by foreign students of the Soviet system.

A test case [38] has indicated that even without a written employment contract workers are entitled to the full benefits of the Code of Labour Laws relating to the employment relationship. Suit was brought by a group of five persons who had been a brigade of boiler makers in the Petroleum Supply Trust in the Georgian Republic. They were dismissed after completing a job, but were denied severance-pay and compensation for vacations. They sued to recover these benefits guaranteed to permanent employees by the Code. The trust defended successfully in the trial court on the ground that the men had not been part of the permanent staff and had stopped work because the job for which they had been employed had been completed. The College for Civil Cases of the Supreme Court of the U.S.S.R. reversed on the ground that the facts in the record should have been interpreted as indicating that the men had been part of the permanent staff and, therefore, were entitled to the benefits provided by the Code. They had been working for the defendant for nearly two years in riveting a metal water tank and large boilers, and had certainly become part of the staff. The absence of a written contract was considered as no basis for depriving the plaintiffs of their rights under the Code.

[38] *Belousov, Karesev, Kryuchkov, Liskonov, Zubchenko* v. *Azneftesbyt* [1939] 3 Sov.Yust. 76.

Examination of the Code and the multitudinous statutes amending the 1922 vehicle so as to make it fit the conditions of universal State employment for which it was not drafted originally, suggests that the body of labour law has been developed with two major aims in mind: increasing production and maintaining the good-will of the workmen by protecting them in that relationship which is paramount in their survival, namely their job. The first of these aims has been evidenced most dramatically of recent years. The measures designed, apparently, to increase production have been characterised by severity since Hitler's legions marched across the plains of Poland. They have attracted the attention of the world.

REDUCING LABOUR TURNOVER

In the first decade of life of the Code of Labour Laws a low rate of labour turnover and maximum production at the job was achieved, in part, by the threat of unemployment held over those who fell below the standards required or who failed to appear for work for specific periods of time. Article 47 of the Code permitted the employer, whether he was a private entrepreneur or a State manager to dismiss an employee who failed to appear at work for more than three days in succession, or more than six days in a month without satisfactory reason; in the event of complete or partial liquidation of the enterprise, office or business, or in the event of reduction in its work; in the event of work stoppage for more than one month for reasons of a production character; in the event that the employee evidenced his unsuitability for the work; in the event that the employee systematically, and without acceptable reasons failed to perform his duties, established either by contract or the disciplinary rules of the enterprise; in the event that the employee committed an act punishable under the criminal law directly connected with his work and established by a court sentence, and in the event that the employee was held under guard for more than two months; in the event of failure to report to work as the result of temporary loss of capacity to work for a period of two months from the day the capacity was lost; in the event of failure to return to work after loss of capacity to work because of pregnancy or birth for two months in excess of the four-month period established by law; and in the event that in the position occupied by the employee an employee formerly occupying the position is reinstated as a result of a court order or an order of the grievance committee.

So long as unemployment threatened the workman who violated any of these provisions, there was pressure against laxness of discipline, but unemployment fell gradually. By 1930 the growth of the industrialisation of the country under the stimulus of the five-year plans and the investment the State was making in capital construction, had absorbed all of the floating labour.[39] It did more than absorb the floaters. It resulted in an acute shortage of skilled labour from which it became possible for workers to better their position by moving from one employment office to another. Although all of the employment offices by this time were State agencies, they felt no obligation to refrain from outbidding each other in seeking to fill their employment requirements. The result was a heavy turnover in the labour force, from which great waste occurred. Skills acquired at the expense of training and spoilage of production were lost to an industry as a workman moved on, only to be replaced by another inexperienced youth just arrived from a peasant village.

In 1932 a step was taken towards strengthening labour discipline. The Code was amended[40] as it related to absence from work to provide that not three days of unexplained absence but one day was sufficient reason for dismissal of a worker, and to make this meaningful in an era of full employment it was provided that the dismissed worker should be deprived of his ration coupons and of any living quarters which might have been made available to him. Both of these sanctions had teeth in them, for non-rationed food was many times more expensive than the rationed goods, and housing was almost impossible to acquire.

In spite of the efforts to instil responsibility to society through the medium of sanctions which could cut deeply into the economic life of the individual, there were still reports of heavy wastage as the result of labour turnover. Efforts were then made to eliminate opportunities for re-employment after

[39] Baykov, *The Development of the Soviet Economic System* (1947) p. 213.
[40] Decree of November 15, 1932, [1932] 1 Sob.Zak. SSSR, No. 78, item 475, incorporated in Code of Labour Laws of the USSR, Art. 47 (1) by decree of November 20, 1932, [1932] 1 Sob.Uzak. RSFSR, No. 85, item 371.

leaving a job. A regulation in April, 1934,[41] required managers to record in a labour book to be carried by workmen any penalties for absenteeism. Four years later the concept of a personal labour record for each citizen in enterprises and offices was expanded by a decree of December 20, 1938,[42] requiring all such persons to carry a 'labour passport', into which a record of their employment was to be entered. This book would put State employment officials on notice of an applicant's record when he sought another job.

A week later a decree[43] provided that an employee might be dismissed not only because of absence but because of tardiness for three times during any month or four times during two consecutive months. Still labour discipline remained lax, perhaps partly because it had not been common for the Russians to count the minutes in the past. A different value has been placed on time for generations than the value placed on it in the highly industrialised and money-minded west.

A blow fell on June 26, 1940, immediately after the fall of France, when the prospect was opened up of a German march to the east in spite of the 1939 Nazi-Soviet pact. The 1940 decree[44] denied to workers the right to leave their jobs without having obtained permission from the administration. The administration was instructed that it was required to give permission only in the event of ill-health or withdrawal on admission to a technical training school. In other cases it might withhold permission at its discretion. The penalty for withdrawal without permission was to be from two to four months' imprisonment, after trial by a court to determine the facts. The director of an enterprise or chief of an office who hired persons and concealed the fact that they had departed without permission from their last job was ordered to be tried by a court. Thus, the policy-makers of the U.S.S.R. attempted to prevent labour turnover and also to counter-balance the inducement to labour turnover which had been afforded by the willingness of labour-short managers to hire any one who came into their office. The

41 [1934] Byull. Fin. i Khoz. Zak., No. 13, p. 37.

42 Decree of December 20, 1938, [1938] Sob.Post. SSSR, No. 58, item 329.

43 Decree of December 28, 1938, s. 1, par. 5, [1939] Sob.Post. SSSR, No. 1, item 1.

44 Ved.Verkh.Sov. SSSR, No. 20, 1940. A decree of October 19, 1940, Ved.Verkh.Sov. SSSR, No. 42, 1940, required engineers and technicians to accept transfer from one enterprise to another on pain of prosecution under the decree of June 26, 1940.

severity of the June 26, 1940, decree was increased within less than a month by an order of the Prosecutor and the Minister of Justice of the U.S.S.R. declaring that 'unexplained absence' within the meaning of the statute was to include tardiness in excess of twenty minutes in arriving for work in the morning or after the luncheon recess, or department for luncheon or at the end of the shift so early as to cause more than twenty minutes working time to be lost.[45] This interpretation was placed in the new factory disciplinary laws six months later.[46]

To speed prosecution of offences under the June 26, 1940, decree, a series of measures was taken to amend criminal procedure. The Supreme Court of the U.S.S.R. ordered that the usual preliminary investigation before trial be eliminated in such cases.[47] The bench was reduced in size to a single professional judge sitting alone without the two lay assessors usually required in trial courts.[48] Directors of enterprises were ordered to notify the court not later than one day after a violation of the law of June 26, 1940,[49] and the courts were ordered to try the case within five days after receipt of the notification.[50] As a consequence of these measures a man who was more than twenty minutes late on Monday morning would have been convicted by the following Monday.

The Soviet leadership seems to have been shocked by the turn of events in the war and to have determined to increase production by preserving the strictest discipline.

The German Army marched into the U.S.S.R. on June 22, 1941. Within six months an even more severe law was enacted providing that persons who left military industries without permission were to be considered on a par with deserters from the military services and sentenced by courts for a period of from five to eight years.[51] Labour in war industries was thus 'frozen' in its place of employment. The period for beginning trials was ordered to be shortened to forty-eight hours for tardiness and seventy-two hours for unauthorised departure from a job.[52]

45 Order of June 22, 1940, [1940] 13 Sov.Yust. 5.
46 Order of January 18, 1941, [1941] Sob.Post. SSSR, No. 4, item 63.
47 Order of Supreme Court USSR, July 15, 1940, [1940] 13 Sov.Yust. 5.
48 Decree of August 10, 1940, Ved.Verkh.Sov. SSSR, No. 28, 1940.
49 Order of August 21, 1940, [1940] Sob.Post. SSSR, No. 22, item 543.
50 Order of Minister of Justice, USSR, August 26, 1940, printed as annotation to *Code of Criminal Procedure RSFSR* (1943 ed.) p. 199.
51 Decree of December 26, 1941, Ved.Verk.Sov. SSSR, No. 2, 1942.
52 Order of Minister of Justice, USSR, October 22, 1942, printed as annotation to *Code of Criminal Procedure RSFSR* (1943 ed.) p. 200.

SOCIAL EDUCATION SEEMS INADEQUATE

To those who had anticipated that the new social attitudes to be expected with the advent of socialism would reduce the necessity of disciplinary laws, the steps leading to the labour situation existing in 1941 must have been a disappointment. Social change was being brought about by time-honoured severity rather than the educational measures anticipated by many of those who had fought the revolution. What consolation there was could have been found only in a scanning of the news of the day. Hitler had almost conquered the Soviet capital. The regime was thought by many throughout the world and in the U.S.S.R. itself to be tottering. It was not a time when even the most ardent educators would have claimed any possibility of success for the reasoned approach among a people who had not yet shown much aptitude for accepting arguments alone.

The 1940 decree 'freezing' employees in their jobs seemed to provide that, except in the two special instances given (health and advanced schooling), the administration was entirely free to decide whether or not an employee could leave his post. There was no indication that the reasonableness of the denial of a request to be permitted to leave was reviewable, but the courts soon built up a practice on the subject. Some cases will indicate what happened.

One Nikitina had been an inspector in a rubber factory. She left her job without permission and was prosecuted, found guilty and sentenced to four months' imprisonment. On review by the College for Criminal Cases of the Supreme Court of the U.S.S.R. the conviction was set aside because the refusal to grant permission to leave was thought to have been unreasonable.[53] The record showed that the woman had five children, the youngest of which was but three months old. She asked for permission to depart after return from pregnancy leave on the ground that she could not abandon her nursing child and her other children, but the permission had been denied.

One Bereznitskaya had been convicted of the same offence and sentenced to two months' imprisonment. Her conviction was also set aside on review by the College for Criminal Cases of the Supreme Court of the U.S.S.R.[54] From the record it was

[53] *Case of Nikitina* [1940] 19–20 Sov.Yust. 43.
[54] *Case of Berezhnitskaya* [1940] 11 Sots.Zak. 67.

evident that the woman had left work because she had two children, aged seven and one, who were to be left without care because her domestic worker had suddenly left. The woman thought that she could leave properly in spite of the refusal of her employer, a bank, to release her, because her trade union's Provincial Committee chairman had given her an opinion that she was not under the 1940 law, having been employed for only a trial term.

Prosecutions for tardiness also show that the courts established a rule of reason in the application of the statute, although no such rule was incorporated in the precise wording of the statute. One Madzaeva had been convicted for tardiness in returning to work after a brief permitted absence and had been sentenced to two months' deduction of salary of 5 per cent and loss of seniority for the period. The College for Criminal Cases set the conviction aside as being a perversion of the statute.[55] The record showed that she had been a worker in the factory for seven years with a record of no violations of discipline. She was one of the leading producers in her shop. She had been permitted four hours' absence from work to place her child in a kindergarten, but the child had been denied admission to the kindergarten because it was ill with an infectious intestinal disease, and she had had to take it home and could not return for work that day.

One Batmanov fared badly before the trial court because the court failed to pay attention to the facts before it. He was accused of tardiness in returning to his post after a business trip. Under his travel orders he had been required to return on July 5, 1940, by virtue of the fact that his assignment ran from June 21 to July 4, 1940, inclusive. He reached his home town on July 4 early in the morning in what was described as a very untidy condition after two weeks of travel. Having put himself in order he reported for duty at noon on July 4. Since this was three hours after the usual opening of the plant, he was reported late, and prosecuted on this basis. The Supreme Court pointed out that he had not been required to report on July 4, and so he had really arrived at the office half a day early instead of half a day late. The prosecution was ordered to be terminated.[56]

55 *Case of Madzaeva* [1940] 19–20 Sov.Yust. 43.
56 *Case of Batmanov* [1940] 11 Sots.Zak. 68.

From such cases as these it appears that Soviet higher courts have believed it to be their duty not only to make certain that the severe laws were applied only to cases which fell within the provisions of the laws, but also to mitigate the severity of the law when it was applied unreasonably by the administration of an enterprise to the undoubted disturbance of the morale of the factory population. In the U.S.S.R. as in other lands there would be many who knew of the situation in which the distressed mothers had found themselves, and a system of law which left them in prison would have done much to offset the propaganda efforts of the government to claim for itself credit for its great concern for the workers.

Some lower courts seem to have thought that there was an opportunity to enforce labour discipline through the law of torts. A State enterprise brought suit to recover damages for a period of idleness of a machine tool caused by the unexplained absence of its operator. The plaintiff claimed that damages should be in the amount of the value of the product which could have been produced by the machine had the operator been present. The College for Civil Cases of the Supreme Court of the U.S.S.R. found it necessary to set aside the judgment on the ground that there was no basis in law for such an action.[57]

DISMISSALS FOR INCOMPETENCE

Dismissals from work for lack of capacity to perform a job are said to have given rise to one of the two most litigated types of disputes within the realm of labour law. The other most litigated subject is wages. The policy is set forth by Article 47 of the Code to which reference has been made, but the application of policy is obviously one requiring the exercise of judgment. Lack of capacity to perform one's duties is not often measurable in terms of demonstrable units which have not been produced.

To determine the reasonableness of managerial decisions that an employee is incompetent, two procedures are provided: one a procedure before a grievance committee on which both management and the employee's trade union are represented, and the other before a court. The court is denied jurisdiction

[57] *Case of Shuvaeva,* September 9, 1943, Sbornik Post. Pl. i Opr. Koll. Verkh. Suda SSSR, 1943 (1948) p. 271. For commentary, see Karinsky, 'The Concept of Real Injury in Cases Concerning the Liability of Workers and Clerks', [1950] 10 Sots.Zak. 37.

in this type of case until the grievance committee has had an opportunity to establish the facts.[58] If the two sides on the committee cannot agree on the correctness of the decision, the dismissed employee has a right to appeal to the court. If the two sides agree, the dismissed employee may still present his appeal to the court, but it need not respond. It has only a post-audit function, with the right to review a case if it thinks the decision has been taken wrongly. Some court decisions will indicate the reasoning adopted.

An electrician was dismissed because the management believed him to be incompetent. The trial court denied his suit for reinstatement, and the Moscow Provincial Court affirmed the denial. When reviewed by the College for Civil Cases of the R.S.F.S.R. the dismissal was reaffirmed. The record showed that the man had rung the fire alarm by mistake when attempting to find the light switch in the shop in which he was working. The Supreme Court was of the opinion that his actions were negligent in view of the fact that he had worked for a long time in the factory and could not have failed to know the difference between the fire alarm and the light switch, and he had not denied that the fire alarm was in a separate box from the light switch.[59]

An elderly woman sued for reinstatement in her position as the chief of a village medical clinic. She was dismissed by the District Health Department for poor rendering of medical aid and for careless storage of medicines at the clinic. Her argument was that no proof of these charges had been presented. The grievance committee had upheld her employers. The woman took her case to court, at which point management presented a derogatory report of medical experts on her work at a previous post in another clinic. The trial court upheld the decision of the grievance committee, and the Provincial Court affirmed. The woman then petitioned for review by the College for Civil Cases of the Supreme Court of the R.S.F.S.R., and her petition was granted. The dismissal was set aside, because the Supreme Court found that not one witness had confirmed the allegation of the insanitary condition of the clinic and the improper execu-

[58] Decree of December 12, 1928, as amended, s. 10 (*c*). Kisilev and Malkin, *Sbornik Vazhneishikh Postanovlenii po Trudy* [*Collection of the Most Important Statutes on Labour*] (1936) p. 309.

[59] *Barenblat* v. *Moselektrik* [1930] 8 Sud.Prak. RSFSR 19.

tion of duties. All of the evidence had related to a prior position, and it was not pertinent to dismissal from the position held at the later time. The case was remanded for rehearing to determine whether there was any evidence relating to the specific dismissal in issue.[60]

The presentation of evidence in support of a charge of lack of capacity has had to meet rather strict standards since the war, if two cases reported in 1950 are to be accepted as representative. In the first of these,[61] a teacher in a children's nursery school had been dismissed on two counts: frequent absence and lack of professional competence. Both the trial court and the appellate court found the dismissal valid, and even the Supreme Court of the R.S.F.S.R. through its College for Civil Cases supported the finding.

On a review initiated by the Prosecutor General of the U.S.S.R. the College for Civil Cases of the Supreme Court of the U.S.S.R. set aside all of the decisions below as lacking support in the evidence set forth in the record. It was noted that for all of the incidents listed by the lower courts as supporting the management's charge of frequent absence, disciplinary fines had been levied. The woman had not been dismissed until after she had returned from her vacation. The Supreme Court concluded that the absences had not seemed important enough at the time to merit more than fines, as evidenced by the fact that employment had been continued for a considerable time in spite of the absences.

Evidence in support of a finding of professional incompetence was also thought inadequate. The Supreme Court's College declared that lack of professional competence should be considered by the grievance committee representing the trade union and management before the matter is taken to court. It remanded the case to the Voronezh Provincial Court, from which it had come, and ordered that evidence must be produced at the trial in the manner required by law.

A teacher in a trade school sought reinstatement in the second case after having been dismissed as unfit for his job because of inability to teach discipline; of overgrading students

60 *Weinstein* v. *Mozhaisk District Health Office* [1938] 9 Sov.Yust. 23.

61 *Bondarevskaya* v. *Gryazinsk Combine of Food Concentrates* [1950] 1 Sots.Zak. 61.

and of teaching without any organised syllabus. While the trial court and the Supreme Court of the R.S.F.S.R. upheld the dismissal for incompetence, the Supreme Court of the U.S.S.R. through its College for Civil Cases ordered a new trial.

Again the reasons for the reversal were inadequate examination of the facts of the case. An order of December 25, 1941, issued by the Supreme Court was cited under which lower courts were advised not to permit dismissals for incompetence unless it has been manifested by systematic failure of the employee to perform assigned tasks, and unless disciplinary penalties had not achieved the desired results.

The Supreme Court concluded that the evidence in the record was inconclusive on these points, for it did not indicate that the teacher had been given the task of teaching discipline to the students. On the contrary, this task seemed to have been placed upon the director. Evidence in the record also suggested that the dismissal had really occurred because of the director's desire for revenge. There had been a letter to *Pravda* written by the teacher, following which the communist party's Provincial Committee had been asked to make an investigation. The Supreme Court noted that the trial court had not investigated the text of the letter or the results of the investigation, nor had it taken into account an investigation of the school by the responsible Ministry, following which the school director had been censured.[62]

Failure of management to appreciate that dismissal for failure to perform assigned tasks must no longer occur unless there is repeated failure seems to have brought forth a second order from the Supreme Court. On January 11, 1952, the rule was repeated that dismissals for such a reason will be upheld by the courts only if the disciplinary measures applied to the employee have had no result, indicating that his retention would be harmful to production.[63]

The responsibility placed upon the managerial authorities in making dismissals was demonstrated by a suit brought by a workman dismissed from his job for inability to cope with his work. He had been reinstated by the court which heard his

[62] *Vertogradov* v. *Usmansk Trade School* [1950] 5 Sots.Zak. 59.
[63] Pasherstnik, 'Strengthen Socialist Labour Discipline—One of the Most Important Tasks of Soviet Law' (1952) 10 Sov. Gos. i Pravo 45 at p. 61.

complaint, and judgment had been given for the loss suffered by virtue of his period of enforced idleness against the manager who had dismissed him illegally. The judgment against the manager was protested by the Prosecutor of the U.S.S.R., who thought it wrong. The College for Civil Cases of the U.S.S.R. agreed that it should be set aside, but for the reason that the manager had not been made a party to the suit, and the amount awarded against the manager exceeded the three months' wages permitted by law.[64]

DISMISSALS FOR SUNDRY REASONS

Dismissals for reasons other than incompetence have also been litigated. A teacher in an engineering institute was relieved of his position just before the term opened in September because there was insufficient need for him. He sued, not to recover his position, but for the wages he had expected to obtain during the first term at the Institute, and recovered. The Provincial Court altered the judgment from an award of full wages of 1,785 roubles to severance pay of 249 roubles 90 kopeks. The College for Civil Cases of the Supreme Court of the R.S.F.S.R. reinstated the judgment for full wages on the ground that the teacher had been informed after the beginning of the term that his services were not required.[65] Under the law he had, therefore, a right to his full wages for the term.

Some cases indicate that dismissals have occurred for reasons other than those permitted by the Code of Labour Laws. Thus a manager of a co-operative society sought relief when dismissed from his position in 1937 on the ground that for a large number of years he had refused responsible positions offered to him, and that his father had been a merchant in 1924. The grievance committee agreed to the dismissal, and the trial court refused to reinstate him, saying that he was an 'alien' element, the son of a man deprived of civil rights as a merchant, and that he should have been dismissed as a precautionary measure at a time when there was being conducted throughout the co-operatives a campaign against embezzlement. The Supreme Court of the R.S.F.S.R. ordered reinstatement and damages for the period of

[64] *Afonin* v. *Kirin* [1939] 8–9 Sots.Zak. 100.
[65] *Bodungen* v. *Leningrad Institute of Industrial Transportation Engineers* [1938] 2 Sots.Zak. 107.

enforced idleness, on the ground that the reasons for dismissal were not those permitted by Article 47 of the Code of Labour Laws. The court added that the Commission of Soviet Control had issued an order specifically forbidding dismissal of employees on grounds of social origin and the like.[66]

A piano teacher was dismissed because her local trade union requested it. She appealed to the grievance committee, which upheld the dismissal. She then went to the Central Committee of the Trade Union, which found that the dismissal was illegal, and she filed suit in court, but both the trial court and the appellate court refused to reinstate her. Both courts accepted the dismissal as legal within the provisions of Article 49 which adds to the list of reasons for dismissal given in Article 47 the request of a trade union. The Supreme Court of the U.S.S.R. ordered a new trial because it believed that the ruling of the Central Committee of the Trade Union that the dismissal was illegal indicated that the requirements of Article 49 had not been complied with, and there was no evidence in the record to support a dismissal for any of the reasons given in Article 47.[67]

Not all employees can obtain redress through the courts in the event of dismissal. A case indicates that there are reserved areas in which management is given complete discretion to dismiss an employee without the necessity of justifying the dismissal. These areas might be called the 'sensitive' areas, and are so called in some other countries.

A teacher in the department of the history of the communist party in the All-Union Law Academy brought suit for reinstatement in his position after dismissal in 1937. The grievance committee denied his complaint, and the trial and appellate courts agreed with it. The College for Civil Cases of the Supreme Court of the U.S.S.R. took the matter for review at the request of the President of the Court who was of the opinion that the court had no jurisdiction in the matter. The court on the review agreed that there was no jurisdiction in the court because a special procedure had been established by the Council of People's Commissars of the U.S.S.R. and the Central Committee of the communist party in 1936. This procedure placed

[66] *Belyaev* v. *Medyn City Consumers' Co-operative Association* [1938] 9 Sov.Yust. 22.

[67] *Gardt* v. *Stalinabad College* [1939] 1 Sov.Yust. 75.

full responsibility for appointments to Professorial Chairs and to the position of readers, in the highest educational administrative agencies, and in no one else. Any appeal against dismissal could be only to the Division for Educational Institutions of the Ministry of Justice of the U.S.S.R.[68]

PRODUCTION AT ALMOST ANY COST

Examination of the functioning of Soviet labour law suggests that the leadership is determined to raise production, if need be by the enactment of the most severe measures, to force workmen to remain at their post, and to perform their services conscientiously. Yet, at the same time, there is ample indication in the work of the courts that there is a procedure in use which mitigates the severity of the statute in cases which represent severe hardship, and which would certainly be taken by the populace as examples of manifestly unfair application of the statute, if the penalties were permitted to stand.

The increase in severity of the labour law has accompanied the development of planning, but it also has accompanied the rise in international tension prior to the second world war. Some have attributed the increase in severity to the natural inclination of the planner who begins with planning the distribution of materials and then, seemingly quite naturally, seeks to plan the distribution of human resources.[69] Others have laid emphasis upon the war situation and have thought that the increase in severity of the statutes was a result of the near-panic faced by the leaders as they surveyed the potential of their productive plant to meet the needs of war.

Proof of the primacy of one or the other of these theories was expected after the war. If the severe disciplinary laws were relaxed, one might suppose that the reason for their original enactment had been military preparedness. If they were not relaxed, one might suppose that the master-planners had caught up human beings in their plans and thought it necessary to direct their distribution and their very lives, at least so long as the inducements presented by varied wage scales and appeals to patriotism failed to achieve the results required by the expansion

[68] *Topalov* v. *All-Union Academy of Law* [1940] 2 Sov.Yust. 41.
[69] M. T. Florinsky, 'Stalin's New Deal for Labour' (1941) 56 *Political Science Quarterly* 38.

of the economy. Since the end of World War II there has been no publication of any decree repealing the law of June 26, 1940, 'freezing' workmen in their jobs. It seems, however, no longer to be in force. It has been removed from its accustomed place as an appendix to the Criminal Code of the R.S.F.S.R.,[70] and the principal Soviet writer on labour law does not include it in an article on the problems of the present time.[71] On the contrary, he emphasises the necessity of instilling in the workman a sense of discipline out of appreciation of social duty rather than fear of criminal sanctions.

While there may now be developing some relaxation in the severity of labour law, it is clear that until recently there had been a trend in the opposite direction accompanying the progressive regimentation of the national economy and the development of the present-day social structure of the U.S.S.R. Soviet leadership seems to have moved far from the readiness exhibited in the early years to rely primarily upon the good judgment of the bench workman to get the job done.

As production has increased, laws and educational campaigns have multiplied to develop a new sort of 'good judgment'. The concept of service to the community in enlightened self-interest has been fostered by every means. The trade unions have been enlisted in this effort and deprived of any independent existence from which they might organise pressure-groups to challenge the programme of the leaders. Labour law has been used by the leaders to strengthen their hands for the tasks ahead. The lessening of the severity of sanctions which seems now to be developing appears to be but a cautious experiment in a change in emphasis. The fact that the step has been taken without publicity suggests that the Soviet leadership is far from believing that it has yet been successful in moulding the disciplined and devoted Soviet workman needed to accomplish its purposes.

70 Cf. *Criminal Code RSFSR*, edition of 1950, containing the law of June 26, 1940, on pp. 157–160, together with subsequent decrees and orders interpreting it as well as a decree of December 28, 1940, applying the rule to students in the labour reserve schools, with *Criminal Code RSFSR*, edition of 1952, which prints none of this material at the point where it had appeared in 1950, namely, between the law of November 21, 1929, and the law of February 10, 1941.

71 Pasherstnik, 'Strengthen Socialist Labour Discipline—One of the Most Important Tasks of Soviet Law' (1952) 10 Sov. Gos. i Pravo 45.

Chapter 8

THE INDIVIDUAL HAS A NICHE

Production and education—these have been the declared immediate goals of Soviet leadership. Without the goods to meet the needs of the people and indoctrination in the new social patterns the achievement of communism has been thought impossible. Law is assigned a role in preparing the way.

Previous chapters have indicated how the base has been laid by nationalisation of the productive resources and centralisation of control over their use. Exemplary producers have been rewarded, and those deemed recalcitrant and slothful have been disciplined. Community organisation of production has been encouraged where it has not existed previously. Political leadership has been reserved for a selected few, and their hand has been progressively strengthened by the silencing of those who have given or might give false counsel. But social change is not wholly the result of such basic measures.

The imaginative individual has his niche. It is he who through the novel, the drama, the opera, the ballet, the painting, the symphony, the poster and the poem can transmit the vision of the future to the pedestrian elements of the community. It is he who through the imaginative arrangement of machines and the rationalisation of productive processes can make each working hour contribute more to the common good.

Law has been given its place in encouraging imagination, yet its rewards are reserved for those who use their imagination in a fashion deemed by the leadership to have social value. In the phrase of a Soviet textbook, 'The Soviet author's right has the objective of protecting to the maximum the personal and property interests of the author. But at the same time it has as its aim the widest distribution of the product of literature, science and the arts among the broad masses of the toilers'.[1] In other words, law has had to balance the interests of the individual with those of the community.

[1] All-Union Institute of Juridical Sciences, 2 *Sovetskoe Grazhdanskoe Pravo* [*Soviet Civil Law*] (1951) p. 336.

Soviet law has reflected this balancing of interests from the outset. A year after the revolution[2] it was decreed that the Ministry of Education might declare to be the property of the Republic any published or unpublished scientific, literary, musical or artistic production. Royalties were ordered to be paid in accordance with a fixed tariff to the authors of any works appropriated in the fashion established by the decree.

Works which were not nationalised remained under the complete control of the author for his life and under the control of his heirs for six months after his death. The heirs received no royalties, however, as a matter of course. In accordance with the policy against inheritance existing at the time and discussed in Chapter 1, only needy relatives had the right to receive maintenance from a decedent's estate. The decree stated that royalties could be paid over to heirs only in accordance with the general principle established by the law of inheritance.

A similar policy was adopted for invention in the following year.[3] Any invention found by the Patent Committee to be useful to the State might be declared to be the property of the Republic by the Supreme Council of National Economy. Patent certificates were to be issued by the Patent Committee to inventors. Royalties were to be paid on patents declared the property of the Republic, while holders of patents on inventions not appropriated were, apparently, left free to get what they could from their invention by the usual open market process. The decree incorporated by reference the provisions of the earlier copyright decree concerning inheritance of royalties.

With the coming of the New Economic Policy the attitude toward copyright and patent had to be developed to accord with the restoration of private enterprise. It was becoming possible again to manufacture one's own invention or to assign patent rights to others with the expectation of profit. The decree of May 22, 1922,[4] concerning the protection of property rights to be introduced by the New Economic Policy included copyright among the rights to be protected, but no new copyright law was adopted until January 30, 1925.[5] This law, adopted after the

[2] Decree of November 26, 1918, [1918] 1 Sob.Uzak. RSFSR, No. 86, item 900.
[3] Decree of June 30, 1919, [1919] 1 Sob.Uzak. RSFSR, No. 34, item 341.
[4] [1922] 1 Sob.Uzak. RSFSR, No. 36, item 423.
[5] [1925] 1 Sob.Zak. SSSR, No. 7, item 67.

formation of the federal government, introduced most of the provisions which are fundamental to the law still in effect, in particular the extension of copyright protection on literary productions for fifteen years after the author's death. It declared, further, that the heirs had a right to royalties without limitation in amount, as an exception to the then existing policy of limited inheritance. The final article of the decree preserved in the State the right to purchase any production without the consent of the author whether published or not, so long as the work had taken concrete form.

A patent law for the conditions of the period of the New Economic Policy was adopted on September 12, 1924.[6] Said to have been patterned upon German law[7] it adopted familiar principles. Persons who held pre-revolutionary patents issued after January 1, 1910, were required to apply for reissuance of the patent if they desired protection. Earlier patents were considered as having expired. Those applications which were based on earlier patents were to be reviewed for novelty as of the date of filing the original patent claim. Any reissue of the patent was to be for the standard term of fifteen years, but it was to be considered as having commenced on the date of issuance of the pre-revolutionary patent. Under this provision little life would have been left in patents issued by the old regime.

With the gradual decline of the New Economic Policy, Soviet law relating to copyright and patent assumed new features reflecting the increased emphasis upon community. No longer could the imaginative individual be permitted to manufacture his own invention on any scale other than that of the artisan. No longer could he license its manufacture to a private producer. To have permitted private exploitation of invention would have been a concession of a grave nature to the individual. It would have upset the balance for which the leaders had struggled in the early days of the revolution and to which they had returned with the introduction of the five year plans. Whatever rights the inventor was to be given to induce invention needed to be fitted within the scheme of State production and distribution.

The author, dramatist, composer, painter, photographer and poet was still to be permitted to work as a free-lance artist in his

[6] [1926] 1 Sob.Zak. SSSR. No. 9, item 97.
[7] Gsovski, 1 *Soviet Civil Law* (1948) p. 593.

studio. He was not to be required to accept a salaried position in any 'art factory' producing for the State. Yet, if he wished to obtain social rewards from mass distribution the interests of the community raised their heads.

It was the thesis of the law that the State must be permitted to reserve unto itself the right to intrude upon the privacy of the artistic producer and appropriate for the use of the community that which the artist was not prepared yet to release. This principle, enshrined in all earlier legislation, was restated in the final article in the statute, which put the author on notice that he could not be capricious and withhold from the world artistic creations which the leaders thought necessary to the world's cultural development. Yet, while the right was reserved, the leadership felt it desirable, however, not to emphasise its existence until after the author had permitted the first public disclosure.

COPYRIGHT BALANCES INDIVIDUAL AND COMMUNITY

A general pattern of copyright was established by statute on May 16, 1928,[8] by the federal government to supersede earlier laws. This federal statute was subsequently carried into the law of each Republic.[9] At the outset the statute made it clear that it was not attempting the difficult task of protecting the Soviet works abroad. It said simply that it was to protect only artistic works existing in objective form within the U.S.S.R., whether the creation of Soviet citizens or foreigners. Works existing abroad, whether of Soviet citizens or foreigners were not to be protected unless a treaty had been negotiated with the foreign State concerned.

The provisions relating to the right of the State to intervene in the decision of the author to publish are the most arresting to the outsider. Generally, the principle is recognised that the individual is the best judge of the point at which a work is ready for public view. It may be thought likely to inhibit further production if a work is snatched from the hands of an author before he feels that he is proud of it. Whatever the reason, the State has held its hand and declared its general policy to be one of freedom to the author to choose his own time for publication. Yet, it reserves and states in no uncertain terms its right to step

8 [1928] 1 Sob.Zak. SSSR, No. 28, item 246.
9 Decree of Ocober 8, 1928, [1928] 1 Sob.Uzak. RSFSR, No. 132, item 861.

in as soon as the author gives the first indication that he is satisfied with what he has created. This is found to be stated in provisions concerning certain classes of artistic productions. Thus, when a manuscript of a dramatic, musical, operatic, pantomimic, choreographic or cinema production has been performed in public before it has been printed, the author may lose control of its future production.

Loss of control does not mean that the work is expropriated and the author deprived of any right to royalties. It means only that the work may be judged to be a national treasure in the opinion of the Ministry of Education of the Republic concerned. Thereafter, the Ministry may license performances even without the consent of the author. The latter can claim only the royalties accruing under the statute for such performances.

Curiously enough, the procedure for attributing the public interest to manuscripts not yet in print is not extended in express words to novels and poems. Yet, even for these works the paramountcy of the public interest seems to have been preserved in less precise language by the final article of the statute, to which reference has already been made. It reserves to the federal government and to the various Republics the right to require the owner of a copyright to sell it to the State. Presumably the price is set by the State, and thereafter the author has none of the means of influencing the use of the work provided him by statute.

The fact that some types of artistic productions are listed specifically while others are not suggests that appropriation in the public interest was expected to occur more usually before printing with the types listed than with the other types, for which only the general clause was provided. Neither the Soviet press nor common knowledge of those residing in the U.S.S.R. has indicated that such appropriation has occurred with any notable regularity against the author's will, so that the question may be only hypothetical.

For the work not appropriated in the public interest protection attaches in the form of a monopoly right to publish and license production. It applies both before publication, when a manuscript or sketch lies in the author's study, and after publication when it has become known to the world. The term of such protection varies in accordance with the character of the work. For choreographic productions, pantomimes, cinema scenarios and films the period of protection is ten years. Should the author die before the expiration of the period, his heirs have the right to royalties during the unexpired balance of the period. Photographic works in collections are extended the same period of protection, but for individual photographs the period is set at five years. Periodicals and encyclopædiæ are protected also for a term of ten years. All other works are protected for the life of the author and an ensuing fifteen years.

THE PROPERTY RIGHT IS LIMITED

While copyright has been referred to in the textbook cited earlier as incorporating a 'property' interest of the author, it is a limited one in Soviet law. Not only is it subject to expropriation in the public interest in the manner indicated, but there is a considerable number of situations listed by the statute in which reproduction is not considered an infringement. These indicate the points at which public interest is believed to outweigh individual interest. Some of the most important situations bear examination.

No translation is considered a violation of the copyright law. It has been explained by Soviet authorities that the social progress of the various minority peoples of the Soviet Union toward socialism and communism, especially those with small populations, requires that artistic productions become available to them at minimum cost. In consequence the payment of author's royalties to any but the translator is not required. In practice, however, royalties have often been paid even to the accounts of foreign authors, although Ministry of Finance restrictions on the transfer of currency has prevented their utilisation anywhere except in the U.S.S.R.

Selections may be published without payment of royalties or the consent of the author, up to forty lines of poetry or 40,000 printed characters of other materials, and subsequent authors may 'borrow' from the work. In this fashion the publication of anthologies for mass distribution is reduced in cost and facilitated and the dissemination of ideas is encouraged. Public speeches may be reproduced freely, as may newspaper articles not having a literary character. Photographs and sketches appearing in like manner may also be reproduced.

Schools and groups specialising in the study of the subject

may reproduce or perform works of art without requesting consent of the author and without payment of royalties, provided that no special admission charge is made of those who attend. Drawings and photographs may be used by artisan groups in the production of their wares without the consent of the artist or photographer, but only upon the payment of royalties.

With the exceptions listed, a copyright owner may exercise some of the rights of an 'owner', in that he may alienate the 'property' right to a State publisher, but not to any one else. He may designate in his will any one or more of those entitled to inherit his estate as the sole heir of his rights for the fifteen years after death permitted by law. An author may prevent any one during his lifetime from altering a work by adding to it, or cutting it and the heir receives the same right. He may recover damages under the Civil Code for violation of the right and is excused from paying a court fee.[10] He may instigate criminal prosecution if the violation was with criminal intent.[11] Damages are computed in the event of violation on the basis of the regulation of the Ministry of Education of the R.S.F.S.R. at 150 per cent of the established tariff for royalty payments.[12]

The distinction drawn in Soviet law between what are called 'property' and 'personal' interests of an author is illustrated by the following case.[13] Suit was brought on behalf of two translators of a Ukrainian epic poem to obtain supplementary royalties because the edition of the work had exceeded the publisher's expectations at the time of making the publishing contract. Judgment was given for the authors, but it was set aside by the College for Civil Cases of the Supreme Court of the U.S.S.R. when reviewed at the request of its President.

Grounds for reversal were that the authors had transferred to the publishing house all of the 'property' interest in the work. This was entirely legal. They had received as compensation a fee which exceeded that which would have been paid normally

10 *Code of Civil Procedure,* RSFSR, Art. 43.

11 *Criminal Code,* RSFSR, Art. 177.

12 Regulation of June 8, 1930, [1930] Byulleten Narkomprosa, No. 19. The standard tariff is set forth in a decree of July 12, 1944, [1944] Sob.Post. SSSR, No. 8, item 43. Both this decree and the regulation on punitive damages are published in Gorodetsky and Rozovskaya, *Spravochnik po avtorskomu pravu* [*Manual of Copyright*] (1948) pp. 73–78.

13 *Administration for the Protection of Authors' Rights* v. *Institute of Language and Literature, Azfan* [1940] Sbornik Post. Pl. i Opr. Koll. Verkh. Suda SSSR, p. 283.

under the standard royalty tariff for the size of the edition originally contemplated. In consequence, they had no standing in court. The Supreme Court noted that the 'personal' rights of the authors were inalienable, for even the publishing house could not obtain by contract the author's right to control alterations in the work and to withhold consent to performance or reproduction unless this had been withdrawn by the Ministry of Education in accordance with the procedure already set forth.

Further clarification of the nature of the 'personal' right in a literary production is to be found in a circular letter of the R.S.F.S.R. publishing house, 'OGIZ' issued on September 15, 1943.[14] At a time when the disruption of the war made it difficult if not impossible to obtain the consent of authors to reprinting of their work by provincial publishing houses, it apparently became necessary in what was thought to be the interest of the community to find a way out of the difficulty.

The circular indicated that under the law the 'personal' right of an author included the right to refuse permission to reprint a work. The circular letter, in its effort to follow the law without hampering the work of the provincial press, declared that no work should be reprinted by the provincial publishers without preliminary communication with the author, and without conclusion of a publishing contract. Yet, if the author could not be reached directly in the normal way the provincial publishing house might inform the author of its reprinting plans in a letter addressed to the author at the publishing house which had presented the original work, or at the office of the Soviet Writers' Union. A copy of the communication was to be sent to the All-Union Administration for the Protection of Authors' Rights. A royalty was always to be paid, and if the All-Union Administration held a power of attorney from the author, the royalty was to be forwarded immediately to it.

The circular letter of OGIZ indicated again the extent to which the Soviet leadership seems to feel the desirability of preserving for the authors not only the right to receive royalties, but also the right to control the use to be made of their productions. Yet at the same time there is always in the background the interest of the community, as interpreted by the leadership,

14 Gorodetsky and Rozovskaya, *Spravochnik po avtorskomu pravu* [*Manual of Copyright*] (1948) p. 15.

and this may require what amounts to 'substituted service of notice' when the times are such that direct communication is impossible.

No formalities are necessary on the part of the author to effect copyright within the U.S.S.R., except for the photographer. He must place his name or that of the publisher with an address in the corner of each photograph, together with the year of publication. The publisher and not the author has the obligation of depositing copies of the work in the designated depository libraries of the U.S.S.R., of which there are many.

Royalties are fixed by statute to accord with the type of work and the size of the edition. The form of the publishing contract is also prescribed by the statute, so that the parties have little to bargain about. Some variation may occur, however, in the time set in the agreement for publication, although a maximum is set for each of three categories of publication: the quickest being periodicals and brochures of five printer's sheets (200,000 printed characters), for which a maximum period of six months is allowed; the middle category being other literary publications having up to ten printer's sheets, for which the maximum period is set at one year; while for longer works the maximum period may be two years. Once the period has been set, the publisher is held to it on pain of payment of damages in the full amount of royalties due under the contract if delay occurs. After a second period of one half the time permitted in the contract for publication, the author has the right to demand the return of the manuscript.

As has already been indicated in the discussion of the censorship rules in Chapter 3, a judicial decision refused royalties to an author when it appeared at the trial that the work has not passed the trade union's reviewing department because of its ideological deficiencies, and for this reason it had not been published in accordance with the provisions of the contract.[15]

SUITS AGAINST PUBLISHERS

An author who had no such ideological problem was successful in obtaining full royalties when his work was not published for reasons thought by the Court to be beyond his control.[16] The

[15] *Solonevich v. Publishing House 'Our Newspaper'* [1931] 15 Sud.Prak. RSFSR 4.

[16] *Kirpichnikov v. Peat Institute* [1940] 9 Sots.Zak. '77.

author had completed for the Peat Institute in 1936 two articles, 'The Economics of Drying Peat' and 'Literature on Chemical and Technical Reworking of Peat'. The contract provided for a royalty of 300 roubles per printer's sheet. 50 per cent of the royalty had been paid when the work was accepted, but the balance had remained unpaid and the work had never been published.

The Peat Institute won the decision on a mistake of law in the trial court. It also argued that the work was substantially a copy of articles by another man. While the argument of plagiarism was not accepted, the trial court held that when a work was not published, the royalty need be only the 50 per cent which had already been paid. The Supreme Court of the U.S.S.R. pointed out the error of law and ordered payment at the full amount set in the contract.

The copying of the materials used in the work does not always prevent protection of an author. Thus, an author of a book of charts with explanatory text depicting the construction and operation of a Soviet tractor was successful in obtaining royalties, even though experts testified that the diagrams were only copies of the blueprints of factory models and the text only the specifications for the blueprints, slightly rewritten. The court explained that such copying would prevent the granting of a patent, but not the protection of copyright.[17]

Two cases have indicated that absence of a written publishing contract does not prevent protection of an author's rights. In the first case[18] a translator had made a written contract to translate an Ossetian epic poem into Russian for a fee of 2,000 roubles. Subsequently, by oral agreement the time limit for delivery of the translator's work had been extended to permit rewriting in Russian verse. The publisher refused payment of 7,000 roubles claimed by the translator as a supplemental fee for the versification, and suit was brought. While judgment was denied in the Supreme Court of the Ossetian Republic, the Supreme Court of the U.S.S.R. remanded the case for trial to determine by oral testimony the precise terms of the supplementary oral agreement and judgment in accordance with its terms.

17 *State Scientific-Technical Publishing House 'Mashgiz'* v. *Morozov* [1944] Sbornik Post. Pl. i Opr. Koll. Verkh. Suda SSSR, p. 333.

18 *Tsagolov* v. *Administration for Artistic Affairs of the Northern Ossetian Republic* [1942] *ibid.*, at p. 203.

Similarly, a publishing house fought a suit for royalties on an unpublished manuscript entitled 'Glaciers of the Lake Balkhash Basin', partly on the ground that it had been prepared during working hours of the author at the publishing house, but also because there was no written contract. The Supreme Court's College for Civil Cases declared that the lower court had correctly rejected both arguments because no written contract was required by law and because the evidence in the record indicated that the principal part of the work had been performed outside of working hours.[19]

Both of these cases discussed an additional point, for in both the defendant publishing house had argued that the authors had published identical materials in another place. In the second case, the Supreme Court's college stated that the trial court had not investigated the evidence submitted on this point, but that on retrial if such were found to be the case, there could be no recovery.

The first case was more complicated. To reply to the publishing house's defence of identical materials elsewhere, the author charged that the publishing house had delayed so long in printing his book of tractor charts that they had become out of date. In consequence he had made a contract with another State agency under which he had prepared a second manuscript. Further, the second manuscript had been offered by its purchaser to the publishing house which had contracted for the first. The second manuscript contained 800 drawings, while the first had but 120.

The court ordered careful comparison of the two manuscripts on retrial and declared that if they proved to be charts of the same model of tractor, the two contracts should be treated as one. Payment under the second contract should be computed by deducting the advance payment made under the first. If, however, the manuscripts contained charts of different models, the two contracts should be treated separately, and recovery might be had on each independently.

An author, suing under the law in existence prior to the present statute, was successful in obtaining the return of his manuscript when the publishing house to which it had been

19 *Gorbunov* v. *Alma Ata Administration for Gidrometshluzhba* [1942] Sud.Prak. SSSR 27.

delivered under a contract was liquidated. The liquidating commission argued that the manuscript had become a part of the assets of the publishing house, and also that the author had already received part payment on account of the royalty. The Supreme Court of the R.S.F.S.R. held for the author and declared that the manuscript could not be assigned against his will to another publisher by the liquidating commission.[20]

Some judicial decisions indicate that disputes arise as to whether employees of enterprises have written a work as a feature of their employment or as an outside endeavour for which the protection of the copyright law applies. Two cases suggest the variations on the theme which may arise. In the first of them [21] the manager of State Soap Rendering, Candle and Chemical Factory No. 1 was ordered by the director of the enterprise to prepare a statistical summary entitled 'Five Years of Work', telling the story of the factory's activities. The work was completed, printed and distributed, and the manager sued for royalties at the fixed rate for such brochures. At the trial an expert testified that the brochure was not merely a factory report but an economic essay of original merit. The director argued that it was no such thing, and also that other persons in the factory had participated in its preparation. The court gave judgment for the manager as plaintiff, finding that he had copyright in the work as an original contribution.

The fact that the manager was chairman of a factory team of writers; that he was obligated to prepare official reports; and that there was no publishing contract were considered as evidence by the Supreme Court to support its conclusions that the manager had performed his work in the line of duty. It seemed to the Supreme Court that the plaintiff had no copyright in the brochure.

Another author under nearly similar circumstances was also unsuccessful in establishing copyright.[22] He worked as a specialist in the administration of the State Bakery Inspection Office of the Ministry of Trade of the U.S.S.R. He had been commissioned by the Ministry to prepare a handbook with Instructions con-

20 *Rozin* v. *Publishing House 'School and Book'*, No. 34,813 [1929] 8 Sud.Prak. RSFSR 7.
21 *Vinogradov* v. *State Soap Rendering Candle and Chemical Factory No. 1*, No. 32,435 [1929] 1 Sud.Prak. RSFSR 8.
22 *Sokolov* v. *State Bakery Inspection Office* [1929] 8 Sud.Prak. RSFSR 7.

cerning the way in which pests might be eliminated from grain and its products. The brochure had been accepted and printed by the Ministry and distributed at 75 kopeks a copy.

When the author sued for royalties, an expert testified in his behalf that the work was not an instruction of the Ministry in the precise sense of the word but a popularised brochure about a scientific subject. The trial court did not accept the expert's opinion, feeling that the matter was really a Ministerial instruction book, even though not in the form of a Ministerial order, and that it had been written in the line of duty. The appellate court agreed with the trial court that a Ministerial instruction could take a form other than one which is 'bureaucratically dry'. Also it considered important the fact that there was no publication contract. It was prepared, however, to uphold the author's right to a premium for the work, to be distinguished from copyright, since it found that there had been an agreement to give 150 copies of the work to the author, and since this had not been done, the money equivalent could rightfully be ordered in the amount of 150 roubles.

The extent to which an author may 'borrow' from other works without violating the copyright has been indicated by a case involving a dictionary.[23] A German-Russian Technical Dictionary had been published before the revolution, and in several reprints up to the year 1934. It was a large three-volume work of 183,000 words. In the case at bar the two authors brought suit against the State publishing house and the two authors of an abbreviated one-volume *Technical German-Russian Dictionary,* published in 1931 and reprinted in 1932 and 1934.

The authors of the older work claimed that the major part of the abbreviated work corresponded with the earlier work. Experts were called by both sides. The expert for the plaintiffs stated that four-fifths of the new volume were borrowed from the plaintiffs' volumes, even to the extent of copying all of the errors. The expert for the defendants explained that any compiler of a dictionary would have to use all earlier dictionaries, including that of the plaintiffs, but that the percentage of translations which were identical with those of the plaintiffs was not over twenty five, and since it was a short dictionary the selection process also had to be taken into consideration.

[23] *Saltanov* v. *Erasmus and Soviet Encyclopedia* [1937] 17 Sov.Yust. 51.

While the trial court reached the conclusion that the borrowing had not been critically performed and hence did not constitute an original contribution, it agreed that the number of words and definitions borrowed was only 25 per cent. The defendants were ordered to pay jointly damages of 2,500 roubles and an additional 990 roubles as the expenses of the plaintiffs' expert. The Civil College of the Supreme Court of the R.S.F.S.R. set aside the judgment, arguing that under the copyright law, not only may one borrow from the works of others but one may reprint small excerpts. Under the circumstances it thought that the compilers of the small volume had not exceeded the amount of borrowing permitted by the statute.

The case suggests that the borrowing which may be permitted in the interests of the community may be more extensive than in other systems of law, yet it contains the implication that the borrowing may not be excessive without violating the law. The amount which will be deemed excessive is, presumably, for the court to decide in each case in which an author feels sufficiently aggrieved to take the matter to court.

The form of reproduction was brought into the defence of a publishing house, which argued that it owed no royalties to a Professor of Geology for the part of a textbook which had been lithographed.[24] Royalties had already been paid on the part which had been printed. The Supreme Court's College for Civil Cases cited the law in support of its decision that the form of reproduction was not a bar to recovery of royalties. Its suspicions were aroused, apparently, for it ordered an examination on retrial of the reasons why the second part had not been printed.

Some suggestion of a procedural bar which must be kept in mind when suing for royalties is offered by a case involving suit for a fourteen year period during which the author had been in exile under an order of the Special Board of the Ministry of Internal Affairs. On his return to Moscow in 1947 he claimed accumulated royalties which had been paid by the publishing house to the Administration for the Protection of Authors' Rights. The trial court dismissed his suit for 74,674 roubles and 34 kopeks, but the Supreme Court of the U.S.S.R. ordered retrial, saying that the exile had not included confiscation of property.

[24] *Dzhavakhishvili* v. *University Press* [1940] Sbornik Post. Pl. i Opr. Koll. Verkh. Suda SSSR 281.

In consequence, his royalties did not escheat, but there had to be consideration on the retrial of the statute of limitations, and this would limit recovery to that part of the fourteen year period which did not exceed the three year bar of Article 44 of the Civil Code.[25]

MUSIC AND PHOTOGRAPHS

Music and photographs have provided the subject matter for two decisions and a court order concerning copyright. The suit involving music arose because a cinema with an orchestra was playing the author's compositions in the foyer without payment of royalties in the amount which the Administration for the Protection of Authors' Rights thought appropriate. An order of the Ministry of Education of the R.S.F.S.R. had established two rates for the payment of royalties when music was played in the foyer of a cinema. One applied when fees were charged separately for the musical performance in the foyer, and the other when no separate fee was charged. In accordance with Soviet cinema practice the performances of a cinema occur at fixed times, and no one may enter the auditorium after the performance has begun. Reserved seats are sold for all performances. To fill the interval between performances, an orchestra often plays in the foyer, and those who plan to attend the cinema arrive early or stay late to hear the concert.

The trial court held for the plaintiff at the rate of 1½ per cent of the receipts, but the plaintiff appealed saying that the rate referred only to music played at cinemas showing silent films. After several retrials, the College for Civil Cases of the Supreme Court of the R.S.F.S.R. upheld the first trial court's decision on the ground that a separate fee was charged for the concert, and that was the sole governing factor.[26]

The court order was issued in 1933,[27] with the declaration that the courts in an unnamed Republic had been making errors in determining the rights of composers whose compositions were recorded on phonograph records. It stated that the law protected

25 *Mass* v. *Administration for the Protection of Authors' Rights, ibid.*, at p. 284.
26 *Administration for the Protection of Authors' Rights* v. *Theatre Aurora* [1937] 13 Sov.Yust. 51.
27 Order of October 20, 1933, Sbornik Deistv. Post. Plenuma i Direkt. Pisem Verkh. Suda SSSR (1941) p. 82.

generally any form of reproduction of a copyrighted composition, and there was no specific exclusion of phonograph records in the article listing various circumstances in which royalties did not accrue. In consequence, composers had rights to royalties.

The second case [28] involved a photographer who discovered that a photograph of one of the Soviet leaders had been produced on bronze and sold throughout the country without payment to him of any royalty. The trial court rejected the photographer's suit for royalties on the bronze because he had not placed his name and the date on each photograph as required by the statute for protection, and further the term of protection had already expired. The College for Civil Cases of the Supreme Court of the R.S.F.S.R. agreed that no protection could attach in the absence of the designation of name and date on the photograph and said that all other questions were irrelevant in consequence.

A suggestion that the number of suits for royalties has been large and that they have been handled to the dissatisfaction of the authors is to be found in an order of the Supreme Court of the U.S.S.R. The order, dated 1933,[29] stated that there had been much delay in the payment of judgments for royalties, and ordered the court executioner to levy upon the cashier of the entertainment enterprise or its bank account immediately after receipt of the judgment.

INCOME TAX IMPLICATIONS

Authors have found themselves courted in increasingly munificent fashion if one may believe reports of high incomes which are being paid to them in the U.S.S.R. Credence is lent to these reports by the income tax law.[30] In the form adopted in 1943, this law contains a special chapter devoted to the incomes of literary people and artists. Unlike the tax on those earning wages as workmen or clerks, the chapter listed nineteen brackets within which an author would be placed in accordance with the amount of royalties. These began at 1,800 roubles per year, as did the tax on the wages of workers and clerks, and it proceeded at the same rate of tax, bracket by bracket until the bracket

28 *Tolchan* v. *Publishing House 'Moscow Worker'* [1929] 7 Sud.Prak. RSFSR 7.

29 Order of October 20, 1933, Sbornik Post., Raz. i Direktiv Verkh. Suda SSSR (1935) p. 129.

30 Decree of April 30, 1943, Ved.Verkh.Sov. SSSR, No. 7, 1943.

beginning at 12,000 roubles per annum was reached. The table for workmen and clerks, which would include factory directors, had no brackets above this point, but indicated a tax at 13 per cent on the excess above 12,000 roubles. The table for authors continued to list further brackets up to 300,000 roubles per year, above which the tax was set at 55 per cent of income.

It would seem a reasonable presumption that the top bracket would not have been listed if no one had fallen within it. It would also seem a reasonable presumption that no high brackets were listed in like manner for the workmen and clerks because none of them could have dreamed of reaching them. Clearly, the favouring of authors over other members of the community in terms of income received had become a policy of the Soviet leadership. The one reminder of past policies looking toward egalitarianism in the wage structure was the high rate of tax. In some measure it served to reduce the incomes of those receiving the largest royalties.

Yet, even this reminder was dropped in 1947, when the Ministry of Finance of the U.S.S.R., acting under the authority conferred upon it in the 1943 income tax statute to issue instructions, changed the approach to the taxation of authors and artists.[31] In its explanation relating to the application of section 16 of the 1943 statute, it said simply, 'the income of literary persons and artistic workers, including income from the public performance and distribution of their works, is subject to tax in accordance with the tariff set in section 16 of the statute, except that income in excess of 12,000 roubles shall be taxed at the rate of 13 per cent'.

By this instruction the authors and artists seem to have been shown additional favouritism, for their income above 12,000 roubles became taxable at a flat rate of 13 per cent instead of at the scale of rates graduated up to 55 per cent to which the high incomes had been taxable previously. The wooing of authors to the cause of the regime seems to have become intense in the post-war period. The leadership has evidenced its dependence upon the talented individual to put in attractive and moving terms the social changes demanded by that leadership.

[31] Instruction of March 27, 1949, 3 *Spravochnik po Zak.* (1949) p. 111 at p. 122.

FAVOURING THE INVENTOR

Examination of the law relating to inventors indicates much the same favouring of the imaginative producer. There is also preserved for the State the opportunity to appropriate any invention it may need.

With the expansion of State-owned industry under the five year plans and the abandonment of the private enterprise of the New Economic Policy, the change in attitude toward the protection of invention was evidenced by a decree which declared in its preamble, 'The patent legislation existing up to the present time, preserving the interests of the inventor by means of allowing him exclusive rights to his invention, already is out of accord with the aspirations of the leading inventors, those who are conscious of their position as the builders of a socialist society'.[32] While this preamble probably put words into the mouths of most inventors, it can be presumed to represent the attitude of the leadership seeking to effect a change in social attitudes in the interest of the community. A new concept was developed, the concept of the 'author's certificate'. While the concept of 'patent' was left in the law, and remains there today with the current statute of March 5, 1941,[33] it was pushed to the background. It has been said that not a single Soviet citizen now seeks protection under the provisions of the statute relating to patent. They all demand the 'author's certificate'.[34] Only the foreigner now requests a patent, often only for prestige purposes to be able to claim that his idea is 'protected throughout the world'.

What is new about the 'author's certificate'? Under the 1941 statute, it is declared that the right of exploitation of an invention for which an author's certificate is issued belongs to the State. In consequence the inventor loses forever control over his invention as soon as he discloses it. He assigns automatically to the State the right to exploit or not to exploit an idea, reserving for himself the right to remuneration and the privileges set forth in the statute.

Considering that the Soviet pattern of economy permits no private enterprise beyond that of the artisan, this automatic

32 Decree of April 9, 1931, [1931] 1 Sob.Zak. SSSR, No. 21, item 180.
33 [1941] Sob.Post. SSSR, No.9, item 150.
34 Bratus, Grave, Zimileva, Serebrovsky and Shkundin, *Sovetskoe Grazhdanskoe Pravo* [*Soviet Civil Law*] (1950) p. 576.

assignment of all rights of exploitation is to have been expected. What benefit the inventor is to receive cannot but depend upon the exploitation of the idea in State industry or commerce. The benefits offered the holder of an author's certificate are not inconsequential, however. Under the statute he is to receive a portion of the savings or any other effect produced by the invention or technical improvement upon the national economy. Further, he is exempt from income tax on the first 10,000 roubles received under the terms of the statute for the specific invention. Last, but by no means least under Soviet conditions, the inventor is given a priority in selection for positions open in scientific research and experimental institutions and enterprises related to the field in which the invention was made.

The portion of savings accorded the inventor varies in accordance with the type of suggestion and the amount of the savings. By an instruction of November 27, 1942,[35] issued under the authority of the general statute of 1941, a scale of payments is established for the three classes of inventive activity distinguished by the 1941 statute: (1) invention of a completely new tool, instrument or process, (2) a technical improvement of an existing tool, instrument or process, and (3) a proposal for 'rationalisation' of production.

The percentage of savings up to 1,000 roubles in the year selected are 30 per cent, 25 per cent and 12½ per cent respectively. If the savings exceed 1,000 roubles, the percentage paid the 'author' is reduced on a progressive scale so that at the level of from 50,000 to 100,000 roubles the three categories would receive (1) 6 per cent plus 2,500 roubles, (2) 3 per cent plus 1,650 roubles and (3) 1½ per cent plus 850 roubles. At the top bracket of savings, namely when the savings exceed 1,000,000 roubles, the percentage to be paid to each of the three categories would be (1) 2 per cent plus 21,000 roubles but not to exceed 200,000 roubles, (2) 1 per cent plus 11,000 roubles but not to exceed 100,000 roubles and (3) ½ per cent plus 5,500 roubles but not to exceed 25,000 roubles.

Payment under the statute is computed on the basis of one year's savings to industry. For a technical improvement or proposal of 'rationalisation' the period is the first twelve months after its introduction. The inventor of a completely new tool,

35 [1942] Sob.Post. SSSR, No. 10, item 178.

instrument or process is treated more favourably, probably because the maximum savings cannot be expected to appear in the first year after introduction of the invention into industry. The instruction provides that the inventor shall be paid the percentage of savings under the established tariff during the first year of use of the invention. Thereafter, he will receive additional payments so that at the end of the five year period he shall have been paid the appropriate percentage of savings for the best single year of the five year period.[36]

The 1942 instruction represents a slight change to the advantage of the inventor over the rule existing prior to 1942. Under the instruction,[37] issued under the 1931 statute, the inventor received a percentage only on the savings of the best of the first three years of exploitation of his invention. The 1942 instruction also improved the position of two of the three categories of persons who qualify for royalties under the act. It doubled the top permissive amount of payments payable to those who effected savings to industry of over 1,000,000 roubles. This change in the decade between 1931 and 1942 probably reflected in part the inflation which occurred in the U.S.S.R. during the decade, but it may also reflect an attitude seen in the field of wages generally, namely the attitude of reliance on high wage incentives to stimulate production.

Interest in encouraging certain types of production is also revealed by the 1942 instruction. Thus, payments of double the amount provided by the instruction may be made for an invention opening up a new field of production, or creating new kinds of valuable materials, or substitutes for non-ferrous metals, or machines and instruments not previously produced in the U.S.S.R. Under this provision any inventor of means of utilising atomic research, or the discoverer of substitutes for copper would benefit handsomely.

A suggestion as to the amount of earnings from 'author's certificates' is offered by the report of the Minister of the Food Industry to the 1952 meeting of the Supreme Soviet of the R.S.F.S.R. He explained that 6,000 proposals for rationalisation of production, technical improvements and inventions had been

[36] Section 16c.

[37] Instruction of Council of Labour and Defence, October 7, 1931, published in *V Pomoshch Izobretatelya* [*In Aid of the Inventor*] (1936), p. 105.

accepted in 1951 with a resulting saving to his industry of 30,000,000 roubles.[38]

The rewards for invention to the holder of the author's certificate are to be compared to those offered the recipient of a patent. Under the statute the latter obtains the monopoly right to control the patented invention, in that no one may use it without his agreement. Since he cannot exploit the invention himself, except as an artisan, this right of control means that he may license it to a State producing agency upon the best terms he can get. If he is unable to reach agreement with the State enterprise upon the terms of the licence, the State reserves to itself the right through the Council of Ministers to decree the compulsory alienation of the patent or the compulsory licensing of the invention to the interested State agency. In such event, the Council of Ministers sets the remuneration to be paid the inventor. The patent is issued for fifteen years from the date of filing the application.

To establish the right to a patent or an author's certificate, the inventor must satisfy the technical experts of GOSTEKHNIKA[39] that the idea is novel, and this requires claiming its novelty not only within the U.S.S.R. but throughout the world. The Soviet patent authorities subscribe to the patent journals of all countries, and scrutinise them to determine whether an idea presented for patent or author's certificate is really new. Reports from foreigners who have sought to obtain patents indicates that this scrutiny is meticulous, and the examination of the experts severe.

PROBLEMS OF ADMINISTRATION

The number of disputes over payment of royalties for an invention which reach the printed reports of judicial decisions is few. Whether this is because there are few such disputes, or whether the agencies of the law which report judicial decisions feel that

[38] Report of V. N. Sokolov, *Zasedaniya Verkhovnogo Soveta RSFSR, vtoraya sessiya, stenograficheskii otchet* [*Session of the Supreme Soviet of the RSFSR, second sitting, stenographic report*] (1952) p. 77.

[39] Established by decree of January 9, 1948, as the State Committee for the Introduction of Advanced Techniques in the National Economy. The decree was announced only when approved by the Supreme Soviet of the USSR, June 17, 1950, Ved.Verkh.Sov. SSSR, No. 15 (630), June 29, 1950. Previously each Ministry had issued its own certificates. Gostekhnika was abolished February 17, 1951, Ved.Verkh.Sov. SSSR, No. 4 (661), March 7, 1951. No indication has yet been given as to where the certificating authority has been placed.

no decision sets a general rule since each concerns only the unique characteristics of a single invention is not known. It may well be that no generalisations are possible, and for that reason the technical details of each case are thought of too little importance to merit space in the public journals. The few reported decisions discovered suggest the type of problem presented. The two cases reported in 1940 indicate that the Supreme Court of the U.S.S.R. was concerned at the time with serious ignorance of the law on inventions on the part of two important Provincial Courts. The decisions attempted to state the fundamental principles governing the work of the courts in this field.

The most elemental problems had been raised in the first case.[40] Suit had been brought by a Leningrad public corporation to recover from a workman 1,443 roubles paid as royalty for the use of a technical improvement. The corporation argued that the payment had been made in error, since the workman had not made a novel suggestion but had borrowed his idea from a design for a brake tyre then in process of manufacture for the Ministry of Railways. The trial court had given judgment for the corporation, and the Leningrad Provincial Court had affirmed it.

In setting aside the judgment the Supreme Court's College for Civil Cases indicated that it did so on two procedural grounds either of which was sufficient, namely that the defendant had not been present at the trial because of illness, and secondly, because the record indicated that the defendant alone had not received the money but had shared it with a whole group of persons, all of whom should have been joined as defendants. The Supreme Court's College then seized the opportunity to discuss the substantive law, indicating that it had a message for the lower courts.

The message was that in a suit concerning technical improvements the court must determine first whether the patent authorities have passed upon the claim and granted an author's certificate, and secondly whether the improvement has actually been put to use. If this simple formula had been followed, the Supreme Court indicated that the trial court would have been able to determine the inventor's rights in this case and could have rejected the corporation's claim for repayment immediately had the facts of recognition of the novelty of the invention and of its use been established.

40 *Kirov Factory* v. *Kryuchkin* [1940] Sud.Prak. SSSR 292.

In the second case[41] two persons filed competing claims for royalties against a public corporation. Each argued that the corporation was using an attachment for holding a thread cutter on a machine tool which was his invention. The Kharkov Provincial Court had given its decision in favour of one Kiyashko, and had denied the claim of Ryzhenko. This decision had been affirmed by the Supreme Court of the Ukrainian Republic, but the President of the Supreme Court of the U.S.S.R. brought the case before his own College for Civil Cases for review.

In ordering retrial the Supreme Court's College again explained the role of the Court in such matters, when competing claims are filed. It noted that Ryzhenko, whose claim had been denied, already had an author's certificate from the patent authorities, while Kiyashko whose claim had been upheld by the court had no such certificate because it had been denied him on the basis of his description. This fact had not been considered sufficiently by the trial court in the opinion of the Supreme Court. Secondly, the trial court had not adequately determined whether the attachment in use by the corporation was like the claimed invention of either or both of the claimants. Finally, the court had not pressed its technical experts to give a conclusive answer to the question of whether Kiyashko's claim infringed Ryzhenko's invention.

A third case[42] suggests that the authorities are determined not to let an inventor claim that his idea has been utilised in such a large field that his share of the savings to the State would make him extremely wealthy. The case arose in connection with a claim of a man who had devised a new way to place refrigeration coils in a cold room to obtain lower temperatures. The inventor claimed that the idea had been utilised widely throughout many branches of industry, and that he had a right to a return from this wide use.

The College for Civil Cases of the Supreme Court of the U.S.S.R. reviewed the decision of the trial court and the affirmance of the appellate court which gave the claimant all that he claimed. The Supreme Court's College pointed out that this was not a new invention but a technical improvement, and

[41] *Ryzhenko and Kiyashko* v. *Machine Tool Factory* [1940] Sud.Prak. SSSR 288.

[42] *Kulbin* v. *People's Commissariat of the Food Industry of the USSR* [1940] 8 Sov.Yust. 34.

that such improvements were to be protected only within clearly defined limits, depending upon the person to whom the proposal for technical improvement had been addressed. The Supreme Court's College found that the proposal had been made only for the meat refrigeration plants, and that there was a co-inventor. It ordered that the decision be revised to limit the payments to savings in the meat refrigeration plants and to state the person who was recognised as the co-inventor.

If this decision is representative, it suggests that the authorities are concerned with limiting royalties and do not relish the thought of the emergence of a group of men who claim a share of the income of large segments of the industrial plant of the U.S.S.R.

Within the limits set, however, the policy of the leaders is indicated to be the favouring of the ingenious individual who improves the productive process and makes possible important savings to the State. There is also an indication that the leaders realise that a wholly State-owned industry may present difficulties to inventors seeking the adoption of their ideas with attendant lack of progress in the industry. It is obvious that an inventor, who can realise upon his invention only if a bureaucrat in State industry finds the idea valuable, lacks such pressure as may be possible in private enterprise economies in the threat of private exploitation and competition.

The evils of bureaucracy in the utilisation of inventions was the subject of an order of the Supreme Court in 1933.[43] It declared at its outset, 'Practice shows that in spite of many achievements in the field of mass inventions, bureaucracy, red tape and even wrecking in some places have come to light'. The Supreme Court called upon the lower courts to act promptly upon complaints of such bureaucratic attitudes among officials charged with the utilisation of new ideas, and to hold them responsible under the Criminal Code's provisions relating to crimes committed by officials.

Again, it is the criminal law which is relied upon to assure that the individual inventor obtains a hearing, rather than the pressures possible in private enterprise economies. The inventor is encouraged to develop new ideas from which the community

43 Order of May 22, 1933, Sbornik Post., Raz. i Direktiv Verkh. Suda SSSR (1935) p. 95.

can be expected to benefit, and the means used to encourage him are those of personal reward. This form of incentive is not thought by the Soviet leaders apparently to be too great a concession to make in the interests of the national welfare. Yet, the additional lever upon the bureaucrat which might be possible if the inventor could exploit his invention and compete against the State industries is not to be permitted. A concession of this character might threaten the structure of power which the leadership has been at such pains to erect.

Chapter 9

COMMUNITY ASSUMPTION OF RISKS

Mass craving for security has been heralded as a major phenomenon of the twentieth century. Remedies offered by the traditional legal action in tort or by the purchase of an annuity from an insurance company have been called inadequate to the conditions of an advanced industrial society. Workmen's compensation, social insurance and national health acts have evidenced the response of legislatures to the demands of the population. The Soviet leadership has felt the same pressures and taken many of the same steps as have the policy-makers of other lands.

Soviet development of social insurance schemes has not been a response solely to the demands of pressure groups. Marxist doctrine has favoured a communal solution to the accident problem as well as to other social problems. Further, the expectation that law would wither away at an early date has had its influence upon the development of social security. Some of the early theorists expected the withering process to begin with a substitution of social security legislation for the law of torts.

Even before the revolution Lenin began to formulate the type of social security scheme to be favoured by the Social Democrats. When the Tsarist government enacted a law in 1912,[1] Lenin was ready with his criticism.[2] He wanted no social insurance system built upon the principles of private insurance with the workman paying part of the premium. He argued for an approach in a new direction.

The first Soviet law on social insurance was enacted a year after the revolution.[3] Since that first law, a large body of statutes and regulations has been developed.[4] The new instru-

1 Statute on Industrial Labour, Part 4, 11 Svod Zakonov, Part 2 (1913).

2 Lenin, 17 *Sochineniya* [*Collected Works*] (4th ed. 1948) pp. 426–429.

3 Decree of October 31, 1918, [1918] 1 Sob.Uzak. RSFSR, No. 89, item 906.

4 The first law after federation was that of February 6, 1925, [1925] 1 Sob.Zak. SSSR, No. 8, item 74, creating a federal body to co-ordinate policy in the Republics. There followed the decree of February 26, 1925, establishing a unified tariff for all social insurance premiums, [1925] 1 Sob.Zak. SSSR, No. 14, item 107, and the decree of March 23, 1926, entitled 'Temporary Statute on the Social Insurance Resources', [1926] 1 Sob.Zak. SSSR, No. 19, item 124.

ment has been utilised not only to meet the needs of the masses for protection but to achieve political ends. It is evident that social security has been given its part in moulding the masses in the direction of social change desired by the leadership. Attention will be focused on the law relating to industrial accidents as a major feature of the social insurance scheme.

Soviet law has not limited insurance coverage to employment injuries.[5] The insured may claim benefits for time lost from any injury or illness, even if unrelated to his employment. Thus, the Soviet scheme offers broader coverage than is available under the usual workmen's compensation statutes, but it does not cover as many persons as the present British National Insurance Act. It reaches neither the vast number of persons working together as members of co-operative associations,[6] whether on the farm or in the handicraft groups, nor does it protect the self-employed,[7] except for lawyers, private professional fishermen, private prospectors for precious metals and insurance salesmen. Unprotected persons must rely solely upon a court action in tort to recover for personal injuries.

To facilitate administration of the law, two periods are established in which payments are to be made. The first period commences on the first day of absence from work when there is a presumption that the workman will return eventually to his job. The trade union is the agency which administers the law

[5] The basic principles of the Soviet social insurance law are set forth in Code of Labour Laws, RSFSR, c. 17. Details are provided by the basic statute of February 13, 1930, [1930] 1 Sob.Zak. SSSR, No. 11, item 132, and No. 51, item 520, and in numerous orders and instructions.

[6] A special fund is established for social security purposes under the terms of the collective farm charter of February 17, 1935, [1935] 1 Sob.Zak. SSSR, No. 11, item 82, s. 11 (*c*). For statute on mutual benefit funds of the collective farms, see [1931] 1 Sob.Uzak. RSFSR, No. 34, item 287. Persons who are wage employees of the collective farms, such as bookkeepers, agronomists and barbers fall within the regular social insurance system.

[7] The self-employed group includes those who are classified as private contractors for co-operative and State enterprises, *i.e.*, independent peasants who hire themselves out for brief periods with their horses or without, persons working for an enterprise on their own materials provided that the materials exceed 50 per cent of the value of the completed product, persons who perform occasional jobs for an enterprise without a written contract making them staff members, *i.e.*, watch and machinery repairmen, and persons employed on incidental jobs by private persons. The categories of insured persons were increased in 1932 to include some persons not currently employed, these being former employees temporarily in schools to improve their skills (ordinary students are not insured). See Aleksandrov, Astrakhan, Karnitsky, Moskalenko, *Zakonodatelstvo o Trude Kommentarii* [*Legislation on Labour, Commentary*] (1947) p. 267.

at this stage, ascertaining the facts and ordering payment by the regular disbursing officer of the place of employment. The second period commences at the time indicated by a medical commission [8] which has reached the conclusion that cures have been ineffective, and the workman cannot be expected to return to his job. Payment is made thereafter not by the cashier at the place of employment but by the local office of the Ministry of Social Security in the Republic concerned.[9] The rate of payment is generally reduced when the employee passes from the first period to the second in accordance with a scheme which favours certain categories of workmen.

During the first period when the medical commission has not yet reached its discouraging conclusion that the workman is permanently disabled, the basic principle is maintained that the workman shall receive full wages.[10] This principle applies, however, only to a favoured category, namely those workmen who are trade union members and who have a record of over eight years of service. For those trade union members having less seniority, payments are reduced. Thus, a trade union member with from five to eight years of service receives 80 per cent of his wages; those with from three to five years of service receive 60 per cent of their wages, and those with three years or less of service receive 50 per cent of their wages.

An exception is made for minors who would be prejudiced under the seniority rule. For those minors up to the age of 18 years of age who are trade union members, the payment is set at 60 per cent of their wages, regardless of the time they may have worked in the place from which they are temporarily absent because of a disability.[11]

[8] For the structure and function of the medical labour commissions, see decree of November 5, 1948, [1949] Sob.Post. SSSR, No. 1, item 1.

[9] For the structure and function of the Ministry of Social Security of the RSFSR, see order of May 16, 1947, [1947] Sob.Post. RSFSR, No. 6, item 19.

[10] Order of August 9, 1948, ss. 1–3. 1 *Spravochnik po Zak.* (1949) p. 603. Full wages have been defined as all payments received with the exclusion of overtime, service in any supplementary spare time job, and all non-recurring types of payment. Instruction of July 31, 1937, [1937] 1 Sob.Zak. SSSR, No. 43, item 204. Yet, a bench workman who also has an administrative position for the performance of which he receives a regular premium in accordance with an established system shall receive social insurance benefits on the basis of his full take-home pay so long as the total is not more than double the base pay for the bench work. Instruction of August 9, 1948, s. 3. 1 *Spravochnik po Zak.* (1949) p. 603.

[11] Instruction of August 9, 1948, *ibid.*, at s. 1.

POLITICAL AIMS AND SOCIAL SECURITY

Having established the rate of remuneration for the favoured trade union member with high seniority, the social security statutes provide that persons who are not trade union members shall be paid benefits during temporary absence at a rate which is one-half of the amount they otherwise would have been paid.[12] Another possibility of reduction lies in the nature of the employer. If the workman is employed by a private employer, he receives only 50 per cent of his wages if he does not belong to a trade union, and two-thirds of his wages if he has trade union membership.[13] Such employees of private persons receive an increase in the rate of payment after the first twenty days of absence, if they have been working for more than a year.

Employees of private persons have been reduced to small numbers as a result of the steps taken to discourage private employment, outlined previously in connection with the law relating to property in small business. Thus, the only privately employed persons of consequence today are domestic servants, and those persons who are employed as herdsmen for the privately-owned cattle of collective farm households.

The hierarchy of categories as a result of which not all workmen receive the same treatment during their period of temporary absence from their job because of disability indicates the political ends to which the social security laws are being bent. It is evident that the Soviet leadership is using them to mould society in the image desired, partly because of Marxist doctrine, and partly because of the harsh reality of lessened production when there is large labour turnover. Thus, the hierarchy favours those who join trade unions, those who work for public employers, and those who remain on the job for long periods of years.

The differentiation between categories of persons in paying social insurance benefits to those temporarily disabled seems to have aroused criticism within the U.S.S.R. Soviet writers have found it desirable to explain the phenomenon.[14] They have

12 *Ibid.*, at s. 2.

13 Instruction of Central Council of Trade Unions, dated June 28, 1932, s. 37. This section was not reprinted in 1 *Spravochnik po Zak.* (1949) p. 595. There is, however, no indication that it has been repealed. This excised section may be found in Kats and Sorokin, *Sotsialnoe Strakhovanie* [*Social Insurance*] (2nd ed. 1936) p. 42.

14 Krasnopolsky, 'The Nature of Soviet State Social Insurance', [1951] 6 Sov. Gos. i Pravo 62.

related differentiated social insurance benefits to the progressive wage scales already discussed in connection with the labour law. It is suggested that the same policy which requires the utilisation of progressive wage scales as an incentive to production requires the application of progressive social insurance benefits favouring those who follow patterns believed desirable by the Soviet leadership. Social insurance is indicated as being more than a means of restoring the producer to the assembly line. It becomes an instrument to be used in the incentive programme in which Soviet leaders have professed to see the only hope of achieving the economy of abundance so long promised.

Even basic principles have had to suffer, however, when resources have been inadequate. This fact is evident from a provision of the law to the effect that a limit of 160 roubles a day has been placed upon social insurance payments during the period of temporary absence.[15] This limit applies even if the claimant has been earning in excess of that amount at the job from which he is temporarily absent as a result of having been disabled. Those of the directors who earn in excess of this limit would not, under such a rule, have a claim upon the fund during the period when production may be reduced because of their absence from the directing role.

Payment rules are not normally affected by the source of the injury or illness. Thus, the worker who is kept away from his job temporarily may recover his benefits in accordance with the formula which has been discussed, regardless of whether he broke his leg mountain climbing on vacation or in the shaft of a mine. The benefits continue until he is returned to the job or a medical commission decides that he can never return.

This rule of full payments without limitation in time includes an exception for seasonal workers, part-time workers and persons in the building trades who have not been employed for ten months out of the preceding twelve months.[16] For such persons payment of benefits for temporary absence must stop after seventy-five days, if the absence is due to an injury or illness not connected with the employment. At the end of the period a medical commission is required to decide whether the employee should be placed in the category of those permanently disabled

[15] Order of August 9, 1948, s. 3. 1 *Spravochnik po Zak.* (1949) p. 603.
[16] Instruction of June 28, 1932, s. 19 (*a*). 1 *Spravochnik po Zak.* (1949) p. 597.

to whom the rules of pensions apply. Only when the trade union requests an extension of time will the temporary benefits continue.

So that it may be clear to administrators which injuries may be considered as having been connected with employment, an instruction [17] defines the following to be within the classification: an injury which occurred while performing the prescribed regular duties of the employee, or special duties assigned to him by the employer or his agent; an injury which occurred while performing activities in the interest of the enterprise even when not ordered by the employer or his agent; an injury which occurred while performing public duties relating to the enterprise and also while performing special tasks ordered by the communist party or by the trade union agencies even though the tasks were not related to the work of the enterprise; an injury at the employee's place of work during working hours, including the recess period or during working hours if the place was not 'out of bounds' under the disciplinary rules of the enterprise; and an injury which occurred during travel to and from work.

The Soviet leadership seems to draw a distinction between performance of communist party duties, which it is prepared to consider a function of the job itself and therefore within the full protection of the law when injury results, and an injury suffered in a mustering operation of the armed forces or in civil defence. While these latter injuries are covered by the law exactly as if they were employment-connected, the statute treats them as situations *analogous* to injury on the job, rather than an injury on the job itself. The distinction may indicate that communist party and defence activity, while requiring equal treatment under the social security laws because of their great importance to the preservation of the society within which the citizen lives, have a different relationship to employment. A job cannot be separated into its components of work at a lathe and work in a propaganda capacity in furtherance of communist party policy decisions, while work in policing a threatened part of a city or in digging a trench during a siege is considered of a transitory character, and not a necessary accompaniment of factory labour.

[17] Instruction of July 4, 1928, Kats and Sorokin, *Sotsialnoe Strakhovanie* [*Social Insurance*] (2nd ed. 1936) p. 117.

To facilitate administration the law establishes in a lengthy table the precise types of illness which will be considered as employment-connected.[18] Each designated illness is followed by the types of employment with which they are commonly associated. An example is cancer of the skin, which is said by the statute to be found among miners, workers in the chemical industry and those who clean pipes.

THE PERMANENTLY DISABLED

To be distinguished from the period of temporary disability to which the foregoing remarks apply, is the period of permanent, complete or partial disability. It is the medical commission attached to the social security scheme which determines when a patient passes from the temporary category into the permanent category of invalid. The transfer from one category to another is of great importance to the citizen, for he is generally in receipt of less of a benefit when he becomes a permanent invalid than when he was deemed to be absent only temporarily from his job.

Many of the factors determining the rate of pay within the limits available to the permanently disabled worker are the same as for the temporarily incapacitated worker, but there are some additions.[19] The administrator must determine whether the invalid acquired his incapacity in connection with his job or not, whether the employee had been employed for a long period of time, and what type of employment was concerned. An additional factor is the extent of the disability, it being a fact that the person absent temporarily from his job cannot be expected to engage himself in some other different gainful occupation during a brief temporary absence, while a permanently disabled person may be retained to perform a less skilled or even a more skilled job requiring different senses or members from those affected by the injury.

For the great bulk of employees the maximum monthly pension is 300 roubles. When compared with the wage reported as average in 1951, namely 500 roubles, or the lowest wage in the factory visited by an English economist in 1952, namely 700

[18] Instruction of January 4, 1929, *ibid.*, at p. 141.

[19] The basic statute on pensions for the permanently disabled is that of February 13, 1930, [1930] 1 Sob.Zak. SSSR, No. 11, item 132 and *ibid.*, No. 51, item 528.

roubles,[20] it will be seen immediately that the rate of pension can be expected in almost every instance to be less than the injured person's former wage. Before computing any reductions from the top limit of 300 roubles because of the factors to be discussed below, it is the general rule that the recipient's wage must be levelled to 300 roubles, regardless of what it had previously been.

To the 300 rouble maximum there are some exceptions for industries which are favoured because of the desire of the leadership to induce persons to enter them. Thus in mining and metallurgy, which are believed to be keys to the economy, the maximum monthly pension may be 400 roubles or 500 roubles or 600 roubles, depending upon the activity. The most favoured is coal mining,[21] while the other extractive industries are put in second place with a maximum of 500 roubles per month.[22] Coal miners may even receive above the nominal maximum if their wages exceed the maximum, but they do not in any case receive full wages at amounts exceeding the maximum. An example of the benefits they are to receive is indicated in a textbook sample computation.[23] It states, 'For a coal miner, who has been placed in the first group because of an injury on the job, and who is earning 2,000 roubles a month as wages, a pension shall be computed in the following manner: 100 per cent of his first 600 roubles of wages (in accordance with the generally established rate of pensions for invalids of the first group who have been injured on the job); 20 per cent of the remainder of his wages up to a total of 1,500 roubles (*i.e.* 20 per cent of 900 roubles); no part of the balance of his wages (500 roubles). The total pension will be 780 roubles (600 plus 180)'.

When considered together with the exceptional written contract provided for collective farmers who can be induced to leave their farms and enter the coal mines of the Don basin, the policy of preference to coal miners is indicated to stem from the desire to cause the transfer to coal mining of persons otherwise engaged and to overcome the emotional prejudices against underground work. The inducements for those citizens who

20 See discussion of wage scales in Chap. 1.
21 Order of September 10, 1947, [1947] Sob.Post. SSSR, No. 8, item 149.
22 Order of October 17, 1947, [1947] Sob.Post. SSSR, No. 9, item 153.
23 Aleksandrov, editor, *Sovetskoe Trudovoe Pravo* [*Soviet Labour Law*] (1949) p. 340.

have not fallen foul of the Special Boards of the Ministry of Internal Affairs seem to be primarily monetary, although elements of social pressure are also said to exist. For those caught up in the drag-net of the Ministry of Internal Affairs and forced to work in the mines or in digging canals on the ground that labour cures the recalcitrant opponent of the regime, a very different type of law is applied, yet the social purpose of both is evident. Unpleasant heavy work has to be performed in modern industrial society. The Soviet leadership has devised laws of varying character to see that it is performed, some of this law going well beyond the limits acceptable in the western democracies.

Labour turnover, to which reference has been made earlier as one of the impediments to production in the U.S.S.R., is discouraged by provisions in the law relating to disability pensions. The policy of utilising the social security law to develop a citizen who will stay by his work is not, however, extended to cut down the pension of a man or woman actually injured on the job.[24] It relates only to those who acquire injuries or illnesses not connected with their employment. Humanitarian elements seem to have triumphed over the urgent necessity of encouraging loyalty to the job when the workman has been permanently disabled by the employment itself. Thus, a pension is paid without regard to length of service in such instances, the sole requirement being that the illness manifest itself within two years after 'temporary incapacity' compelled cessation of work, or within two years after termination of payments made on the basis of 'temporary incapacity'.[25]

The reductions established for disability of a permanent character arising from events not connected with the employment vary in accordance with the sex of the applicant, the type of employment and the years at the job. In order to receive any pension for a permanent disability not connected with employment, a man must have been employed prior to the injury for a period of from three to twenty years depending on his age, and a woman must have been employed from two to fifteen years depending on her age.[26]

[24] Statute of February 13, 1930, s. 1, [1930] 1 Sob.Zak. SSSR, No. 11, item 132.
[25] *Ibid.*, at s. 35.
[26] A table of requirements is provided by the decree of December 28, 1938, s. 19, [1939] Sob.Post. SSSR, No. 1, item 1.

So that the State may not be required to pay more than is actually needed and also to induce the invalid to seek productive employment, which is deemed essential to a healthy Soviet society, invalids are examined by medical commissioners before the pension is set. Their lack of capacity is measured and consideration is given to alternative forms of employment in which their reduced faculties might be less of a handicap than in the activity from which they are compelled to retire. The process is codified by an instruction [27] ordering the medical commission to place each applicant within one of three categories: (1) loss of complete capacity to work, (2) loss of capacity to work at the profession for which the applicant was trained or at any other profession but retention of capacity to do work of a general character, and (3) loss of capacity to work systematically under normal conditions for the profession, but preservation of the capacity to work intermittently or during a shortened working day or at another profession requiring considerably less skill.

Applicants placed in the first group deprived of all capacity to work receive their full former wages if the disability arose from the employment, but only up to the maximum amount provided in the law for the industry concerned. This figure is usually less than full wages, as has already been indicated. If a person placed in the first group because of total incapacity, received his injury from a factor outside of employment, the rate of payment is reduced to two-thirds of the former wages.[28] For persons falling within the other categories involving lessened disability the rates of pension are lowered.[29] Yet, they are varied in accordance with whether the disability arose from employment, and in accordance with the social importance assigned to the industry by the policy-makers.

MAINTENANCE OF SURVIVORS

Survivors of a deceased family provider present a problem to the social security administrator. In earlier chapters it has been indicated that the men of the revolution envisaged some broad

[27] Instruction of February 29, 1932, s. 1. 1 *Spravochnik po Zak.* (1949) p. 591.
[28] Statute of February 13, 1930, s. 3, [1930] 1 Sob.Zak. SSSR, No. 11, item 132.
[29] Instruction of February 29, 1932, s. 5. 1 *Spravochnik po Zak.* (1949) p. 591.

system of care for heirs of a deceased, and that inheritance found its way back into the law only as property incentives were strengthened to achieve greater production. With the passage of time the persons who had estates of any magnitude to descend to their heirs were not the entrepreneurs or the rentiers, for such no longer existed, but those persons who had come to represent the social paragon because of their skill in producing more than the average norm. The liberalisation of the inheritance laws in the mid-1920's made it possible for the citizen singled out for a high salary because of his productivity or his work in a key but unpleasant job to assure to his heirs protection beyond the average in the event of his death from injury or illness.

With such liberalisation of inheritance laws it might have been possible for the State to reduce pension costs for survivors of deceased insured employees by reducing pensions in accordance with the amount of property inherited from an exemplary spouse or father, yet the policy-makers seem not to have appreciated their opportunity to effect savings or, more likely, to have appreciated that such a policy would have negated the full value of property incentives which they were seeking to develop. They may even have considered the difficulty of enforcing a means test. They were not, however, unmindful of the relationship of the property status of survivors in establishing pensions for them, as they established a form of means test for the survivor. All payments are related by law to the need of the survivor. There is no concept that an heir shall have a right against the social security fund because of any claim which might have accrued in favour of the estate of the deceased as a result of the accident.

Need is not related to amount of property inherited but solely to ability to work. Ability to work is determined almost automatically, probably to facilitate administration and make it unnecessary to conduct a detailed investigation requiring the use of discretion on the part of the administrator. Thus, need is established satisfactorily if a claimant proves himself to be (1) a minor son or daughter, brother or sister of the deceased, minority being defined for this purpose as less than 16 years of age if not in school, and 18 years of age if still attending school; (2) an adult son or daughter, brother or sister who is incapacitated; (3) a parent of the deceased or a surviving spouse who is over 60 years of age (if a male) or 55 years of age (if a female), or unable to work at a lesser age; or (4) a parent, surviving spouse or brother or sister, regardless of age and capacity to work, if engaged in caring for minor children, brothers or sisters who have not yet reached 8 years of age.[30]

Even with survivor's claims the policy of favouring those who have not contributed to labour turnover is evident. While a survivor who can qualify under the rules receives payment without regard to the deceased's length of employment when the death was related to the employment,[31] a survivor of a decedent who was employed for less than one year can claim nothing when the death was caused by an event outside of the deceased's employment. Should the deceased have been receiving a pension prior to his death in accordance with the social security rules, the qualifying survivors have a right to pensions regardless of the deceased's term of prior employment.[32]

The size of the surviving family affects the amount of survivor's payments. If there is only one qualifying survivor, he has a right only to 50 per cent of the pension the deceased would have received as an invalid of the second category had he lived.[33] If two survivors qualify, the two may receive between them a total of 75 per cent of what the deceased would have received as an invalid of the second category had he lived. If three qualify, the total payment to the three may be 100 per cent of such an amount, and if there are more than three qualifying survivors, the payments to them all may total 125 per cent of such an amount. Remarriage does not deprive a widow or widower receiving a pension as a needy survivor of the right to continue to receive it.

Emphasis upon the community solution to the accident problem is to be found in the system of premium payments devised by those who drafted the law. Actuarial principles are adhered to, in that the accident rate of each industry is studied in setting the premium rates,[34] but no premiums are required of

30 Instruction of July 4, 1928, ss. 62 and 88. Kats and Sorokin, *Sotsialnoe Strakhovanie* [*Social Insurance*] (2nd ed. 1936) pp. 128 and 132.
31 Statute of February 13, 1930, s. 6, [1930] 1 Sob.Zak. SSSR, No. 11, item 132.
32 *Ibid.*, at s. 6, par. 3.
33 Instruction of February 29, 1932, s. 15. 1 *Spravochnik po Zak.* (1949) p. 591.
34 Order of March 23, 1937, [1937] 1 Sob.Zak. SSSR, No. 22, item 88. The table appears in an edited form taking account of mergers among

the employees themselves. The State enterprise alone pays the cost, by forwarding to the agencies of the Ministry of Social Insurance a percentage of the total wage bill for the enterprise, after deducting payments made by the enterprise to those employees certified by the trade union in the plant to qualify for payments as 'temporarily incapacitated'. No payments to the permanently incapacitated are made by the enterprise unless such persons are employed in some capacity in the plant in accordance with the determination of the medical commission that they are still competent to work in positions demanding lesser faculties than their original position. The completely incapacitated receive their pensions from the local agencies of the Ministry of Social Insurance, namely from the department of social insurance of the local soviet.

Since the premium is computed on the basis of the monthly wage bill of the enterprise concerned, the definition of the wage bill is vital to the operation of the scheme. A special bulletin [35] declares that the wage bill shall include in addition to wages for normal work, payment for overloading, commissions paid over and above the guaranteed minimum to certain sales representatives, and the value of any payments in kind to the employees. The wage bill is not to include severance payments, *per diem* payments during business trips, penalties levied against the management for delayed payment of wages, royalty payments to inventors and authors, free transportation coupons provided to the employees, and sums paid to a trade union under such collective bargaining agreement as may have been negotiated.

TORT LAW HAS A PLACE

Examination of the social security laws of the U.S.S.R. indicates that they are not comprehensive, nor do they provide full compensation even to those persons included within their terms. They seem to be devised as a means of maintenance at minimum substance levels of those persons who are incapacitated and the former dependents of a decedent. Their highest payments

the trade unions in 1 *Spravochnik po Zakonodatelstvu dlya Ispolnitelnykh Komitetov Sovetov Deputatov Trudyashchikhsya* [*Manual on Legislation for Use of Executive Committees of the Soviets of Toilers Deputies*] (1946) p. 168.

35 Instruction of September 15, 1933, Kats and Sorokin, *Sotsialnoe Strakhovanie* [*Social Insurance*] (2nd ed. 1936) p. 385.

rarely equal the salaries of the incapacitated person, and certainly are even inadequate to permit him or his former dependents to live in the manner in which he or they had become accustomed.

No precise statement as to the reason for the less than complete protection provided by social insurance has been offered by Soviet authors. The outsider is left to wonder whether the reason is inadequacy of State resources to meet the full needs of those members of the population who are incapacitated or whether there is some more subtle reason. The latter possibility is suggested by an examination of those elements of tort law which have been retained in the Soviet system as the social insurance funds have been enlarged. Statements of Ministers of Finance in recurring budget messages to the Supreme Soviet suggest that it is not inadequacy of funds which causes the social insurance benefits to be maintained at rates less than wages. It is quite possible that they are held purposely at present levels to permit the utilisation of tort law to achieve social purposes. Here again seems to be found a realm of the law which is called upon to help mould the new Soviet society. Complete community assumption of risks would not, apparently, meet the full needs of the community which seeks more than the feeding, clothing and housing of the incapacitated at rates to which their former salaries had permitted them to become accustomed. Examination of the currently, effective provisions of the Civil Code relating to torts suggests that the Soviet leadership has found in it a convenient means of compelling managers of enterprises to be careful.

Appreciation of the potentials of the law of torts in moulding the Soviet man in the image of the careful administrator is a rather new phenomenon on the Soviet scene. The law of torts seems to have been thought of originally as a means of redressing the balance between rich and poor, or perhaps as a means of caring for the incapacitated at the expense of the wealthy employer or tortfeasor until such time as social insurance funds were sufficient to assume the burden. Such conclusions are suggested by the early emphasis of the Soviet courts upon liability without fault.

While the Soviet Civil Code's provisions are declared by the Supreme Court of the R.S.F.S.R. to have been patterned largely upon the French civil code,[36] there was an indication that the draftsmen were prepared to extend the rule of liability without fault well beyond the familiar rule of extra-hazardous activity. An article of the code established the familiar rule by providing: 'persons and enterprises, whose activities present special danger to the persons around them, such as railroads, street cars, factories and mills, vendors of inflammable materials, keepers of wild animals, persons engaged in the erection of buildings and other structures, etc., are liable for injury caused by the source of increased danger, unless they prove that the damage was caused as the result of *force majeure,* or as the result of a wilful act or gross negligence on the part of the injured party'.[37]

For activities outside those classed as extra-hazardous, the code seemed to adopt as its major principle the usual rule of no liability without wilful or negligent action, for it was provided:

'A person who has injured another person or causes damage to his property must make good the damages arising from such acts. A person is exempt from such duty if he proves that he was unable to prevent such damage, or that he was privileged to cause the damage, or that the loss occurred as the result of a wilful act or gross negligence on the part of the suffering party himself'.[38]

While the general principle of no liability without fault except in extra-hazardous situations was made basic to the system of tort law, there was a subsequent article which went far to negate it, for a subsequent provision of the Code declared, 'In circumstances when the person causing injury is not required to repair the injury under the provisions of Articles 403–405, the court may, however, require him to repair the injury, taking into consideration his wealth and that of the injured party'.[39]

Two American lawyers who analysed the early Soviet judicial decisions applying the tort provisions of the Civil Code reached the conclusion that the courts went far toward applying a rule of liability without fault, and that this practice was characteristic of the Soviet approach to tort law.[40] A student of comparative

36 Protocol No. 10, dated June 28, 1926, *Sbornik Razyasnenii Verkhovnogo Suda RSFSR* (4th ed. 1935) p. 77.
37 *Civil Code RSFSR,* Art. 404.
38 *Ibid.*, Art. 403.
39 *Ibid.*, Art. 406.
40 Holman and Spinner, 'Basis of Liability for Tortious Injury in Soviet Law' (1936) 22 *Iowa Law Review* 1.

law has concluded that the Soviet jurists seized upon western European and pre-revolutionary Russian law developing the doctrine of liability without fault and turned it to their own ends.[41] Certainly those ends were made clear by a further provision of the Code which declared, 'In fixing damages the court must in all cases take into consideration the wealth of the injured person and the wealth of the person who caused the injury'.[42]

It was the Soviet use of tort law to reduce the wealth and power of members of the class of persons against whom the revolution was directed that first caught the attention of western lawyers. The Soviet Civil Code seemed to be but a sieve through which the principles of western European law slipped whenever their application would have benefited a person with property. Certainly there was no utilisation of tort law to enforce an obligation of care. While the Code seemed to favour such an approach as the normal one, it was definitely secondary in the practice of the courts.

The wheel began to turn in the early 1930's. The property owners who had acquired their wealth before the revolution or during the period of the New Economic Policy of the 1920's had been heavily taxed and reduced in circumstances by the many hostile measures applied to them. Differentiated wage scales were being applied to build up a new group of persons of moderate wealth. The primary aims of the revolution were being achieved. The enemies who operated from a property base were no more. The private employer of labour for profit had been reduced to the artisan with one hired hand, and even that one hired hand was soon to be denied him. The major sources of injury, namely the factory and transportation systems, were State-owned and in the hands of State managers. It was obvious that a changed attitude toward tort law was appropriate, if not required. Soviet leadership seems to have appreciated that fact, if one may judge by the activity of the courts when suits were filed against State enterprises.

TORTS BY STATE AGENCIES

The Code laid the groundwork for decisions in cases involving injuries caused by State agencies, related as they are to the social

[41] Gsovski, 1 *Soviet Civil Law* (1948) pp. 491–500.
[42] *Civil Code RSFSR*, Art. 411.

insurance scheme. Article 413 indicated the rules to be applied in the event that a workman was injured at his job under circumstances in which social insurance benefits were to be paid. It said:

'A person or enterprise paying insurance premiums to protect an injured person under social insurance, shall not be required to repair injury caused by the happening of the event against which the insurance has been purchased'.

By this provision the Soviet Code adopted the usual rule of insurance law that the payment of premiums as a protection against loss shall entitle the agency paying the premium to indemnification if loss occurs. While the injured employee received his benefits regardless of the fault of the employer who had been paying insurance premiums, the latter was not subject to a suit by the insurance carrier to recover the amount of the benefits.

To this basic rule a second paragraph of the Article concerned provided an exception, for it states:

'But if the injury is caused by the criminal act or failure to act of the management of the enterprise, the social insurance agency which satisfies the injured person shall have the right to demand from the management of the enterprise an amount equal to the insurance benefits paid to the injured person [subrogation]'.

By this paragraph the management of the enterprise was put on notice that even though it had insurance against loss, it would be subjected to suit by the insurance carrier if its action were sufficiently negligent to constitute 'criminal' negligence in the eyes of the court hearing the case.[43] Some judicial decisions indicating how the courts approach such a situation will be introduced shortly to clarify application of the article.

A final paragraph in the article extended to the injured person rights in excess of those acquired under the social security laws if an insured employer were so negligent that his actions or failure to act could be established as 'criminal' in the eyes of a court. It states:

[43] 'Criminal negligence' within the meaning of this article is said by a Soviet commentator to be present when there has been failure to take measures to protect labour and to adopt safety techniques. Matveev, 'Cases concerned with damages for injury', [1950] 2 Sots.Zak. 26 at p. 32.

'In the same situation the injured person to the extent that he fails to obtain through the social insurance procedure full recompense for his injury, shall have the right to make a supplementary demand upon the management of the enterprise'.

It is this final paragraph which suggests that there may be a relation between the maintenance of a rate of social insurance benefit generally lower than the average wage of Soviet employees in order to induce injured employees to bring tort actions against employers who are seriously negligent in protecting their employees against harm.

Actions brought by employees against their insured employers will indicate the application of the articles set out above. A wartime case will serve to introduce the practice.[44]

A workman was injured while loading lumber in the yard of a State-owned mining enterprise, as the result of which he was unable to work for nearly a month. He found it desirable, apparently, to sue his employer, who pleaded in defence that as an insured employer he was not liable in the absence of criminal negligence on its part. The trial court held for the defendant, finding that the defendant could not have prevented the injury and so was not criminally negligent. On a review of the record following a protest of the President of the Supreme Court against the decision, the Appellate College of the Supreme Court of the U.S.S.R. found it obvious that the plaintiff had been injured because the employer had never provided instruction in safety techniques, but had offered training only in extinguishing fires. A retrial was ordered to permit reconsideration of the factor of the insured employer's negligence. The appellate court ordered that on the second trial the State labour inspector who is maintained by the Trade Union, be summoned as a witness to inform the court as to whether in his opinion the failure to give safety instruction was sufficiently serious to constitute 'criminal negligence' within the meaning of the Civil Code.

The relationship of a social insurance pension to damages in tort was indicated by a second case.[45] By virtue of having been placed in the second category of invalids by the social insurance medical commission, an employee was granted a social insurance pension of 225 roubles a month, as against his wage of 363

[44] *Sosidko v. Kzyl-Kiiski Iron Ore Administration* [1942] Sbornik Post. Pl. i Opr. Koll. Verkh. Suda SSSR 158.

[45] *Case of Shupaev, ibid.*, at p. 158.

roubles per month before the permanent injury. The employee then brought suit against his insured employer for the difference between his social insurance benefit and the original wage, namely 138 roubles per month.

The action for the difference was decided in the plaintiff's favour in the trial court, but the Prosecutor of the U.S.S.R. protested the judgment in accordance with the right given him by the Constitution to intervene in any case if he believes there has been misapplication of the law. In agreeing with the Prosecutor of the U.S.S.R. the Appellate College of the highest court referred to the requirement that criminal action or inaction must be proved before an insured employer will be held liable in a suit for injury suffered by an employee. The Appellate College thought that there had been insufficient investigation of this factor to permit a final decision, and the case was remanded for further trial of this issue.

THE INFLUENCE OF SPECIAL CIRCUMSTANCES

Some insured employers have sought to avoid liability by pleading special circumstances which they believe should release them from application of the general principles. Three cases will indicate the lengths to which counsel have gone in seeking to escape liability for their clients.

A construction worker who had fallen from a scaffolding and injured his spine brought suit to recover damages in excess of his social insurance benefits.[46] He had obtained a pension of 129 roubles per month under the social insurance system by virtue of having been placed in the second category of invalids by the medical commission. The trial court gave judgment for the worker in the lump sum of 1,592 roubles and 36 kopeks, and ordered that the insured employer give the employee also an all-expense-paid trip to a sanatorium.

A retrial was ordered by the Provincial Court at the intermediate appellate court. On the retrial the lower court heard the argument of the employer that medical evidence showed that the plaintiff had suffered from concealed tuberculosis before the accident, and that the accident had only accelerated his disability. The judgment was reduced in the light of this argument to a monthly pension of 70 roubles for one year, plus a lump

[46] *Gavrilov* v. *Palace of Pioneers* [1940] *ibid.*, at p. 229.

sum of 940 roubles to pay the cost of a trip to a watering-place. The court ordered that the plaintiff be re-examined by experts at the end of the year. The Provincial Court on the second review indicated that it believed the decision on the retrial sound in principle, but it extended the pension for a total of two years and raised the amount awarded for the trip to a watering-place to 1,410 roubles.

The matter was not allowed to rest in this condition, for the President of the Supreme Court found the decision in his regular audit of the work of the lower courts and protested the second judgment, sending the record for review to the Appellate College of his Supreme Court. The review disclosed that the record supported a conclusion that the accident had occurred because of the fault of the employer in that the scaffolding was weak. The record was found to disclose further that the medical evidence had proved the existence of tuberculosis at the time of the injury. Nevertheless, the Appellate College felt that the fact that tuberculosis had existed at the time of the injury was not reason to mitigate damages, since the plaintiff had indicated his ability to work before the accident and had been receiving a wage of 270 roubles a month. There was no medical evidence in the record to support the lower court's opinion that the tuberculosis had reduced the plaintiff's capacity to work by 50 per cent at the time of the accident. The case was remanded for retrial to determine the precise amount for which the defendant should be held liable under the Supreme Court's rulings.

An employee of an insured employer was injured in a second case[47] because of a structural defect in a metal working machine tool as the result of which he lost the thumb of his left hand. He was already partly incapacitated, for he had been blinded during the civil war in 1919 and granted a pension of 65 roubles a month. Yet, in spite of this handicap he had been rehabilitated sufficiently by 1938 to begin work in the machine shop in which he was finally injured. As a result of the new injury the medical commission had placed him in the first group of invalids after the injury, and he had been awarded a social insurance pension of 235 roubles a month.

When the new pension was added to the civil war pension of 65 roubles a month, the plaintiff reached the ordinary maxi-

[47] *Panasov* v. *Emos Factory*, *ibid.*, at p. 228.

mum of 300 roubles a month generally allowed to a social insurance pensioner under the statute. Yet, since the blind man had been earning 447 roubles a month at the time of the loss of his thumb, he sued the insured employer for the difference between his combined pensions of 300 roubles a month and his wages of 447 roubles a month.

The defence attorney argued that since the medical experts had reached the conclusion that the blind plaintiff had suffered only a 60 per cent reduction in his earning capacity as a result of the new injury, the defendant should be liable only for the difference between the social security payments of 235 roubles a month (exclusive of the civil war pension) and 60 per cent of the plaintiff's wages at the time of the injury, namely 268 roubles and 20 kopeks. The defendant argued further that the plaintiff could be expected to earn 40 per cent of his old wage with the 40 per cent capacity left to him in the opinion of the medical experts. Thus, the defendant believed the court should not exact from it a pension of more than 33 roubles 20 kopeks a month (computed by deducting 235 roubles from 268 roubles 20 kopeks). Judgment was rendered in this amount, but shortly afterwards the Supreme Court's President protested.

On review by the Appellate College of the Supreme Court the conclusion was reached that the record supported a finding that the insured defendant had been liable for the injury caused by the structural defects in the machine tools. A retrial was ordered, however, so that further evidence might be taken as to the plaintiff's continuing ability to work. The Appellate College did not believe the medical testimony in the record as to the ease with which a blind man could be taught new skills and ordered this fact to be considered carefully on the retrial.

In ordering the reconsideration of the extent of disability, the court introduced an element not mentioned in previous cases, namely a court review of the medical testimony on the capacity of the injured person to work after the injury. The courts in the other cases of severe injury seem to have accepted mechanically the medical findings and to have given judgment for the difference between the social insurance pension and the former wages without question.

The third case[48] in which special circumstances were urged

48 *Mezhevov* v. *Vykunsky Metallurgical Factory* [1942] *ibid.*, at p. 159.

on the part of the defence arose during the second world war. A workman in a steel plant tripped on a piece of steel while going to the factory restaurant during an air raid blackout at night. He struck his chest in falling and was invalided. Since he did not receive his full wages from the social insurance system, he brought suit against his insured employer for the difference between the social insurance benefits and his wages before the accident.

The suit was rejected by the trial court on the ground that the injury occurred as the result of the workman's own negligence. Under Soviet law, it is the rule that contributory negligence is not a bar to recovery, but must be weighed in determining the extent of the defendant's liability. The court's decision in the case seems, therefore, to have rested upon a finding that the plaintiff's negligence was so gross as to outweigh the defendant's negligence completely. The President of the Supreme Court protested the result, and his Supreme Court's College for Civil Appeals reviewed the record. It reached the conclusion that the accident had occurred because of the obstruction in the passageway and because of the absence of illumination. It felt that the presence of the blackout was no defence because under the regulations blackouts were to be conducted in such a way as not to upset the normal functioning of a factory. The responsibility of the administration to take precautions during blackouts was increased, so that the lack of care could be considered as so severe as to amount to criminal negligence on the part of the employer, making it liable under the Civil Code for injuries suffered by its insured employee as the result of his fall in the dark.

SUBROGATION OF THE INSURANCE CARRIER

The right of the insurance carrier to sue the tortfeasor to recover the pension paid is illustrated in the application of the Civil Code's provision to this effect. The plaintiff has the same burden of proof as in the cases just recounted. He must prove that the negligence of the defendant was sufficiently gross to constitute 'criminal negligence'. A case[49] will illustrate the type of problem faced by the courts in applying the Code.

[49] *All Georgian Republic Committee of the Union of Highway Workers* v. *Inzhstroi* [1940] *ibid.*, at p. 337.

The All-Georgian Republic Committee of the Union of Highway Workers, an insurance carrier, brought suit against a State engineering enterprise for 3,365 roubles and 36 kopeks, alleging that the social insurance agency required this sum to pay social insurance benefits to a typist who had been injured when the ceiling of a room in the engineering enterprise's office fell on her head for want of proper inspection and care by the defendant company. Only 1,683 roubles and 46 kopeks had been paid out to the injured typist at the time suit was brought, but the plaintiff computed that a further 1,781 roubles and 90 kopeks would be required to restore the typist to health. The trial court gave judgment but only in the amount actually expended, namely 1,683 roubles and 46 kopeks.

The jurisdiction of the courts to entertain such a dispute was brought into question on the appeal to the Supreme Court of the Republic of Georgia. This court noted that both of the parties, as the result of the subrogation of the insurance carrier to the rights of the injured typist, had become State agencies. Under the usual rules, a suit involving two State agencies goes before the State Arbitration Tribunal and not the regular courts, if the amount involved exceeds 1,000 roubles. Being of the opinion that the arbitration rules applied, the Georgian Supreme Court dismissed the action.

The Appellate College of the Supreme Court of the U.S.S.R. held that the regular courts retained jurisdiction because of a circular letter issued four years previously by the Supreme Court of the U.S.S.R. and the State arbitration system.[50] It, therefore, restored the judgment of the trial court.

The letter to which reference was made indicates that its authors did not think in terms of subrogation of the insurance carrier to the rights of an individual as the reason for placing jurisdiction in the regular courts. The circular letter places jurisdiction in the regular courts on the ground that suits for personal injury arising in the course of employment are usually closely related to labour law, and also to criminal prosecution of management for negligence in permitting conditions to occur from which injury results. Since both labour and criminal law

[50] [1936] 4 Arbitrazh 32. The rule is also incorporated by the Supreme Court of the USSR in its order of June 10, 1943, s. 21, printed as annotation to *Civil Code RSFSR*, s. 13 (1950 ed.) p. 244.

matters are the concern of the regular courts, a suit by an insurance carrier to recover benefits paid to an injured party remains subject to the jurisdiction of the regular courts even though the parties to the suit have become State agencies.

The court in suits brought against insured employers to recover the difference between insurance benefits and the wages being paid at the time of the injury are denied the right to interfere in the determination of the amount paid as a social insurance benefit,[51] but the court may go beyond the report of the social insurance medical commission and seek its own professional advice as to the extent of the injury.[52] In so doing it may serve as a check upon any insurance decision which it believes to be overly liberal, for it may reduce the amount recoverable from the employer in accordance with its finding that the injury suffered was not, in fact, as incapacitating as thought by the social insurance experts. By keeping the total social insurance benefit at a rate considerably lower than the average monthly wage of Soviet employees, the Soviet policy-makers may well have desired to provide the court with this opportunity to correct any undue liberality on the part of the social insurance administrators.

DISCOURAGING CRIMINAL NEGLIGENCE

A second reason for setting the maximum social insurance benefit at an amount below the average monthly wage may be the desire to stimulate the bringing of an action for damages against an employer who is criminally negligent. Such an action could serve as a deterrent against gross negligence in the future. In addition to the deterrent effect of a possible criminal action brought against the responsible officials of the employing State agency, the judgment for damages in tort has a deterrent effect in that it will be reflected unfavourably in the profit and loss statement of the enterprise. Under conditions of cost accounting, instituted, as explained earlier, in all Soviet State enterprises in the early 1920's to assure quick detection of inefficient administrators, an expenditure of funds to pay such a judgment will constitute a warning signal to the inspectors of the Ministry of

[51] Explanation of Plenum of the Supreme Court of the RSFSR, [1930] 8 Sud.Prak. RSFSR 8, and *Konovalova* v. *District Committee of the Trade Union* (1939] 15–16 Sov.Yust, 70.

[52] *Shavshishvili* v. *Soyuztrans* [1939] 15–16 Sov.Yust. 69.

Finance when they review the periodic statements of the enterprise. Tort law serves in this fashion as an instrument of policy in encouraging State economic administrators to give careful attention to the safety rules.

To the conclusion that tort law is looked upon as serving, under conditions of Soviet socialism, a deterring function rather like that assigned to it in the non-socialist world, a *caveat* must be entered. It is made necessary by the manner in which suits against enterprises engaged in extra-hazardous activities are handled. As has been indicated earlier, such suits are brought under the provisions of an article of the Civil Code which adopts a rule providing for liability without fault, except in cases where the injury resulted from the intervention of *force majeure.*

Most of the actions in Soviet courts falling under the article concerned with extra-hazardous activity are brought against State enterprises engaged in transportation. In such cases, the employees who are insured by their industrial employers but injured while riding to or from work on the vehicles of the transport enterprise bring an action for damages after they have received their social insurance benefits as an insured employee. Under the Code they need prove nothing more than their injury and causation. They are not required to prove negligence in any degree. A case will illustrate the situation.[53]

An insured apprentice, who had been injured in a street railway accident and who had received social insurance benefits, sued the Moscow Transit Company for the difference between her pension and her former wages. No question was raised as to the fault of the defendant, since the operation was classed under the code as extra-hazardous. The court devoted its attention solely to the measure of damages. In giving judgment for the girl the trial court awarded her the difference between the social security benefits and her wages as a student apprentice. The appellate court altered the amount on the ground that although she was actually receiving at the time only the wages of a student apprentice, the formula should have been based on the wages of an unskilled worker at the average rate for unskilled workers then existing. It could be assumed that the girl would have come to earn at least the amount of an unskilled worker and would not have remained at the level of a student apprentice.

53 *Burova* v. *Moscowtrans* [1930] 7 Sud.Prak. RSFSR 11.

Enterprises engaged in extra-hazardous activities are not held responsible without fault, if they cause injury to one of their own employees. A Ukrainian case is cited as an indication of a trial court's failure to understand the distinction to be drawn between an injury to an employee and to a passenger on a railway. A wagon coupler was injured on the Southern Railway in the Ukrainian Republic and sued the management for the difference between his average wage and his social security pension, he having lost a hand.

The trial court gave judgment in the amount of a monthly pension of 958 roubles, and the Kharkov Provincial Court affirmed. The Supreme Court of the Ukrainian Republic set aside the judgment and remanded for a new trial because there had been no effort to establish the criminal negligence of the management, as is required if an insured employer, even one operating an extra-hazardous activity, is to be held liable for injury to its employees.[54]

The rule is not, apparently, fully appreciated by some of the courts, as evidenced by another case in the same Supreme Court.[55] The operator of a chopping machine in a mine was injured and brought suit against the management for the difference between his pension and his former wages. The trial court in Voroshilovgrad Province denied recovery because of the contributory negligence of the injured party. The Provincial Court affirmed, but the Supreme Court of the Ukrainian Republic ordered a new trial, saying that, 'The court may release the defendant from the obligation to pay damages only if it is proved that the injury was caused by *force majeure* or if it occurred as the result of the wilful or grossly negligent act of the injured party'.

A Soviet commentator writes that he cannot agree with the decision of the Ukrainian Supreme Court, because an extra-hazardous enterprise is not responsible at all to its own employees unless it is criminally negligent, as evidenced by its failure to take the required safety measures. No one had charged such failure. The commentator thought that this fact should have been established before any discussion was had of the extent of the negligence of the injured party.

[54] Case reported in Matveev, 'Cases Concerned with Damages for Injury', [1950] 2 Sots.Zak. 27 at p. 29.

[55] *Ibid.*, at p. 30.

DOES TORT LIABILITY ASSURE CARE

Soviet authors are of two minds on the advantages to be gained from utilisation of tort law when social insurance remedies are available to meet the needs of an injured person. Fifteen years ago the standard Soviet textbook on civil law was able to say in criticism of the view that social insurance could replace the action in tort, 'The duty to pay compensation, naturally has preventive importance. Likewise, to the extent that injury is compensated for by means of civil liability, the same purposes are achieved by insurance and social security. But the specific purpose of civil liability is not this relationship, but is the relationship that it establishes between compensation to the injured person and the obligation of the injured person responsible for the injury. The damage falls upon the person who caused it . . .'.[56]

A different view was expressed twelve years later in 1950. Another Soviet author wrote, 'The right of subrogation of the social insurance carrier to the claim of the injured person could well be abolished. In fact it is already rare to encounter any such claims in practice. Whenever such a suggestion of abolition is made, it is replied that it would be dangerous. Management would relax its vigilance and its observance of safety regulations, accidents would increase, and the social insurance system would be overburdened. I think these prophecies unfounded. Safety precautions are enforced quite effectively without this additional stimulus of fear of lawsuits, which in fact already has little significance. If there is any increase in social insurance payments, it is possible to transfer this to managements under a planned system by raising the premiums'.[57]

The 1950 critic is still in the minority, if one may judge by other Soviet literature, but it is significant that his voice has been raised. He may herald a trend away from the use of tort law as a deterrent of wrongdoing by managers of State enterprises. It is suggested that the same effect might be achieved without the delays and costs of a court action by raising the premiums. Presumably a system could be established in which the premiums would not vary from industry to industry as they now do,

56 All-Union Institute of Juridical Sciences, 2 *Sovetskoe Grazhdansoe Pravo* [*Soviet Civil Law*] (1938) p. 389.

57 Matveev, 'Cases Concerned with Damages for Injury', [1950] 2 Sots.Zak. 27 at p. 33.

depending upon the accident rate in an industry, but from employer to employer, depending upon the accident rate within the enterprise administered by the employer. Yet, even with such a system, it is hard to see how it would be possible to utilise the differentiated premium rate solely as a deterrent to negligence, unless some tribunal existed to determine the presence or absence of the negligence factor in each accident for which insurance benefits are paid.

A differentiated premium rate based solely upon the number of social insurance claims paid in each year would reflect only the accident rate without distinguishing between those accidents which could have been avoided and those which could not have been avoided. At present, the court makes the distinction through the tort suit. Under the proposed scheme, the social insurance system would have to set up a tribunal to determine negligence, not in order to determine whether the injured party was to receive a benefit, because he is to receive a benefit under present law in any event if he is insured, but whether the employer was sufficiently negligent to require the raising of the insurance premium payable by the enterprise for which he is responsible.

The Soviet policy-makers have, apparently, felt it undesirable to extend social insurance coverage to all, as has been indicated earlier, yet they have provided a system of tort law which makes it possible for injured persons, even when not insured, to recover damages. Usually such persons have to prove negligence to recover. The article of the Civil Code, inserted in 1922 to catch the wealthy person who causes injury even without fault, is no longer being applied. A 1947 textbook says that under present Soviet conditions it has no further applicability because class differences have been eliminated from society.[58] In consequence, a tort action will be successful only if the tortfeasor has been wilfully or negligently harmful. Thus, tort law serves to enforce care in the community and it serves also to benefit the injured person who does not fall within the social insurance system because he is not employed. By far the greatest number of such

[58] Zimeleva, Serebrovsky, Shkundin, *Grazhdanskoe Pravo* [*Civil Law*] (1947) p. 374. The same comment is repeated in All-Union Institute of Juridical Sciences, 2 *Sovetskoe Grazhdanskoe Pravo* [*Soviet Civil Law*] (1951) p. 314.

persons are children, housewives and collective farmers, and the published decisions of the courts indicate that these people are among those engaged in bringing suits against those who injure them.

EXTRA-HAZARDOUS ACTIVITY AND THE UNINSURED

Sometimes the task of the uninsured is facilitated because they are able to rely upon the provisions of the article relating to extra-hazardous activity.[59] In such cases they need prove no fault. It may not be chance that the sphere of extra-hazardous activity is extended beyond the usual expectation in the west so as to relieve plaintiffs of the burden of proving negligence in a large number of cases even including all cases of injury by automobiles. A few judicial decisions will indicate the problems of the uninsured plaintiff.

A male member of a collective farm broke his leg in the co-operative society's flour mill and brought suit against the mutual benefit fund maintained by the society for the purpose of protecting members in their old age.[60] The trial court gave judgment for the plaintiff. The judgment was protested on various grounds by the President of the Supreme Court of the U.S.S.R., one of the grounds being that under a 1932 order the mutual benefit fund of the society was a distinct entity separate from the society and hence could not be held liable for the torts of the society.

The protest was upheld, the Supreme Court's Appellate College declaring that the mutual benefit fund could not be held liable, but the farm could be held liable in view of the fact that the milling operation was judged to be an extra-hazardous activity. In this instance, however, the court was of the opinion that a hurricane which caused a stone to fall from the mill on to the plaintiff's leg introduced a *force majeure*. By applying the rule of the Civil Code the court released the society from a liability it would otherwise have had to assume.

Suits by minors injured by extra-hazardous activities have introduced a problem as to the manner of payment, whether it be in a pension only for the period of minority to be reviewed

[59] *Civil Code RSFSR*, Art. 404.
[60] *Krivosheev* v. *Mutual Benefit Fund of the Collective Farm named for Kirov* [1940] Sbornik Post. Pl. i Opr. Koll. Verkh. Suda SSSR 232.

when the child reaches the age of majority, or whether it be a pension for life. In one such case [61] action was brought on behalf of a minor against a State street railway company which had cut off his legs. The court held that while the defendant, as the operator of an extra-hazardous activity, was clearly liable, no decision as to the permanent rate of pension could be made until the child reached his majority.

The rule that the judgment establishing a pension must be reviewed when the child reaches his majority served to benefit one plaintiff. In the case concerned [62] a minor was injured in 1928 by a railway and recovered judgment in the amount of 79 roubles and 60 kopeks a month. On reaching his majority in 1934 the plaintiff brought suit again for recomputation of the pension on the basis of the average wage of an unskilled workman plus a lump sum for a special diet, the wages of a constant companion, the purchase and repair of an artificial limb and shoes and three years in a watering-place. The trial court gave judgment in an amount representing the difference between the childhood pension and the average wage of an unskilled workman, plus fixed lump sum amounts to meet the cost of the other items. The judgment was affirmed by the appellate court, but then reviewed by the Supreme Court of the U.S.S.R. on the basis of a protest issuing from the Prosecutor of the U.S.S.R.

On remanding the case for new trial, partly because of its feeling that there was insufficient link in the record between the supplementary expenses and the original injury, the Supreme Court stated that it was prepared to permit an increase in the pension, but only on the basis of a computation based upon the average wage of an unskilled clerical worker, for which the completion of the ten year school by the plaintiff presumably qualified him. The Supreme Court rejected the plaintiff's argument that the computation should be based upon the wage of a chief clerk, since the position of chief clerk required not only schooling but executive ability, and this was not to be acquired from middle school alone but usually required further training in management plus practical experience.

In one case in 1931 [63] the court had sought to reduce the

61 *Magradze* v. *Tbilisi Tramway Trust* [1940] 12 Sots.Zak. 91.

62 *Revason* v. *Azov-Black Sea Railway* [1940] Sbornik Post. Pl. i Opr. Koll. Verkh. Suda SSSR 233.

63 *Baltushkin* v. *Zapolsk Agricultural Artel*, No. 32,659 [1931] 3 Sud.Prak. RSFSR 10.

number of actions necessary for a minor. In a suit brought on behalf of an injured child against a co-operative association, the court held the defendant liable for maintenance of the child until its majority at the age of sixteen, and ordered that on the retrial it be determined what pension would be required thereafter for life, so that a new action would not be required when majority had been achieved.

The fine line as to what is an extra-hazardous activity was the issue in a case involving the injury of a minor by a machine making matzos for the Iranian Jewish Synagogue of Tbilisi.[64] The trial court gave judgment in the amount of 300 roubles as a lump sum. On review by the Supreme Court it was held that a retrial was necessary for several reasons, one of them being that the record did not indicate whether the matzos machine was operated by a motor or without one. If operated by a motor, the operation was within the class of extra-hazardous activity, and the article of the Code requiring no proof of negligence would apply. If the machine had no motor, it was necessary for the plaintiff to prove negligence on the part of the defendants.

INFLATION AND PENSIONS

Payment of damages in terms of pensions, rather than as lump sums, has introduced a problem when the value of the currency fluctuates. In the early years the administrative authorities and the courts seem to have been unrealistic in facing the problem. A plaintiff who had recovered judgment in 1928 against an employer railway for personal injuries in the amount of a pension of 31 roubles and 11 kopeks a month sued in 1939 to have the amount increased.[65] He argued that the wage rate for his former profession of engine cleaner had been increased several times since 1928, and the pension should be recomputed on the basis of the current wage for those engaged in the type of work which had been performed by the plaintiff at the time of the injury. The trial court was moved by the argument and gave judgment in the amount of 143 roubles a month. The Provincial Court remanded for retrial because of lack of a new

64 *Yarolan* v. *Iranian Jewish Synagogue* [1939] 15–16 Sov.Yust. 70.
65 *Kremgolts* v. *Dzerzhinsky Railway* [1940] Sbornik Post. Pl. i Opr. Koll. Verkh. Suda SSSR 231.

medical examination, thus approving, apparently, the principle underlying the plaintiff's case. On the retrial the pension was raised to 163 roubles 35 kopeks a month.

Review was then given the case by the Appellate College of the Supreme Court which ordered a new trial, and gave instruction that the pensions could be computed only on the basis of wages at the time of the injury. The court had no right to use 1939 wage rates to compute damages as of 1928. It is possible that this seemingly unrealistic approach was influenced by action of the Council of People's Commissars in 1938.[66] At that time it was ordered that all social insurance pensions must be raised at least to a minimum of 50 roubles a month for invalids of the first category without dependants and 60 or 75 roubles a month for those with one or two dependants, respectively. Lower minimum levels were set for invalids of the second category and for those who had lost their family provider. Another blanket increase occurred in 1946 for all non-working pensioners living in urban conditions.[67] They were given a rise of 60 roubles a month.

Further relief was given by the reduction in costs of commodities while retaining the same rate of wages and pensions by legislation of December 14, 1947.[68] This law recalled the outstanding roubles, providing for exchange at varying rates, depending upon the amount in the possession of each individual and the form in which it was kept—cash, savings accounts or government bonds, but it ordered that pensions be continued in the new roubles at the rates formerly paid. Yet, even with this action, the pension for persons receiving the minimum of 50 roubles established in 1939 plus the 60 rouble increase of 1946 seems small when compared with the wages indicated in the cases decided during the war and discussed in this chapter.

In reviewing Soviet statutes on social security and the judicial

[66] Order of December 28, 1938, s. 23, [1939] Sob.Post. SSSR, No. 1, item 1.

[67] Although this order is not printed in the official gazette, it is referred to by. Aleksandrov, editor, *Sovetskoe Trudovoe Pravo* [*Soviet Labour Law*] (1949) p. 340. At the same time a general order established a minimum pension for wounded veterans of the war of 300 roubles a month if they were not 'connected with' agriculture and 250 roubles a month if they were. Order of January 28, 1946, [1946] Sob.Post. SSSR, No. 2, item 35.

[68] This law has been discussed in greater detail in Chap. 1 in connection with the crime of speculation.

decisions concerned with tort claims it is evident that Soviet policy-makers no longer think in terms of the replacement of the tort suit by the social security payment, as they seem to have done in the early years when law was expected soon to wither away. An interrelationship has been worked out within which the uninsured is protected by the tort suit, alone while the insured has both a social insurance claim and a right to a tort action, the latter serving as a deterrent for those State managers who are inclined to be grossly negligent. In the extra-hazardous situation, the usefulness of the tort action as a deterrent gives way, apparently, to the greater need for what amounts to complete protection for every individual who is injured, whether he be insured or uninsured, and whether the defendant has been guilty of fault or not.

CHAPTER 10

THE FAMILY AND THE STATE

LEADERS seeking to effect a permanent change in social relationships have often turned their eyes toward youth. Soviet leaders have been no exception. The hope of eventual achievement of communism has frequently been declared to lie in the rearing of a new generation.[1] Soviet programmes have favoured the children over any other element of the community. Their material well-being has been a matter of primary concern, and their education along lines desired by the leadership has been a responsibility assumed by the highest political figures in the land.

The Soviet family code has reflected the changing theories as to the means by which the child is to be reared in the image of the new Soviet man. It is here that the dreams and disappointments have been registered in concrete ways affecting the upbringing of the child. It is here that the outsider has been able to determine what views among the many expressed in the press have finally triumphed. From the days when a prominent revolutionary found it possible to write that the family had outlived its usefulness[2] to the current time when the Supreme Court says that divorce practice must encourage respect in the population for the family and for marriage[3] the law of domestic relations has held a place of vital political importance.

There were undoubtedly many who expected the State to assume primary responsibility at the time of the revolution for the care of the child. Grandiose schemes for the development of children's institutions to liberate the womenfolk from the drudgery of the home were made the subject of much speculation. Community nurseries, kitchens and laundries were planned to release the housewife from all cares. In these plans many saw an appeal for support from those elements which had little political reason for joining the ranks of the revolutionaries.

[1] Aksenenok, 'The Role of the Court in Strengthening the Family in the Soviet State', [1949] 3 Sots.Zak. 3 at p. 8.

[2] Kollontai, *Communism and the Family* (1920) p. 9. An English translation of this work and other contemporary views is available in Schlesinger, *Changing Attitudes in Soviet Russia: The Family* (1949).

[3] Order of September 16, 1949, 3 *Spravochnik po Zak.* (1949) p. 497.

The new Soviet leaders relied also for support on elements with other interests. Under the law of the Russian Empire, the law concerning marriage and divorce was the province of the various religious groups. The Church, the Mosque and the Synagogue established their own law, and maintained ecclesiastical courts to administer it. While the Synagogue, the Mosque and some of the Protestant sects were often anything but strict in preserving marriage bonds against the will of the parties, the Russian Orthodox Church, to which the great majority of the population belonged, administered a policy of preservation of marriage relationships with few exceptions once they had been assumed.[4] In consequence there had developed among the population, particularly among the intellectuals, some measure of support for a regime which would relax the strict rules of the Church and offer a secular procedure for the dissolution of marriage. To this group the new revolutionary leadership could appeal with a radical change in the law of domestic relations.

The interest in gaining support from the elements of the population seeking liberation from the strict rules of the Church coincided with a political interest of a longer range nature. It was the interest of the leadership in moulding a new society, which would abandon traditional concepts of property ownership and accept the new loyalty to the community which was proposed as a replacement for all narrower loyalties. To the new leaders a major source of opposition, and a source which was largely beyond their reach through ordinary police measures used in ferreting out enemies was the home. It was here that the mother and father could rear their children to revere virtues which they believed to be eternal. It was here that the concepts of the preceding regime could be revived in spite of all that might be done during the less impressionable hours in school.

BREAKING UP THE FAMILY

While Lenin was prepared to criticise those of his Party who favoured irresponsible sexual relationships, he sanctioned the drafting of radically new family laws as some of the very first acts of the new revolutionary government. On December 18,

[4] A summary of the pre-revolutionary ecclesiastical law may be found in Berman, 'Soviet Family Law in the Light of Russian History and Marxian Theory' (1946) 56 *Yale Law Journal* 26.

1917,[5] but little more than a month after the revolution, a decree abolished the ecclesiastical control of the past over the marriage relationship. Thereafter only civil marriage concluded before secular authorities was to be given legal force. On the following day another decree[6] permitted divorce at the request of one or both of the parties without regard to the reasons. The following year a code incorporated all of the law relating to the family in one place.[7] It lasted through the principal years of the New Economic Policy when codes were emerging for the first time to govern other forms of legal relationships. Not until 1926 was it replaced with a fuller code in the R.S.F.S.R.[8] Codes were enacted also in the other Republics.[9]

The 1926 code went further than the earlier family laws of the revolution. It sanctioned both marriage and divorce without the necessity of registration at all.[10] While registration was urged upon the population in the interest of statistics and the simplified handling of legal matters such as those relating to inheritance from a deceased spouse,[11] it was not required. Judicial decisions followed to declare without question that this provision was really meant. In 1927 the Supreme Court of the R.S.F.S.R.[12] declared that a factual wife was not required to prove that she was a dependant of the decedent to be recognised as his heir. The marriage relationship, unregistered though it be, was sufficient to qualify her as a wife and hence an heir within the provisions of the inheritance rules of the Civil Code. In 1929 the Supreme Court went even farther to permit two women with whom the decedent had been maintaining the relationships of factual marriage at the time of his death both to qualify as heirs to his estate, even though it would have been a situation which might logically have fallen within the prohibition against bigamy, had the decedent's status reached the ears of the prosecutor during the decedent's lifetime.[13]

Unregistered divorce was also reaffirmed in 1929 as having

[5] [1917] 1 Sob.Uzak. RSFSR, No. 11, item 160.
[6] [1917] 1 Sob.Uzak. RSFSR, No. 10, item 152.
[7] [1918] 1 Sob.Uzak. RSFSR, Nos. 76–77, item 818.
[8] [1926] 1 Sob.Uzak. RSFSR, No. 82, item 612.
[9] [1926] Sob.Uzak. Ukrainian SSSR, Nos. 67–69, corrected in *ibid.*, No. 72.
[10] Arts. 1 and 3.
[11] Art. 2.
[12] Code of Laws on Marriage, the Family and Guardianship, RSFSR (1937 ed.) p. 43.
[13] *Ibid.*

been permitted by the Code when the Supreme Court had to determine the legal spouse of a woman who had been living with a married man for sixteen years prior to his death. In seeking to establish his status as the husband of the decedent the claimant had proved that he had long ago ceased marriage relationships with the woman to whom he was still registered as married. The Supreme Court reversed the trial court who had refused to find the second marriage valid on the ground that it would have made the husband bigamous in violation of the Criminal Code. To this argument the Supreme Court said, 'In life, situations are often met when marriage relations of spouses who are still registered as married are in fact terminated, but there has been no registration of divorce, while at the same time one of the spouses has established factual marriage relations with a third person. The refusal by the court to establish this fact because the law forbids bigamy would not only be contrary to law but also contrary to simple logic'.[14] The law to which the court referred was the provision of the 1926 code permitting the recognition of factual divorce without the formality of registration.[15]

While the code and the courts' interpretation of it seemed to free the men and women of the new society from the necessity of maintaining a home longer than both of them wished, it did not permit a father or mother to ignore a child whether born in or out of wedlock. The family environment did not have to be maintained for the good of the child in the event that the parents did not wish to live together, but they could not escape the duty of support.

THE CHILD BORN OUT OF WEDLOCK

From the time of the 1918 code it had been legislative policy to remove all legal difference between persons born in or out of wedlock.[16] Social stigma was to be wiped out of the community as well, and it was the duty of the courts to see that the effort succeeded. This task of the court was emphasised in a prosecution for murder brought in a remote Siberian Province. The fact that it occurred as late as 1934 suggests the slow progress of the new ideas across the plains of the East. The defendant was the

[14] *Case of Gromoglasov*, No. 31,325 [1929] 20 Sud.Prak. RSFSR 8.
[15] Art. 20.
[16] Code of 1918, RSFSR, Art. 133.

mother of a child born out of wedlock. She had been deserted by the child's father who had refused even to support the child. In desperation and in shame she had killed the baby. The trial court had found her case pathetic and had given only a conditional sentence. The Supreme Court of the Republic reversed the decision, saying that she was clearly guilty, although because of her ill health no penalty attached to the reversal. The Supreme Court used the occasion of the reversal to read a lecture on the new social relationships to the people within its jurisdiction. It declared 'The reasoning to the effect that the crime was committed by the accused out of fear "of the severity of her parents, her disgrace before them and before her brothers and also false shame before the neighbours" conflicts sharply with the new conditions of life, and with the expanding culture of the workers and collective farmers of the Soviet Union, the more so since the accused was economically completely independent of her parents, and was sufficiently mature herself. Such a sentence does not mobilise the masses to destroy the survivals of capitalism in the mind of man'.[17]

To assure assistance to an unmarried mother from the father the 1918 code gave the mother a special privilege. She might declare before a court the father of the child, but only up to three months before delivery.[18] Notice had to be sent to the person named as the father, and he was allowed two weeks to contest. With the 1927 code[19] the mother was granted an extension of time to file her claim, for she was permitted to file her declaration at any time before or after birth of the child. The putative father was given one month to contest, and if no protest was received the child was registered as his own, and he was held responsible from that moment on. His right to contest was not terminated finally, for within one year he might bring an action to have the record set aside, but meanwhile he was required to pay maintenance charges.

The authorities seem to have been more interested in finding a person against whom charges might be levied for maintenance of the child than in establishing incontestable paternity. The 1918 code provided that when several persons had had relations

[17] *Case of Krivozubova*, Order of June 9, 1935, [1935] 22 Sov.Yust. 24.
[18] Code of 1918, RSFSR, Art. 140.
[19] Art. 29.

with the mother during the period of conception, the court might declare that all of the persons were liable for support both jointly and severally.[20] A Soviet expert declares that practice showed the system to have been defective because none of the men named in this fashion felt wholly responsible.[21] The 1926 code recognised the shortcomings of the earlier rule by demanding that the court select one of the named persons as the father, and presumably the one who really was the father.[22]

The procedure used in designating one of two potentially responsible youths as the father was illustrated in a case begun in 1928.[23] The woman stated in her complaint that during a drinking party at a friend's home she had permitted herself to have relations with one Vinogradov, and then immediately following with one Lebleu. When a child was born, she asked the court to name one of the two men as the father, saying that she did not know which of the two had been responsible. The trial court found that Vinogradov should be declared the father and the Provincial Court affirmed the decision. The Supreme Court of the Republic reviewed the finding and reached the conclusion that it was appropriate to the circumstances, but in doing so it said, 'The court took into consideration both the interests of the mother and her difficulty of presenting evidence, and also the interests of the child, which must assuredly be protected, at least as to its minimum needs. In such circumstances the defendant is not free of the duty of proving the circumstances negating his parentage'. While the burden of proof was on the mother to make her case well enough to implicate the possible fathers, the court seemed to feel that it had sufficient authority to choose between them, and the person chosen had the burden of disproving his parentage.

Inadequacy of State funds to care for children born out of wedlock seems to have been one of the reasons for placing the duty of support upon the father. There has never been a suggestion that the duty to pay maintenance was established as a deterrent against casual intimate relationships, although such may have been the result of the legislation. Certainly it was not

20 Art. 144.
21 Brandenburgsky, *Kurs po Semeino-Brachnomu Pravu* [*Course in Family and Marriage Law*] (1928) p. 109.
22 Art. 32.
23 *L. v. Vinogradov and Lebleu*, No. 358 [1930] 10 Sud.Prak. RSFSR 19.

described as a penalty for those who participated in such relationships. Since the requirement to pay maintenance was neither a planned deterrent nor a penalty, it was presumably but a transitional means of caring for the unwanted child until the State could assume the burden. Not until 1944 did legislation take a turn which seemed to support such an interpretation of the early legislation.

The 1944 legislation abolished the duty of support which had formerly been placed on the father of a child born out of wedlock.[24] The legislation also recounted the measures taken to increase the institutions for juvenile care. The State assumed the former obligation of the father of the child born out of wedlock by paying the mother's requirements for the child. While this fact might seem to support a conclusion that the State was not interested in the extra-marital conduct of its citizens, other developments to be discussed below suggest that such a conclusion would not have been justified.

What might seem like rather remarkable attention to vested rights was evident at the time of the 1944 legislation relieving a father of a child born out of wedlock of the obligation to pay its maintenance. A decree of 1945[25] established the rule that if a child was born out of wedlock before the 1944 decree relieving a putative father of responsibility for maintenance, he would remain responsible for maintenance, and the child would have all inheritance and pension rights attaching to children of the father. The policy of making the extra-marital child the responsibility of the State and not of its father seems not to have carried over to relieve those fathers whose obligations accrued before the date of the promulgation of law reflecting the new policy. It seems almost as if the child had acquired a vested right against its father before 1944 of such strength that it could not be destroyed.

While such a conclusion might seem lawyer-like, it is risky to assume its validity in the Soviet lawyer's eyes. Vested rights acquired by the passage of time are not revered as such under the Soviet system of law. Soviet authors have explained that a right is created and protected only because it has political importance

24 Law of July 8, 1944, s. 20, Ved.Verkh.Sov. SSSR, No. 37 (297), July 16, 1944.

25 Decree of March 14, 1945, Ved.Verkh.Sov. SSSR, No. 15 (342), March 25, 1945. Also 3 *Spravochnik po Zak.* (1949) p. 493.

in the eyes of the leadership. When circumstances require a change, the change is made. In the light of this approach to rights it is probable that while the State was prepared to assume responsibility for the children to be born in the future out of wedlock, it was not financially or technically able to maintain or place in institutions the hordes of children born out of wedlock in the past. It simply lacked homes for the children that might have been presented by despairing mothers had the fathers stopped paying maintenance. For such children the old means of support were to be continued.

Some judges seem not to have realised that the new law had reversed the policy of the preceding years. It has been reported that some courts have continued to require a putative father to pay maintenance of a child born out of wedlock. Thus, a child born on October 26, 1944, was awarded maintenance, and the Moscow Provincial Court affirmed the decision. A child born on November 19, 1944, obtained maintenance from its unregistered father in the Ulyanovsk Province, and similar errors were made by the courts in the Altai Province, in Novgorod Province and in Vladimir Province.[26] The misunderstanding seems to have been widespread.

JUVENILE DELINQUENCY FORCES A CHANGE

1935 stands out as the year of revolutionary change in the official attitude toward the family. The Institute of Criminal Politics in Moscow had begun a survey of juvenile delinquents in the preceding year.[27] Of the 1,001 juvenile delinquents studied in Leningrad in 1934 and 1935, 90 per cent were found to have spent their leisure time in an unorganised way outside the family, while only 7 per cent of the offenders had spent their recreation hours within the family circle. The remaining 3 per cent played in parks and playgrounds in an organised way during their unoccupied moments. The 2,111 cases examined in Moscow during the same period showed a similar situation. Of this group 88 per cent spent their leisure in an unorganised way outside the home, while 7.7 per cent spent their free time

26 Khoklov, 'Inadequacies in the Work of Certain Courts in Cases Concerned with Suits for the Maintenance of Children', [1950] 5 Sots.Zak. 22 at p. 23.

27 Nakhimson, 'More on the Question of Struggling with Juvenile Crime' (1935) 3 *Problemy Ugolovnoi Politiki* 81.

with the family. The balance played in an unorganised way in parks and playgrounds. Of the group which remained in the home during leisure hours, 46 per cent came from families where the mother and father were both employed. Grandmothers, older children or housemaids were left in charge.

Statistics on children in correctional labour institutions showed that of some 2,894 children 54.8 per cent had previously lived with their families, 3.8 per cent had lived in children's homes, 6.4 per cent had supported themselves in their own establishments without parents, while 35 per cent had been homeless waifs. Of this homeless group of 1,013 children, 13 per cent had been on the streets up to a period of six months, 11 per cent up to one year, 15 per cent from one to two years, and 56 per cent over two years. The statistics do not account for the remaining 5 per cent.

The campaign against juvenile delinquency began with the order of May 31, 1935.[28] It required four Ministries to take measures to care for the groups of homeless children from whom the greatest percentage of criminals came. The Ministry of Education was ordered to establish children's homes for the normal children who had no maintenance of any kind, as well as for those who had no homes but received maintenance payments from parents. The Ministry of Health was ordered to establish institutions for the children who were in need of long periods of medical care. The Ministry of Social Security was ordered to provide special homes for the permanently invalided children, while the Ministry of Internal Affairs was ordered to establish reception points, labour colonies and isolation places for the hardened juvenile delinquents. The guardianship agencies of the local soviets were ordered to take great care in the speedy naming of guardians for orphans, and criminal penalties were ordered to be enforced against guardians who assumed the responsibilities for pecuniary motives, or who failed to give proper attention to their wards.

The local village and city police were ordered to take vigorous methods to prevent street brawls, and authorised to fine parents up to 200 roubles when their children were disobedient to the police in the streets or participated in acts of vandalism. Parents were to be made liable for civil damages in the event that

28 [1935] 1 Sob.Zak. SSSR, No. 32, item 252.

their children committed harmful acts. Finally the Cultural-Educational Section of the Central Committee of the communist party and the Councils of Ministers of the various Republics were ordered to give special attention to the supervision of children's books and cinemas, with authority to forbid any which might have a harmful influence upon the child.

The Republics amended their criminal and civil codes shortly thereafter to reflect the requirement that the parent pay a fine if his child was rowdy in the street while under the parent's care [29] and pay damages for any injury he might cause.[30] A law was also enacted to punish more severely a parent who deliberately encouraged his child to commit crime.[31] Failure adequately to enforce this article called forth later a circular from the Supreme Court and Prosecutor's Office of the U.S.S.R.[32]

While the first attack against juvenile delinquency came as an effort to strengthen discipline in such homes as there were, and to create institutions adequate to the needs of the homeless children, the second attack was made against the parents who failed to pay the maintenance charges required by law with which the parent who retained custody of the child might maintain a home environment. Under date of June 27, 1936, a law required both parties to appear when a divorce was granted so that there would be greater opportunity to assure that maintenance for the child might be paid.[33] Further, the amount of maintenance was set rigidly in the new law, as one-fourth of wages if there were one child, one-third of wages for two children and one-half of wages if there were three or more children. Subsequent failure to pay the amount ordered by the court subjected the defendant to an increased penalty of two years' imprisonment. The court had been required by law in 1923 [34]

[29] Decree of November 25, 1935, s. 4, [1936] 1 Sob.Uzak. RSFSR, No. 1, item 1. Introduced into *Criminal Code RSFSR* as Art. 158 (1).

[30] Decree of November 25, 1935, s. 6. *Ibid.* Introduced into *Civil Code RSFSR* as amendment to Art. 405.

[31] Decree of April 7, 1935, [1935] 1 Sob.Zak. SSSR, No. 19, item 155. Introduced into *Criminal Code RSFSR* as Art. 73 (2).

[32] Circular of July 21, 1935. Published in *O Rassledovanii i Rasmotrenii Del o Nesovershenoletnikh* [*Investigation and Hearing of Cases Concerning Minors*] (1937) p. 34.

[33] [1936] 1 Sob.Zak. SSSR. No. 34, item 309, s. 31.

[34] [1923] 1 Sob.Uzak. RSFSR, Nos. 46–47, item 478, s. 113, effective September 1, 1923.

to assist in collecting evidence in such suits so that the full burden might not fall on the mother, who was the usual plaintiff. This provision continued to apply to assist a plaintiff.

DISCOURAGING DIVORCE

The law of 1936 went farther than the provisions to facilitate collection of maintenance payments. It attacked for the first time those who broke up the family through divorce without adequate thought to what they were doing to their children. It stated that the obligation placed upon both parties to appear in a divorce proceeding was set 'with the objective of struggling with light-minded relations to the family and family obligations'. In the following paragraph of the law there was introduced for the first time a measure which seems to have been intended to discourage divorce. It was primitive, being merely a graduated scale of fees for divorce, the first one to cost 50 roubles, the second 150 roubles and the third and subsequent divorce 300 roubles.

It was reported that in 1937[35] there were some 1,000,000 persons in the whole U.S.S.R. who were under a court order requiring them to pay maintenance costs of their offspring. This suggests that there were several million children without a home environment provided by two parents. Of the total under court order some 100,000 were said to have evaded payment.

In spite of providing graduated fees for successive divorces the campaign to strengthen the family had not yet moved in the direction of impeding any one who sought separation from a spouse. The 1936 law left with the registration bureau power to register a divorce when the request came only from a single spouse. While the other spouse had to be served in accordance with the new requirement, he did not need to appear personally but could make substituted appearance. When appearance had been made, the registration bureau recorded the separation and the plan of distribution of property and custody of children as agreed upon by the parties. If the parties were unable to reach an agreement, the decision on these questions was thrown into a court, although the divorce was registered immediately, there being no hearing on the merits of that question.

35 'Preliminary Reports on the Application of the Law of June 27, 1936', [1936] 4 Sov.Yust. 17.

If the absent spouse failed to make personal or substituted appearance the divorce was recorded and distribution of property and custody of children ordered as the party present desired.

While the legislators were making a change in the seriousness to be required of those severing the marriage relationship, the courts were also taking measures which differed sharply from those of the late 1920's. A 1935 report[36] of the work of the Supreme Court of the R.S.F.S.R. included a case with facts not unlike those in the case of 1929, in which the court had reached the conclusion that although bigamy was recognised as a crime this did not prevent the recognition of a subsequent factual marriage following a registered marriage which had been terminated factually but not formally by a recording of a divorce. In 1935 a woman claiming to be a second wife of the deceased sought to establish her status. At the time of the deceased's death he had been registered as married to another woman. The trial court had found that both women might share the property, as the existence of two marriages at the same time could not be considered as bigamy. The Supreme Court said that such a conclusion was wrong, and ordered a new trial, saying that 'the court was required to raise the question of whether the registered marriage had factually terminated since a court has no right to recognise the existence of factual marriage relationships while a registered marriage exists at the same time, and a court must give a precise answer to the question as to which of the contesting parties is actually the heir of the deceased'.[37]

The decision of the court continues the interpretation of early years by leaving open the possibility that in 1935 the second factual marriage might still be held valid, if there had been factual severance of the marriage ties of the first marriage but in no event could both marriages be considered valid at the same time. When the basic principle of the case was put into one sentence for insertion as an annotation in the code itself, the editors extended its rule beyond the words of the full decision by selecting for repetition only a part of the sentence of the opinion. The official annotation reads, 'A court has no right

36 Abstracted in Rostovsky, *Sovetskii Zakon o Brake, Seme i Opeke* [*The Soviet Law on Marriage, the Family and Guardianship*] (2nd ed. 1935), p. 15.

37 *Sokolova* v. *Sokolskaya* [1935] 31 Sov.Yust. 24.

to recognise the existence of factual marriage relationships when a registered marriage exists at the same time'.[38] Perhaps the annotators were influenced by the new policy to discourage divorce, for they seem to have found it possible to depart not only from the true holding of the case, but from the wording of the code itself which had not yet been altered in its provision for the recognition of unregistered divorce. As short a time before as 1934 the Ministry of Justice had issued a circular to the effect that a second marriage following a first marriage which had been factually terminated without registration might be held valid, even though the parties concealed the first marriage when registering the second.[39]

The laxity with which the code was being applied[40] was curbed in some measure by a series of decisions which made it clear that no mere casual relations were sufficient to constitute factual marriage.[41] Failure to prove a common home would prevent one from establishing his or her case.

The codes in the Republics other than the R.S.F.S.R. were uniform in requiring no court contest prior to the registration of divorce.[42] The will of only one party was required for a divorce, and no court participated in the process, which was reserved to the registration office.

The attack upon juvenile delinquency beginning in 1935 was not limited to strengthening the family. A law of April 7, 1935,[43] placed jurisdiction over juvenile crime in a special sitting of the regular criminal courts, as opposed to the commissions for juvenile cases previously existing, and provided that any

[38] Code of Laws on Marriage, the Family and Guardianship, RSFSR (1937 ed.) p. 43.

[39] Circular of October 26, 1934, Code of Laws on Marriage, the Family and Guardianship, RSFSR (1936 ed.) p. 54.

[40] Art. 12 of the Code of Laws on Marriage, the Family and Guardianship, RSFSR had established the types of evidence accepted to prove *de facto* marriage. They were maintenance of a common home, maintenance of a joint bank account, declaration before third persons, in documents or on lists that marriage relations existed, mutual support and joint care of children.

[41] See cases abstracted by Krylenko, 'Socialism and the Family', [1936] 18 Bolshevik 65 at p. 74.

[42] Code of Laws on Marriage, the Family and Guardianship, Byelorussian SSSR (not in official gazette) (1922) Art. 25. Code of Laws on Marriage, the Family and Guardianship and Acts of Civil Status, Ukrainian SSR, [1926] Sob.Uzak. Ukrainian SSR, Nos. 67–69, Arts. 119 and 120. Code of Laws on Marriage, the Family and Guardianship, Uzbek SSR (not in the official gazette) (1928) Arts. 14 and 121.

[43] [1935] 1 Sob.Zak. SSSR, No. 19, item 155.

child from the age of 12 who committed larceny, rape, bodily injury, mutilation, homicide or attempted homicide was subject to punishment under the regular provisions of the Criminal Code relating to such crimes. There were current at the time reports of children who had taunted persons from whom they had snatched pocket books with the remark that the law did not apply to them. Perhaps they had been tutored by criminals who were using them in a gang of thieves. For offences other than those listed the age of responsibility began at 14.

Discipline was also fostered through the youth organisation associated with the communist party, namely the Komsomols. The Programme of the Komsomols was revised in 1936 to include among its provisions the aim of fighting bad behaviour among children, and strengthening discipline in the schools.[44] The nearly 6,000,000 members of the organisation at the time were enlisted in the fight against rowdyism and delinquency.

Measures were taken at the same time to provide for stricter enforcement of the provisions relating to the deprivation of parental rights. The Code of 1926 had provided that a parent who was adjudged neglectful of a child might be deprived of the right to care for the child in his home, and in extreme cases might be denied the opportunity even to see the child.[45] The duty of the parent to provide funds for the maintenance of the child continued. Under the new law enacted on May 31, 1935,[46] establishing criminal penalties for the neglectful parent, the Ministry of Education or the local police were ordered to advise social organisations such as the trade unions at the parent's place of work of any absence of parental supervision over a child. Such a provision was obviously designed to bring into play the important force of social pressure which has been developed into a factor of considerable importance within the U.S.S.R. A parent whose record as a father or mother was reviewed in public by his trade union and fellow workers might well have felt embarrassed if not ostracised.

If public censure through the trade union failed to cause a parent to mend his ways, the 1935 law required the Ministry

[44] A translation of the programme as revised at the Tenth Komsomol Congress held on April 11–21, 1936, is published in Rappard *et al.*, Source Book on European Governments (1937) pp. v.–53 *et seq.*

[45] Art. 46.

[46] [1935] 1 Sob.Zak. SSSR, No. 32, item 252.

of Education to raise before a court the question as to whether the child should be separated from its parents and placed in a children's home at the parents' expense.

FOSTER HOMES FOR THE HOMELESS

Foster homes were sought for children whose parents provided none. Various legal institutions were utilised to create for the child a status which could not be changed once it had been assumed. Campaigns were begun urging that homeless children be adopted. The legal institution of adoption had been placed in Soviet law only by the law of March 1, 1926,[47] following eight years during which the institution of adoption had been prohibited.[48] Immediately after the revolution the institution had been in disfavour for three reasons, (1) adoption was thought to be an institution used under bourgeois law as a means for the exploitation of children: (2) mass institutional care of children was expected to develop so rapidly that the homeless waif would not require a foster home: and (3) the draftsmen of the 1918 Family Code wished to avoid all possibility of violation of their policy against inheritance as it then existed. Adoption would have permitted outsiders to qualify under the one exception authorising members of the family to keep the immediate chattels of the deceased if they did not exceed in value 10,000 roubles.

With the withdrawal of the Civil Code's restrictions on inheritance in 1926, one reason for opposition to adoption was removed, and the institution of adoption was restored, but not without safeguards designed to avoid what were believed to be the excesses of the Tsarist period. Only persons under the age of 18 might be adopted, and only if the consent of any living parents had been obtained. Such consent was not required if the parents had been deprived of their parental rights. If the child was over 10 years of age, his own consent was also required. Not all persons were permitted to adopt, but only those who could qualify as guardians. Thus, the law excluded those who were themselves under guardianship; those who had interests in conflict with the interests of the ward, and those deprived of their rights as citizens. If it developed after adoption that the new status was proving harmful to the child, appeal was per-

[47] [1926] 1 Sob.Uzak. RSFSR, No. 13, item 101.
[48] Code of 1918, Art. 183.

mitted to a court to set aside the relationship. A request to be permitted to adopt had to be approved by the guardianship agency of the local soviet, and registration had to follow at the bureau for registering acts of civil status.

An adopted child is given all the rights and is subject to all of the duties of natural children, including the right of inheritance, and maintenance during minority or while unable to work after coming of age.

In 1928 the code had been amended to formalise an additional institution of a little less sweeping character than adoption but providing legal protection for the homeless child.[49] It was called 'dependency'. The status does not involve the incidents of adoption such as possible change of name, inheritance rights and support under the usual rules. It provides less protection than adoption, yet it is more than guardianship, for the child taken as a dependent is protected to a greater extent than is the ward. If a child's natural parents have died or have insufficient means to support him, the person who has taken the child into his home as a dependent is thereafter bound to continue to provide care and education even if he would like to abandon the relationship, so long as the child remains a minor or is unable to work.

A dependent also has rights against the estate of a decedent if the latter leaves no will. As has already been indicated in the chapter on the law relating to property, any individual who can prove that he was unable to work and was in fact completely dependent upon the deceased for a full year prior to the latter's death has an equal right in the estate with the surviving spouse and the children of the deceased. By law in 1936[50] it was provided that if a will omits any dependent who is a child, those receiving legacies are required to share proportionately to the size of their legacy in any maintenance which may be necessary. Thus, the law relating to dependency, which antedated the campaign against juvenile delinquency, was fitted to the purposes of the new programme to provide homes for the homeless, even when their benefactor turned against them in his last will and testament.

49 Law of November 29, 1928, [1929] 1 Sob.Uzak. RSFSR, No. 22, item 233, introduced into Code of Laws on Marriage, the Family and Guardianship, RSFSR as Art. 42 (3).

50 *Ibid.*, introduced into Code of Laws on Marriage, the Family and Guardianship, RSFSR as Art. 42 (2).

The year 1936 was the occasion for another change in the law to benefit the homeless child, for at that time there was introduced the institution of *patronat,* formerly known to Roman law.[51] The institution was designed to induce persons with homes, who were reluctant to assume continuing obligations, to open them to the homeless children. Under the new law a person might take a child between the ages of 5 months and 14 years into his home under contract. The Ministry of Health was authorised to make the contract if the child was under 4, while the older children were subject to the jurisdiction of the Ministry of Education. The relationship, which had to begin before the fourteenth birthday, had to terminate at the sixteenth birthday. In the country districts the contract was to be executed by the president of the village soviet acting as agent for the Ministry of Social Insurance or for the collective farm's fund for mutual assistance. Under the terms of the contract the patron is paid monthly by the contracting agency.

Since the contract is the sole source of law relating to the *patronat,* the child obtains no right of inheritance or maintenance by way of parental duty. The child may not even qualify as a dependent in the event of the death of the patron as the child is dependent not upon the patron but upon the agency which has made the contract for his care. The patron is, however, ranked as a guardian in other matters by the law, and may be held criminally responsible if the child is left without supervision or support while in the patron's care.

THE WORLD WAR INCREASES THE HOMELESS

With the coming of the second world war and the consequent destruction of families, homeless waifs appeared in numbers not seen since the civil war some twenty years earlier. Campaigns were conducted in the press and through the social organisations to encourage persons to adopt children, or take them into their homes on some less permanent basis. Within the framework of the various kinds of relationships made possible by the legislation of the late 1920's and that surrounding the campaign against juvenile delinquency begun in 1935, large numbers of homeless children were placed in homes. The continuing effort to provide an environment suitable for the child is reflected in some of the judicial decisions of the time.

51 Law of April 1, 1936, [1936] 1 Sob.Uzak. RSFSR, No. 9, item 49.

A post-war case[52] concerned the custody of a child transferred to a Lithuanian by a Jew during the German occupation when the German policy of extermination of the Jews seemed to threaten the three-year-old's life. The child's mother had been killed before the child was transferred by its father, and finally the father was killed. When the war was over and the territory had returned to Soviet control, the child's aunt sought custody of the child, but was denied it by a court. Later the aunt heard that the woman who had assumed responsibility for the child planned to leave for what had been a part of Poland. The aunt petitioned the Ministry of Education of the Lithuanian Soviet Socialist Republic to transfer the child to a relative on the basis of *patronat*. The request was granted and the little girl was given to the relative to be reared.

The *patronat* seems to have been short, for the child was soon adopted by two residents of Moscow, and the appropriate entry was made in the books of record. In 1946 the wartime guardian in the Lithuanian Soviet Socialist Republic brought suit against the adopting parents to regain custody of the child, and obtained judgment in her favour, which was affirmed by the Supreme Court of the Republic. The judgment was then set aside by the Supreme Court of the U.S.S.R. on the ground that the decision had not been in accord with the requirements of Article 44 of the Family Code under which solely the interests of the child must govern in disputes over children.

The Supreme Court thought that the trial court had not compared sufficiently carefully conditions in the homes of the two parties. It noted, further, that the wartime guardian was a Roman Catholic and had educated the child in a Roman Catholic school, while the adopting parents were sending the child to a Soviet school in which she was doing well and were preparing her for a musical career. The new conditions were described as follows, 'The Kavins have means, have a good apartment, are cultured people, and, as was concluded by the Inspector, Shelli Margolis has found what amounts to her own family with the Kavins where all the conditions for her rearing are present'. The Supreme Court also thought that the child who was now nine years old should have been asked her opinion although the law does not require it. Finally the R.S.F.S.R.

[52] *Margolis* v. *Mikshta*, No. 36/628 [1946] 9 Sud.Prak. SSSR 3.

courts had jurisdiction and not those of Lithuania where the plaintiff resided. The case was remanded to the Supreme Court of the R.S.F.S.R. to sit as a trial court, and the Prosecutor was ordered to be present at the rehearing.

While the case indicates the emphasis placed upon the family environment, it suggests that there are various additional considerations of importance, one of these being the presence or absence of a religious upbringing. The implication is clear that the Roman Catholic school was looked upon less favourably than the regular Soviet school, although the fact that the child was a Jewess may have accounted for some of the critical tone which crept into the court's opinion.

A demobilised soldier sought return of his child in another case.[53] During his absence at the front his wife had found it necessary to reduce her cares because of her illness. She put one of her three children in a children's home, from which he was transferred to a family by the director without the consent of the father. In resisting the suit, the defendant produced his certificate of adoption. The trial court held for the plaintiff, but the appellate court ordered that the child be left with its foster-parents. The Supreme Court restored the judgment of the trial court on the ground that the consent of the parents is necessary to adoption, and this consent was not obtained. Further, return to his parents was in the interests of the three-year-old child, for the conditions of poverty and illness which had caused the mother to relinquish the child in the first instance had been reversed, and conditions of life were now entirely normal. The Supreme Court seems to indicate that when two homes appear to be equally good, the natural parents will be preferred, and certainly so if the child was adopted without their consent.

THE IDEAL SOVIET HOME

The type of home preferred by Soviet policy-makers as the environment for a child is suggested by a series of cases concerning the custody of a child of separated parents. Preference is shown unmistakably for a home maintained by the child's mother. A father brought suit for custody of his child against its mother who had continued to live with her parents after the

[53] *Orel* v. *Krinzberg* [1946] 9 Sud.Prak. SSSR 5.

birth of the child.[54] The trial court in applying the usual rule preferring the mother felt, apparently some sympathy for the father for it ordered the mother and the grandparents to permit the father to take the child to his home twice a week, to meet with the child at any time and to concern himself constantly with the growth and proper development of the child. The appellate court affirmed the decision, but the Supreme Court of the U.S.S.R. eliminated from the order the right of the father to take the child to his home maintained with his parents on the ground that this would create two different regimes for the rearing of the child, and this was undesirable, as the mother should have all responsibility for rearing the child. The father was to be permitted to exert influence as the father upon the child's upbringing, but only in agreement with the child's mother. A cautionary remark was inserted at the end of the decision to the effect that 'It goes without saying that if the mother departs from a reasonable upbringing for the child, the father has the right at any moment to bring a new suit against the mother to obtain custody of the child'.

The warning of the Supreme Court that the father may be preferred in special circumstances has been indicated as meaningful in several cases. Some were obvious, such as that in which a divorced husband was permitted to regain custody of a child awarded to its mother at the time of the divorce because the mother had been committed subsequently to a psychiatric hospital.[55] The case had one difficult feature in that the child had been cared for adequately by the mother's parents during the first two years of her illness and was not, therefore, without a good home.

Another mother was denied custody of her child when it was proved that the father had been given the child by the divorced mother in 1942 with the statement that the mother was not in a position to care for it and did not wish to do so.[56] The father cared for it in what the court found to be good circumstances for two years before the mother brought suit to regain its custody. The Supreme Court stated that the considerations which should govern were these: if the mother had resources

[54] *Kvartshav* v. *Redkova,* No. 36/677 [1946] 9 Sud.Prak. SSSR 4.
[55] *Krimov* v. *Polishchuk* [1939] 14 Sov.Yust. 70.
[56] *G.* v. *K.* [1946] 4 Sud.Prak. SSSR 7.

but abandoned her ill infant child to the father in the middle of winter and thus refused to rear it, she should not regain it, but if she had given it to the father only because of her limited experience and lack of resources, she should be permitted to regain it. The Supreme Court was of the opinion that the first situation had been supported by the evidence, and so it decided that the father should be permitted to continue to care for the child.

The political maturity of the father was not found sufficient reason in another case to deprive the mother of custody.[57] The father was Assistant Professor and Deputy Director of the Kutais Pedagogical Institute in the Georgian Republic. The mother was a student in the Institute. The trial court awarded custody of the child to the father on the ground that he could provide it with 'a responsible communist upbringing', which seemed impossible in the home of the very youthful mother. The Supreme Court reversed the decision, saying, 'The court must consider solely the interests of the child. In doing so the court must bear in mind that the interests of the child are not secured solely by the material conditions necessary for its upbringing. Better material conditions of a father are not reason for taking a two-and-a-half-year-old child away from its mother'. The court continued to point out that the child was being well cared for by its mother, grandmother and grandfather, and to deprive the mother of her child would be to 'deprive the child of necessary maternal care and a normal upbringing'.

The emphasis placed upon preservation of the family, begun in 1937 with the introduction of a graduated scale of fees for divorce, began to be reflected in the textbooks on family law soon after. The standard text to appear in 1938 declared that Soviet family law was creating new forms of community living, a new way of life. It stated 'In this society real human relationships between man and woman are being strengthened, and the family is being strengthened as a socialist form of home'.[58]

Dramatic posters in colour began to appear on billboards behind railway platforms and along the wharves of the Volga depicting a father and mother, in a family group surrounded by their children, and bearing the inscription 'Long Live the Soviet

[57] *Khazhalia* v. *Shvangiradze* [1944] 6 Sud.Prak. SSSR 31.
[58] Volfson, *Semeinoe Pravo* [*Family Law*] (1938) p. 5.

Family'. Novels and cinemas were enlisted to guide the population in the direction of the new approach. The public was being urged to abandon its light-minded approach to marriage and to preserve the family bonds.

With the advent of war new measures were introduced. The most startling was a tax on childless persons, enacted in 1941,[59] followed in 1944 by a tax on persons with not more than two children.[60] In both cases there were exceptions for students, the ill and spouses separated by the war. Foreign students of Soviet conditions saw in these tax measures an attempt to advance the birth rate to make good the losses of the war. Other measures were used, such as the awarding of the Order of Motherhood for mothers of ten children with other orders for those with less.[61] These latter measures were part of the most far-reaching and revolutionary legislation, the law of July 8, 1944.[62]

A REVOLUTION IN FAMILY LAW

The law of 1944 rewrote the Code as it related to marriage, divorce and the treatment to be accorded children born out of wedlock. The latter feature has been discussed already in this chapter, abolishing as it did the right previously accorded the mother to obtain maintenance from the father and giving her instead a claim against the State. The other features were equally surprising to a population which had not been entirely prepared by the campaigns in posters, novels and the press.

Registered marriage was declared to be the sole form which was to be recognised thereafter as having legal consequences.[63] The factual marriages recognised previously by the codes were to be no more. If persons living in such unions wished them to have legal consequences they were ordered by the 1944 law to register them immediately and to state the period of co-habitation. The new requirement was soon reflected in the reported judicial decisions. A peasant woman was unable to obtain a share in the division of property of a peasant household, because her alleged marriage with one of its members had not been

[59] Decree of November 21, 1941, *Pravda*, No. 326 (8734), November 24, 1941.

[60] Decree of July 8, 1944, ss. 16–17, Ved.Verkh.Sov. SSSR, No. 37 (297), July 16, 1944.

[61] *Ibid.*, ss. 12–15.

[62] *Ibid.*

[63] Art. 19.

registered. In recompense for the work she had contributed to the household during the period in which she had lived under its roof, she was informed that she might demand payment for its value.[64]

The divorce procedure was radically changed by the 1944 legislation.[65] A procedure was established with the primary aim of reconciling the parties and restoring the home. For this purpose, the trial court was given jurisdiction over divorce but authorised only to make an attempt to reconcile the parties. It could not grant a divorce under any circumstances. To bring the matter to the notice of the community, and presumably to attract social opprobrium, notice of the proceedings was ordered to be published in the local newspaper at the expense of the spouse filing the petition, and a filing fee of 100 roubles was charged in addition. The defendant was ordered to be summoned to permit the court to determine the course of the proceedings and what witnesses would be required.

If efforts to reconcile the parties failed, the case might be taken by one of them to the appellate court, which was authorised to grant the divorce if it found it necessary to dissolve the marriage. No grounds were set forth in the law, it being left for the courts to determine in each case what they believed to be required by the particular circumstances.

Even after the appellate court grants a divorce, its decision must be registered at the civil registry office before legal effect attaches to the separation. This provision of the statute[66] was enforced in a 1949 case which presented a conflict of social interests. A mother sought to establish the fact of adoption of her son by one Burgaft, who had since died. Presumably, the matter of inheritance was paramount in the mother's mind. The Supreme Court of the U.S.S.R. found that Burgaft had obtained a divorce before his death, but that he had failed to register it as required by the code. In consequence, the court held that he had died a married man, and the adoption had not been effective because he had not obtained the consent of his wife, as required by the Family Code relating to adoption.[67]

In the case reviewed the interests of the child appear at first

[64] *Vardush Gosyan* v. *Agit Gosyan,* No. 48 [1948] 4 Sud.Prak. SSSR 24.
[65] Arts. 23–27.
[66] Art. 27.
[67] *Case of Plotnikova* [1950] 1 Sots.Zak. 59.

glance to have been sacrificed on the altar of procedural law, which seems to have been applied with unexpected harshness. Possibly the rationale was that the wife would have suffered a reduction in her share of the estate if the adoption were recognised, and this was impermissible without her consent. Since the boy had been born on August 25, 1947, he was, however, able to qualify for the benefits paid to mothers of children born out of wedlock, and denial of inheritance rights as an adopted son did not mean that the child would be destitute.

A series of judicial decisions appeared in the reports soon after promulgation of the statute indicating the practice of the appellate courts in deciding the cases brought before them. Four of those reaching the Supreme Court in 1946 indicate the first reaction to the new law. In the first[68] the intermediate appellate court had refused to grant divorce because it found that the parties could resume relationships, but the Supreme Court was of a contrary opinion. It pointed to the fact that the parties had actually terminated relationships in 1944, had divided their marital property and agreed to give two children to the father.

A couple, aged 49 and 51 years respectively at the time of their marriage, sought a divorce on the ground that after their marriage they had continued to live in separate homes and had never had conjugal relationships.[69] This was explained by an allegation that after marriage 'such a difference in personality and habits had become evident that life together and family relationships had become impossible'. Witnesses had confirmed the conflict, and the Supreme Court was prepared to agree that it was too deep-seated to permit a normal marriage.

The termination of a marriage by the intermediate court was affirmed by the Supreme Court[70] when the record indicated that marital life had actually terminated in 1941, and the husband had remarried after the lower court's decision in his favour. The Supreme Court said that under such circumstances it must be realised that re-establishment of marriage relations is impossible of achievement. The sole child was awarded to the mother.

[68] *I.* v. *S.*, No. 36/753 [1946] 9 Sud.Prak. SSSR 7.
[69] *Chakhunashvili* v. *Andrievskaya* [1946] 9 Sud.Prak. SSSR 7.
[70] *Case of G. and K.* [1946] 4 Sud.Prak. SSSR 6.

A divorce was likewise granted when it was proved that the parties had actually separated in 1942, the husband creating another family by living with a woman who bore him two children, with whom he now maintained a home.[71] The court found that during the first marriage from 1926 to 1942 there had been constant fights and noisy squabbles.

In the cases in which divorce was allowed, the parties seem to have separated before the new law of 1944 was published. This fact may have influenced the decisions of the court. Some colour is lent to this conclusion by a contemporary case of 1946 in which marital relations had been continuing although with some unpleasantness.[72]

Divorce was sought by a husband married in 1923 to a woman who had borne him two children in 1924 and 1929. In seeking the divorce the husband declared that 'it was impossible to continue family life because of perpetual squabbles which the defendant started out of jealousy'. His reasoning won a decree in his favour in the lower court, but the Supreme Court set the decree aside, stating that not a single witness confirmed the fact of squabbles before 1941. The squabbles had begun only after the wife learned in 1943 that the husband had been unfaithful to her with another woman at the front. After the war the husband had returned home and had resumed family relations.

STRICT POLICIES APPEAR IN THE COURTS

Reluctance to grant divorce is evidenced in increasing measure in later years. In 1949 the Supreme Court refused to acquiesce in the divorce granted by the intermediate court because the strained relationships which had caused the husband and father of three minor children to complain, were his own fault, he having taken up with another woman.[73] The Supreme Court said, 'The relationships which were created in the family for which the plaintiff was himself responsible, cannot serve as the basis for divorce. The decision of the court in this case sanctions in substance the clearly amoral relationship of V to his family duties, and it cannot be accepted as correct'.

The attitude of the courts derived from the several published

71 *X.* v. *X.* [1946] 9 Sud.Prak. SSSR 9.
72 *K.* v. *K.*, No. 36/830 [1946] 9 Sud.Prak. SSSR 8.
73 *V.* v. *V.* [1949] 4 Sots.Zak. 61.

decisions is confirmed as existing generally by a Soviet author reviewing the work of the courts in 1949. It was reported that in the Chernigov Province in the Ukrainian Soviet Socialist Republic reconciliation had been achieved in 54 per cent of the cases heard in the first court, while in the Rozen Province reconciliations had occurred in 56 per cent of the cases.[74]

The Supreme Court issued an order on September 16, 1949,[75] to all courts handling divorce cases saying that many courts did not understand the political implications of the 1944 law introducing a new procedure to be followed in granting divorce. The lower courts were criticised for granting divorces for reasons contrary to the principles of communist morals. Examples of the wrong approach on the part of the lower courts were given as the granting of divorces because a husband had left his wife and found another woman, because the husband had been absent for years in the army, and because the husband fought with the wife over her relatives. The Supreme Court said that it noted in some courts a willingness to accept the desire of the parties for divorce as binding upon the court. The lower courts were also criticised for not taking the necessary time to try and effect a reconciliation, and for failing often even to ask the questions necessary to determine the possibilities of reconciliation. The courts were instructed not to grant a divorce in the future unless they were convinced from the circumstances of the case that proceedings for divorce had been commenced only because there were deeply considered and well founded reasons and that continuation of the marriage would conflict with the principles of communist morals and could not create the conditions necessary to family life and the rearing of children. The courts were ordered to go beyond the material presented by the parties and explore the circumstances on their own initiative.

The attitude of the trial court judges themselves is suggested by the report of the President of the Astrakhan Provincial Court. He pointed out that the very omission of grounds for divorce in the statute had required the trial court judges to use their creative ability based upon their own experience with life. They needed to be more than lawyers. They had to be psycho-

74 Aksenenok, 'The Role of the Court in Strengthening the Family in the Soviet State', [1949] 3 Sots.Zak. 3 at p. 7.

75 3 *Spravochnik po Zak.* (1949) p. 497.

logists with training in the political aims of the leadership and with great tact, seeking to find the key to marital peace. Usually only one of the spouses before his courts sought divorce, as evidenced by the fact that in 1949 in his Province but 9 per cent of all applications for divorce were supported by both parties. He criticised some of his trial judges for failure to hear both parties, and called for a clearer policy to be applied when both spouses desire the divorce.[76]

Similar indications of difficulties in applying a divorce law which lists no grounds for divorce have come from a member of the Supreme Court of the Tartar Republic. He declares that he found it necessary once again to begin to study questions of the family, social organisation, and Soviet morals as defined in the Marxist classics, and these helped him to develop correct criteria for evaluating the motives for divorce and the points of view and errors of the parties.[77]

To induce the parties not to bring actions for divorce the 1944 legislation developed further the concept of high fees introduced by the 1936 law. Fees were increased from the schedule of 50 to 300 roubles set in 1936 to a schedule of from 500 to 2,000 roubles. The court was left free to set the amount, presumably at a rate which would be meaningful to a person within the income group to which the plaintiff belonged.

While legislation was seeking reconciliation of parties rushing impetuously into divorce proceedings, other wartime action had been seeking to establish homes for the numerous orphans of the war. An order of January 23, 1942,[78] set up a series of reception points for war orphans under the Ministry of Internal Affairs, to which all homeless children up to the age of fifteen, inclusive, were to be sent. Those under fourteen were to be directed in not more than two weeks through the Ministries of Education to the appropriate children's institutions or placed in homes under the contract of *patronat*. The older children were to be placed in industry or agriculture. The *patronat* was declared to be an especially desirable means of caring for children, and it was provided that families accepting such a con-

[76] Shumilov, 'The Role of the Court in Strengthening the Family in the Soviet State', [1950] 2 Sots.Zak. 21.

[77] Krylov, 'From the Experience of Trying Cases on Divorce', [1950] 5 Sots.Zak. 26.

[78] [1942] Sob.Post. SSSR, No. 2, item 26.

tract would receive monthly maintenance for each child of 50 roubles. The Ministries of Education in the Republics were ordered to set up a system of special inspection of the conditions under which children placed in homes under the contracts of *patronat* were maintained.

The Ministries of Health and Education of the R.S.F.S.R. established the regulations governing the work of their local agents in the local soviets on April 8, 1943,[79] reciting the rules of the Code on the subject of *patronat* adoption and guardianship, and declaring that if a person wished to adopt a child taken under a contract of *patronat,* this should be permitted and the contract terminated.

For one who reviews the course of Soviet law there is apparent a complete turn of the wheel from the relatively strict family legislation of the Russian Orthodox Church to the similarly strict legislation introduced in 1944 by Soviet legislators. The future desired for the child seems to have motivated the development of the law. The conclusion seems obvious that the necessity of developing a child who would respond affirmatively to the plans of the new leadership has been the governing consideration. When the family structure was thought to impede such a response, it was weakened. When it could aid, it was strengthened. Yet there has emerged since the 1944 law a claim that the law's provisions reflect the new element of communist morals.

A NEW MORALITY

With the claim that there has entered an element of morality Soviet leaders base their actions on something more than utilitarianism or 'politics'. Perhaps they are thinking of the admonition of Engels that the family should be a strong monogamous one. Perhaps they are laying the foundation for what they will claim to be a new 'natural law'. Certainly the Soviet people strayed far from the ideal of the monogamous family in the early years, and they were encouraged to do so by the legal institutions established for their guidance. Today the record suggests that the leadership has now found it desirable to move in the direction of Engels' ideal, and the institutions of the lawyer are being utilised to guide society in that direction.

[79] [1943] *ibid.,* No. 3, item 24.

Just as the word 'sacred' is now being used to give a hallowed element to the concept of State-owned means of production, so also are new social relationships being elevated above politics by being espoused as 'moral'. Old words reappear in the vocabulary to serve new purposes and to add new prestige as the Soviet leadership manipulates the formulæ of the law and the institutions of the lawyer to mould society in the image of its dreams. Andrei Vyshinsky has written that it is wrong to declare today that Soviet law is only 'politics' because that conveys an idea of instability.[80] To Vyshinsky law seems to have acquired characteristics peculiar to itself in its implementation of general policy.

80 Vyshinsky, 'Fundamental Tasks of Soviet Law', Speech made to the first congress on problems of the sciences of Soviet State and law, 1938. English translation published in Lenin *et al.*, *Soviet Legal Philosophy* (1951) p. 303 at pp. 329–330.

Chapter 11

LAW AND THE 'CAPITALIST ENCIRCLEMENT'

THE municipal law of the U.S.S.R. is closely related to the international scene, if one may believe the pronouncements of Soviet leaders. On the eve of the revolution during the summer of 1917 Lenin set the theme when he said, 'There is no more erroneous nor harmful idea than the separation of foreign and domestic policy'.[1] In 1939 Stalin forecast the whole future of the Soviet State and its law in terms of the international situation. He declared that the State as an instrument of compulsion would remain even after communism had been achieved if the 'capitalist encirclement' remained, while the State might be expected to 'wither away' in accordance with the prophecy of Engels if that encirclement could be eliminated.[2]

There are those in the west who doubt that the real cause of the severe forms of compulsion found in Soviet law is to be found in any real or imagined danger from the capitalist powers. They believe the danger to have been manufactured by Soviet leaders to justify to a restless people strict domestic policies against which they might otherwise rebel.[3] There are others, such as Arnold Toynbee, who find in the experience of the Russians since the Polish invasions of the seventeenth century cause to believe that they are obsessed with fear of attack.[4] It is argued that Soviet policies must be evaluated in terms of that obsession, even if the danger is unreal.

Whatever the cause, the relationship between domestic and foreign policy seems unquestionably to exist in Soviet minds. It provides reason to discuss the Soviet practice of international law in a volume devoted to Soviet municipal law.

1 Leading article, *Pravda*, No. 18, June 14, 1917. Also published in (1935) 21 *Leninskii Sbornik* 66, with a preface to the effect that while the article was unsigned, it was the work of Lenin beyond the shadow of a doubt. *Ibid.*, pp. 60–61.

2 Stalin, 'Report to the XVIII Party Congress', *Leninism* (English translation, 1942) p. 434 at p. 474.

3 Kennan, *American Diplomacy 1900–1950* (1951) pp. 112–114.

4 Toynbee, 'Reith Lectures, I. The World and the West: Russia' (1952) 48 *The Listener* 839.

International law has always been defined by Soviet authors in similar terms to municipal law, namely as an instrument of policy.[5] At the outset of the Soviet regime, it was thought to be so much a product of the policies of what were termed the 'great bourgeois States' that there was a tendency among some Soviet statesmen to reject it in entirety, but a less emotional view prevailed. By degrees this view has become the official view so that Soviet text writers now unanimously declare that the institutions of international law, or a selection of them, can be used to Soviet advantage.[6]

The Central Committee of the communist party of the Soviet Union seems to have given its pre-eminent support to the thesis that international law can be used to Soviet advantage. In a directive dated October 5, 1946,[7] it ordered that attention be given to international law in legal education, and chairs of international law have been established in the universities. The interest is not simply cultural. Soviet authorities have been nominated and elected to the International Court of Justice and the International Law Commission of the United Nations. After years of boycott of the legal agencies of the League of Nations, the assumption by Soviet citizens of important posts on international legal bodies dramatises the change in attitude toward the place of international law in Soviet politics.

No general acceptance of international law as being derived from reason, Divine guidance or morals is to be found among Soviet authors and statesmen. They pick and choose among the precedents to meet their needs, and they do so quite openly. The leading Soviet textbook on international law published in 1948 declared, 'Those institutions in international law which can facilitate the execution of the stated tasks of the U.S.S.R. are recognised and applied by the U.S.S.R., and those institutions which conflict in any manner with these purposes are rejected by the U.S.S.R.'.[8] In 1951 the whole course of Soviet research in international law was declared by a succeeding textbook to be related to the State's requirements, for the author's wrote,

5 Vyshinsky, 'International Law and International Organisation', [1948] 1 Sov. Gos. i Pravo 1 at p. 19.

6 Academy of Sciences USSR, Institute of Law, *Mezhdunarodnoe Pravo [International Law]* (1951) p. 3.

7 For text, see [1946] 6 Izvestiya Ak. Nauk SSSR, otd. ek. i prava 460.

8 Kozhevnikov, *Sovetskoe Gosudarstvo i Mezhdunarodnoe Pravo [The Soviet State and International Law]* (1948) p. 25.

'Soviet scholarship in international law is organically linked with Soviet activity in the field of international relations'.[9]

To the student of the relationship drawn in Soviet minds between law and power, analysis of Soviet espousal of the principles of international law may be conducted along the same lines as the analysis of the relationship in municipal law, which precedes this chapter. What has been done by Soviet policy-makers with the formulæ of the law and the institutions of the international lawyer can be examined in the light of the contribution made toward preservation of power and the effectuation of social change. The subject is vast, for there is a practice of over thirty years in the many specific fields with which international law has been traditionally concerned.[10] Studies analysing the years leading up to the second world war exist,[11] and new studies of the subsequent period are in preparation.[12] In this volume on law and social change in the U.S.S.R. space limitations require that only enough of the practice be analysed to indicate the probable nature of Soviet thinking.

SELECTING USEFUL PRINCIPLES

Two trends have been apparent in the Soviet selection of principles of international law to meet its needs. Both seem to have been related to the 'capitalist encirclement', in which Soviet leaders appear to see a continuing threat to their existence and to the development of the social patterns which they intend to instil in those whom they rule.

One set of principles selected from the body of international law seems to have been related to the development of a position in international law which would require any State or group of States having hostile intentions toward the U.S.S.R. to appear as the aggressor in international law if it takes hostile action. The other set of selected principles seems to have been related to maintaining and, where necessary, developing a position in

[9] Academy of Sciences USSR, Institute of Law, *Mezhdunarodnoe Pravo [International Law]* (1951) p. 146.

[10] An impression of the many fields in which Soviet authors are writing currently may be gained from Lissitzyn, 'Recent Soviet Literature on International Law' (1952) 11 *The American Slavic and East European Review* 257.

[11] Taracouzio, *The Soviet Union and International Law* (1935).

[12] A study by Margolis is in preparation at the Russian Research Centre of Harvard University.

international law which would legitimise action taken by the U.S.S.R. to overcome or neutralise the governments of States which will not recognise the Soviet leaders as the principal authorities on the path leading to a desirable new way of life.

Up to the present the first set of principles has been evidenced in a more voluminous record than the second. Perhaps this is because of the power relationship which has existed between the Soviet Union and the States who have disliked most of what she has stood for. Until the end of the second world war the U.S.S.R. through her policies had placed herself in a minority position in the world of international politics. She had refused to recognise the financial obligations of former governments, embittering the investors of France, Great Britain and the United States.[13] She had declared religious beliefs anathema, and had disfranchised the priests and monks and confiscated the estates of the Church on which it relied for its maintenance.[14] She had executed as traitors or potential traitors many members of the old regime, including the Royal Family itself. She had confiscated the industrial plants not only of her own nationals but also of many great corporations of the west. She had created a State monopoly of foreign trade, thus antagonising international commercial elements.[15] She had refused to accede to the proposals which the west had made at the Genoa and Hague Conferences of 1922 as the maximum concessions possible to the Soviet regime in restoring the concert of Europe.[16] She had preached and even assisted revolution in other States. For many who looked upon the League of Nations as the hope for peace in the world, her reviling of the League as an instrument of imperialist exploitation gave reason to believe that she would never return to the family of nations.[17]

Having set their country apart from the nations of the west

13 Decree of January 28, 1918, [1918] 1 Sob.Uzak. RSFSR, No. 27, item 353.

14 As to the franchise, see Constitution of the RSFSR, [1918] 1 Sob.Uzak. RSFSR, No. 51, item 582, Art. 65. As to the nationalisation of Church lands, see decree of October 28, 1917, [1917] 1 Sob.Uzak. RSFSR, No. 1, item 3.

15 Decree of April 22, 1918, [1918] 1 Sob.Uzak. RSFSR, No. 33, item 432.

16 See Saxon Mills, *The Genoa Conference* (no date) and Fischer, 1 *The Soviets in World Affairs* (1930) pp. 318–372.

17 Ivanov, 'The League of Nations', quoting Litvinov. 2 *Entsiklopediya Gosudarstva i Prava* [*Encyclopedia of State and Law*] (1925–1926) p. 747 at p. 755.

on issues which they seem to have thought critical to the preservation of power, Soviet leaders turned their attention to the possibilities of protecting themselves from the eventual onslaught which their doctrine told them was inevitable, and which their actions seemed to invite. Military protection was out of the question in the early years on the part of a power defeated disastrously by a crushing German attack of four years' duration and torn asunder subsequently by a civil war which knew no quarter. Not until the New Economic Policy had served its purpose in restoring the economy, and the five year plans had begun to develop a heavy industry on a grand scale could any but the dreamer have hoped to protect the new Soviet Russia by military might.

Protection had to be sought in other forms. Doctrine suggested that a first attempt should be made to woo the workers of the world so that they would not support a military campaign against a State claiming to be their fatherland. The communist international was formed in 1919 to further such wooing, and the effort was not without some signs of success. But Soviet leaders seem to have thought that this was not enough. While the Cominform continued to function for many years, the Soviet leaders also sought such protection as might be offered by international law. They reasoned that if they could not equip an army, perhaps other armies could be disbanded. They undertook a campaign for disarmament.[18]

The first steps toward reliance upon international law for what protection it might be able to give were taken as early as the spring of 1918. Lenin's decision to make a peace with Germany at Brest Litovsk, in the face of criticism by those of his party who saw an opportunity to use the negotiations to arouse the sympathy of the workers of the world, was a first step in reliance upon the principles of *pacta sunt servanda,* so basic to international law. Lenin discarded Trotsky's formula of 'No war, no peace' for a peace treaty which was humiliating and which was abrogated on the first opportunity, but which was a peace treaty nevertheless.[19] It offered protection against further attack only because like all peace treaties it claimed the support

[18] For a Soviet author's review of Soviet activity, see Korovin, 'The USSR and Disarmament' (1933) 292 *International Conciliation* 291–308.

[19] Fischer, 1 *The Soviets in World Affairs* (1930) pp. 48–49 and 60–67.

of international law to give it enduring qualities. Lenin seems by his decision in Brest Litovsk to have accepted the thesis that peace rests on a treaty basis.

During the middle 1920's, relations were resumed with the States of Europe, and diplomatic intercourse restored in accordance with a pledge on the U.S.S.R.'s part to observe the principles of customary international law, so long as those with whom she resumed relations did likewise.[20] Treaties of commerce were negotiated,[21] and some measure of protection achieved in what Soviet leaders thought to be the atmosphere which would be likely to keep the surrounding powers peaceful in their own self-interest, namely the atmosphere of international trade.

SOVIET COMMERCIAL TREATIES

The new commercial treaties presented some problems to the U.S.S.R. Hostility abounded in many States against the new trade delegations which Soviet diplomats established to conduct trade. Their premises were searched, and they were accused of espionage and even of assisting local communists to conduct strikes and political campaigns. Their commercial activities became the subject of suits in the courts of the lands in which they worked. The U.S.S.R. claimed that the State monopoly of foreign trade made necessary a new approach to the commercial activity of a State. It enacted in its domestic legislation a charter for its trade delegations in which diplomatic status was conferred.[22] Then it sought to obtain recognition of this diplomatic status, with its attendant immunities in international law.

Soviet success in obtaining diplomatic status for its trade delegations and immunity from suit on its commercial agreements varied with the countries approached. Those which were small, anxious for Soviet trade, and close to its frontiers, found

[20] See decree of January 14, 1927, s. 2, extending on the basis of reciprocity to diplomatic representatives of foreign states all rights and privileges accorded by international law. [1927] 1 Sob.Zak. SSSR, No. 5, item 48. For an analysis of the extent to which the USSR has departed in recent years from established diplomatic practice, see Schwarzenberger, 'The Impact of the East-West Rift on International Law' (1951) 36 *Grotius Society Transactions for the Year 1950*, p. 229 at pp. 254–259.

[21] For a list of Soviet treaties during the early years, see Taracouzio, *The Soviet Union and International Law* (1935) p. 450 *et seq.*

[22] Decree of September 13, 1933, [1933] 1 Sob.Zak. SSSR, No. 59, item 354.

it expedient to accept most of the Soviet claim, and the commercial treaties included articles granting the status desired.[23] The more independent powers which had no great need for Soviet customers went to the other extreme and refused to have anything to do with a Soviet trade delegation. In the United States to the present time and in England during the early years Soviet trade was conducted through corporations created under English or American domestic law, and therefore subject to regulation and to suit. In the intermediate group of States a compromise was sought. Diplomatic status was granted to the persons of the trade delegates and to the offices they occupied, but their commercial activities were subjected to suit in local courts and to the law of the land, unless the agreement provided specifically to the contrary. It is this form which has become the most widely utilised by the U.S.S.R. in its commercial treaties of more recent years.[24]

Commercial activities of the U.S.S.R. have been carried on not only through trade delegations but by Soviet corporations chartered solely under Soviet law for the purpose of foreign trade. Since the mid-1930's these corporations have assumed responsibility for most Soviet trade in the countries in which they have been permitted to do business. They have raised also the problem of immunity from suit. Up to the end of the second world war it was the rare occasion on which immunity was claimed,[25] and Soviet officials made a point of calming commercial interests who feared that they might be unable to bring suit. Wherever possible, Soviet negotiators sought to include

[23] *E.g.*, see treaty signed August 29, 1931, between Lithuania and the USSR, [1932] 2 Sob.Zak. SSSR, No. 10, item 105. English translation in Taracouzio, *The Soviet Union and International Law* (1935) pp. 431–433.

[24] *E.g.*, see treaty signed June 12, 1946, between France and the USSR, *Journal Officiel*, June 20, 1946. English translation in (1946) 15 *Department of State Bulletin* 533.

[25] Immunity was claimed for a ship in commercial service in 1927. See *Rizaef Frères v. The Soviet Mercantile Fleet* (Provisional Court of Shanghai, 1927), (1928) 55 *Journal du Droit International Privé* 1104. The practice of the Soviet Government when its commercial corporations have been sued in France has been analysed. It is disclosed that pleas of immunity have been entered when suits have been brought against the Soviet Trade Delegation, but no plea of immunity has been entered on behalf of the particular Soviet State trading corporation engaged in the commercial activity from which the claim arose. See Hamson, 'Immunity of Foreign States: The Practice of the French Courts' (1950) *The British Yearbook of International Law* 293 at pp. 309–317.

in any commercial contract a clause providing for arbitration in Moscow under Soviet law before the Foreign Trade Arbitration Tribunal of the All-Union Chamber of Commerce.[26] Since this is a body composed entirely of representatives selected by the Chamber and acceptable to the Ministry of Foreign Trade, it has an official character. Yet in those cases when a manufacturer or trader was sufficiently large and disinterested in obtaining the Soviet orders, agreement on arbitration in Moscow was often impossible, and the rules of commercial law of the country concerned were applied to the agreement. The Soviet negotiators assured their commercial counterparts in the foreign country that there would be no plea of sovereign immunity if suit were brought.

While no such pleas appear to have been filed with courts in which such Soviet public corporations have been sued on contracts to which they are parties, two cases in the past few years have attracted wide attention. One in the United States involved a libel of a Soviet vessel on which a passenger coming to New York had been injured in a storm. The Soviet government pleaded sovereign immunity, and the federal court in which the claim was filed was advised by the Department of State that it must accept the plea.[27] In an English case involving a libel suit against TASS, the Soviet news agency, a similar plea was filed and also accepted,[28] but not without a considerable stir in the House of Commons among those who thought that a State conducting a commercial enterprise should submit itself to local jurisdiction.

PROTECTION OF FRONTIERS

While commercial agreements were the major concern of Soviet

[26] For an example, see *Amtorg Trading Corp.* v. *Camden Fibre Mills, Inc.* (1952) 304 N.Y. 519 and 109 N.E. (2d) 606. Suit had been brought below by Camden Fibre Mills, Inc. to have set aside its agreement to arbitrate in Moscow on the ground that the body named for the purpose was too closely linked to the Soviet government to permit of a fair award. The Court of Appeals of New York State held that Camden had full information available to it at the time of execution of the contract concerning the character of the tribunal and it must be held to its bargain, although it might subsequently resist enforcement when it was attempted under the New York Civil Practice Act on the basis of a Moscow award if the award proved to be unfair.

[27] *Low* v. *Steamship Rossia* (U.S. District Court, Southern District of New York, 1948), (1948) 26 *American Maritime Cases* 814.

[28] *Krajina* v. *The Tass Agency* [1949] 2 All Eng. L.R. 274.

diplomats in the middle twenties, and have remained a matter of importance to the U.S.S.R. ever since, the negotiation of treaties going beyond trade was begun in the late 1920's. Border agreements providing for the settlement of frontier disputes, before they became magnified to serious proportions, went hand in hand with those creating a sea frontier for the U.S.S.R.[29]

A step was taken in 1926 to establish in international law what has come to be known as the 'sector' principle to govern claims in the Arctic. Seizing upon a proposal made in the Canadian Senate in 1907 and adopted, apparently, as Canadian government policy by 1925,[30] that all of the land in the Arctic north to the pole from points fixed at the eastern and western extremities of the Canadian territories be claimed for Canada, the Soviet government made a similar claim to their 'sector'. All land, whether discovered or not yet discovered in the Arctic, if it lay within a triangle made by lines drawn from the extremities of Soviet territory in the Arctic northwards to the pole, was claimed for the U.S.S.R.[31]

Later the reason for this declaration was indicated to have been self-preservation rather than an excess of national pride, for an author in 1930 suggested that the purpose of the declaration was to assure uninterrupted communication along the Arctic coast and the exclusion of other powers from possible landing fields.[32] He suggested further, that the same policy dictated a claim to ice fields in the Arctic, which might serve as landing fields for a hostile power. He was even prepared to develop his argument to the point of claiming that the sovereignty of the littoral State should attach also to the Arctic Ocean within the sectors of attraction. While the claims of the Soviet author have not been espoused publicly by the Soviet government, they have not been disavowed. It is possible that if a threat to the

[29] Treaty between Poland and the USSR on the settlement of border disputes, signed August 3, 1925, (1932) 3 *Sbornik Deistv. Dog.* 55, succeeded by treaty signed June 3, 1933, (1935) 8 *Sbornik Deistv. Dog.* 79 and CXLII LNTS 265. Treaties of similar character are those with Latvia, signed July 19, 1926, (1936) 4 *Sbornik Deistv. Dog.* 30, LIV LNTS 155; with Estonia, signed August 8, 1927, (1936) 4 *Sbornik Deistv. Dog.* 35, LXX LNTS 401; with Turkey, signed August 6, 1928, (1931) 6 *Sbornik Deistv. Dog.* 29 and with Finland, signed September 24, 1928, (1930) 5 *Sbornik Deistv. Dog.* 38, LXXXII LNTS 63.

[30] See Corbett, *Law and Society in the Relations of States* (1951) p. 112.

[31] Decree of April 15, 1926, [1926] 1 Sob.Zak. SSSR, No. 32, item 203.

[32] Lakhtine, 'Rights over the Arctic' (1930) 24 *American Journal of International Law* 703.

U.S.S.R. were to become real from the Arctic Ocean's ice fields or navigable waters, the suggested position might be taken.

Britain signed a treaty concerning fishing rights on May 22, 1930,[33] in which another statement of Soviet policy as it related to the sea frontier was enunciated. While acceding under the pressure of the situation to the English demand that her fishermen be permitted to fish from three to twelve miles from the low water mark along the northern coasts of the U.S.S.R., the Soviet government inserted in the treaty the saving clause that 'Nothing in this temporary agreement shall be deemed to prejudice the views held by either contracting government as to the limits in international law of territorial waters'. The U.S.S.R. then claimed, and has since claimed, jurisdiction over a territorial belt of twelve miles.[34]

The policy of fixing the Soviet sea frontiers in international law, which had begun with the Arctic was later extended in nearly every direction. A treaty with Iran, dated August 27, 1935, closed the Caspian Sea to vessels of any nation except those of Iran and of the U.S.S.R., and provided that neither nation would permit nationals of other States to serve as seamen on its vessels.[35] In this fashion the possibility of espionage in Soviet Caspian ports and of depredations by foreign vessels acting under an Iranian concession was reduced if not eliminated.

After the second world war the expansion of sea frontiers by the U.S.S.R. was speeded, often in contradiction of present international law. The provisions of the Montreux Convention of 1936 permitting a limited number of war vessels of non-littoral States below 15,000 tons each to pass to the Black Sea were ignored by Soviet text writers, who found in the Russo-Turkish treaties of the end of the eighteenth century and of 1806 reason to argue that the Black Sea had become closed.[36] Any non-littoral State to venture upon it with war vessels was to be branded apparently a violator of international law.

The principle of the closed sea was finally claimed even for the Baltic Sea by Soviet international lawyers in 1951. The step

33 (1931) 6 *Sbornik Deistv. Dog.* 43, CII LNTS 103.

34 Decree of May 24, 1921; [1921] 1 Sob.Uzak. RSFSR, No. 49, item 259, and decree of September 25, 1935, [1935] 1 Sob.Zak. SSSR, No. 50, item 420.

35 [1938] 9 *Sbornik Deistv. Dog.* 129, CLXVI LNTS 299.

36 Kozhevnikov, *Sovetskoe Gosudarstvo i Mezhdunarodnoe Pravo* [*The Soviet State and International Law*] (1948) pp. 210–211.

was taken only after the announcement of careful research, performed by a Soviet student in the form of a doctoral dissertation,[37] which had brought forward for renewed public view a proposal made by the Soviet delegation to the Rome Disarmament Conference of 1924 to close the Baltic Sea to warships of non-Baltic powers. While the Soviet graduate student was cautious in making the suggestion that such a policy should be declared, he thought it necessary, because German experience during the second world war had been disastrous when the Baltic was used as a route by the Allies to attack Germany's coast. His professors were prepared, however, to be dogmatic. In their 1951 textbook, they said simply, 'The Black and Baltic Seas must be placed among the closed seas'.[38]

While a claim of protection under international law is of course mere verbiage in the absence of supporting custom or treaty, the claim is important to this study since it evidences Soviet intent to make as many people as possible believe their position to be legal. Coupled with the other measures taken to push outward international legal protection of the sea frontiers of the U.S.S.R. on all shores except the Pacific, the attitude taken on the Baltic and Black Sea becomes part of a pattern. It can be interpreted as being an effort to fix a line over which no power can sail its warships without subjecting itself to the charge that it has violated international law.

Even the Pacific coast has been brought within the orbit of protection by other means. Laying claim to the Kuriles islands at the end of the war with Japan, Stalin remarked that never again would they serve as a means of blocking ingress and egress to the U.S.S.R.'s major Pacific ports.[39] He might have added that with these islands in its hands, the U.S.S.R. had a chance of excluding any fleet attempting to go through them to reach the beaches of Siberia. No power with the islands in its hands would have to worry much about Siberian coastal waters as Japan had demonstrated in blocking lend-lease shipments to Soviet Siberian ports during the second world war.

[37] Molodtsov, 'The Regime of the Baltic Straits in International Law', [1950] 5 Sov. Gos. i Pravo 61.
[38] Academy of Sciences USSR, Institute of Law, *Mezhdunarodnoe Pravo* [*International Law*] (1951) p. 309.
[39] Stalin, 'Declaration to the People', September 2, 1945, *Pravda*, No. 211 (9982), September 3, 1945, p. 1.

While the presently existing principles of international law have had to be tortured to provide sea protection in some regions, the problem of gaining protection in the air through international law has not been so difficult. For long the rule has been generally recognised that the State has sovereignty over the air space above its territory to the outer atmosphere. The Soviet Air Code of 1935 incorporated this principle in its opening article.[40] The U.S.S.R. has resisted all attempts to change this principle in the interests of international air navigation. It has refused to accede to the International Civil Air Organisation, and even to attend the 1944 sessions at which the question of freedom of air navigation was to be discussed as one of the five air freedoms.[41] It has refused to its closest collaborators, for example, Czechoslovakia, the right to fly Czech planes with Czech pilots over the commercial air route between Moscow and Prague.[42] One of the Czech negotiators has recounted that this refusal was explained as resting on the experience with the German pilots who had flown the air route Berlin-Moscow before the war. The U.S.S.R. would no longer risk the return of commercial pilots in bombers of their own or a third country should international relationships change to bring war.[43]

OUTLAWRY OF WAR

While specific measures have been taken to close the sea and air frontiers to foreign powers, general measures have been attempted to write into international law principles which might protect Soviet territory from other forms of attack. In 1928 the U.S.S.R. evidenced impatience at the speed with which the Pact of Paris outlawing war as an instrument of national policy was being put into effect and negotiated a Protocol with some of its western neighbours to bring the Pact into effect immediately between them and the U.S.S.R.[44]

A series of treaties in which all of the neighbours of the

[40] Decree of August 7, 1935, [1935] 1 Sob.Zak. SSSR, No. 43, item 359.
[41] See Chernomordik, 'Air Space in International Air Law', [1948] 4 Izv. Ak. Nauk SSSR, otd. ek. i prava 243.
[42] Agreement signed July 25, 1946, (1949) 27 UNTS 231.
[43] Kašparek, 'Negotiating the Czech-Soviet Agreement' (1952) 11 *The American Slavic and East European Review* 207.
[44] Protocol of August 27, 1928, signed by Estonia, Latvia, Poland, Rumania and the USSR. Turkey adhered on April 1, 1929. For text, see (1930) 5 *Sbornik Deistv. Dog.* 8.

U.S.S.R., except Japan, agreed not to aggress upon the U.S.S.R. was negotiated in the early 1930's.[45] In the course of negotiating this series of non-aggression treaties, the U.S.S.R. also negotiated a pact defining aggression, signed at London on July 3, 1933, and adhered to by nearly all neighbours of the U.S.S.R.[46]

With the pact defining aggression Soviet diplomacy sought to bring to the defence of the U.S.S.R. international legal protection against not only the obvious forms of attack across land and sea and through the air. It indicated that there were other forms of activity which were equally perilous to its continued existence. The definition was drafted to forbid these more subtle forms of warfare as well as the military campaigns.

The article of the treaty defining aggression which attracted wide attention was that which forbade the following, 'Support to armed bands, which having been organised on its territory move on to the territory of another State, or refusal, in spite of the request of a State opposing the invasion, to take on its own territory all measures available to it to deprive the aforementioned bands of all aid and comfort'.

In its resumption of diplomatic relations with the United States, also in 1933, another form of aggression was made the subject of an exchange of notes. On the initiative of the United States' Department of State, the Soviet representative, Litvinov, signed a letter agreeing for his government 'not to permit the formation or residence on its territory of any organisation or group—and to prevent the activity on its territory of any organisation or group, or of representatives or officials of any organisation or group—which has as an aim the overthrow or the preparation for the overthrow of, or bringing about by force of a change in, the political or social order of the whole or any

[45] For collection of these treaties, see *Traités de neutralité, de non-agression et de procédure de conciliation entre l'Union des R.S.S. et les états étrangers* (1934). English translations of the treaties are published in (1933) 27 *American Journal of International Law,* Supplement, pp. 167–195. The text of the treaty dated August 21, 1937, with China is printed in *Izvestiya,* No. 203 (6365), August 30, 1937.

[46] The treaty and the accompanying convention were adhered to by Poland, Rumania, Afghanistan, Iran, Estonia, Latvia, Finland, Turkey, Czechoslovakia, Yugoslavia and the USSR. For text with dates of adherence, see (1935) 8 *Sbornik Deistv. Dog.* 27. For English translation, see (1933) 27 *American Journal of International Law,* Supplement 192, 194 and 195.

part of the United States, its territories or possessions'.[47] The United States gave a reciprocal undertaking.

It was the purpose of the United States to bring the protection of international law to its side in its struggle with the communist international, but the U.S.S.R., apparently, had no intention of withdrawing its support and protection from the world body established by Lenin in 1919 to foment revolution and provided not only with headquarters in Moscow by the Soviet government but with the guidance of some of the most active Soviet revolutionaries. This was made clear in 1935 when a congress of the communist international was held in Moscow with members of the American communist party in attendance. The U.S.S.R. rejected the protest of the United States that the convening of the congress on Soviet territory violated the obligation assumed by Litvinov for his government in 1933.

Years later, in 1952, when the political situation had changed markedly, the U.S.S.R. seems to have concluded that the 1933 agreement could serve its purposes in much the same way as the American negotiators had once looked upon the agreement. A Soviet protest was filed in Washington against an item in the budget of the United States to aid in supporting refugees from Eastern Europe, who, in Soviet opinion, were preparing to develop a revolutionary movement against Soviet domination of the Eastern European countries.[48]

In the face of the growing threat of Hitler, the U.S.S.R. found it desirable to embrace the League of Nations in 1934 as the international protector of international law. Here again, Stalin said very frankly that the reason for the reversal of the Soviet position was not a newly-found love of the League or the principles for which it stood, but a desire to obtain such support as was available, even if it amounted only to a hillock in the path of the rise of Hitler's power.[49] There followed the assumption of the position of proponent of collective security.

[47] Department of State, Eastern European Series No. 1, *Establishment of Diplomatic Relations with the Union of Soviet Socialist Republics* (1933).

[48] The Soviet protest was dated November 21, 1951. For the United States reply rejecting the protest, see 'Soviet Charged Against Efforts of Free Nations to Achieve Collective Security' (1952) 26 *Department of State Bulletin* 28.

[49] Stalin, 'Interview with Walter Duranty', December 25, 1933, quoted in Pope, *Maxim Litvinov* (1943) pp. 335–336. Also Stalin 'Report to Eighteenth Party Congress', *Leninism* (English translation, 1942) p. 434 at p. 443.

Litvinov's voice rang out at Geneva in support of principles which sounded strange from a State which had criticised the League of Nations' system for many years. He declared peace to be indivisible and aggression to be indivisible,[50] and urged that all States standing to benefit from the system of international relations existing in the late 1930's unite and demonstrate their vigorous solidarity and determination to protect those relationships by supporting established international law by more than words.[51] Support was urged for the articles of the League Covenant in the spirit in which they were originally conceived, a spirit with which the Soviets had had no truck at the time of conception.[52]

Mutual assistance pacts were entered into with Czechoslovakia in 1935[53]; with France,[54] once thought to be the archenemy, in 1936, and with the Mongolian People's Republic in the same year.[55] All were designed to preserve the *status quo* against those who would upset the existing pattern of international relations established in international law.

In her enthusiasm for strengthening international law to protect herself against Hitler, the U.S.S.R. even took a step away from her long-standing refusal to accept arbitration of political disputes. At the Hague Conference in 1922 when the new Russia's position in the family of nations was being debated, Litvinov had expressed the doubt that a third party could ever be found who would be impartial to the non-Soviet State in a dispute with the new Soviet Russia.[56] This principle of resistance to attempts to bring the U.S.S.R. into any system of compulsory arbitration had remained a cornerstone of Soviet policy ever after. Again and again the preference for conciliation or diplomatic negotiation over the third party umpire has been expressed.[57] With the rise of Hitler, the U.S.S.R. offered to

50 Litvinov, declaration to representatives of the French press, July 7, 1933, *Vneshnyaya Politika SSSR* [*The Foreign Policy of the USSR*] (1935) p. 256.

51 Litvinov, *Czechoslovakia and the World Crisis* (1938) p. 6. A speech before the Assembly of the League of Nations, September 21, 1938.

52 *Ibid.*

53 [1935] 2 Sob.Zak. SSSR, Nos. 14–15, item 130.

54 [1936] 2 Sob.Zak. SSSR, No. 7, item 72 and (1936) 30 *American Journal of International Law,* Supplement 177.

55 [1936] 2 Sob.Zak. SSSR, No. 23, item 213.

56 Litvinov, Statement at The Hague on July 12, 1922, quoted in Taracouzio, *The Soviet Union and International Law* (1935) p. 296.

57 Institute of Law of the Academy of Sciences USSR, *Mezhdunarodnoe Pravo* [*International Law*] (1947) p. 475.

submit to the Council of the League of Nations its dispute with Uruguay when diplomatic relations were suspended in 1936.[58] The offer was exceptional and never again to be made.

THE LAWS OF WAR

Rights as a neutral were claimed in support of Soviet assistance to the Spanish Government in its civil war with the forces of General Franco who was being aided at the time by troops and supplies from Mussolini's Italy and Hitler's Germany, and again to send arms to China in the early days of her fight with Japan.[59] When the Italian aggression against Ethiopia was successful, the U.S.S.R. joined with other States in refusing to recognise such a seizure.

Yet the war came, and the U.S.S.R. found itself without the formal protection of the Hague Conventions to protect her prisoners of war and her populations caught behind the lines. She had never formally affirmed her adherence to the Conventions which had been signed and ratified by the Tsarist Government. Having denounced many Tsarist treaties at the time of the revolution, and signified its intention to be bound only by specified ones, the U.S.S.R. could not claim protection with full assurance of being accorded such protection as a successor State. Yet, claim such protection she did, and to make her claim more likely of acceptance she declared herself prepared to grant the right established by the Hague Conventions to the enemy.[60]

In claiming protection of the Hague Conventions, Soviet authorities felt it necessary to make some explanations. The Soviet army handbook on international law[61] pointed out that the Conventions were much out of date, being almost fifty years old, and that they did not reflect the actual military State of affairs of the second world war. They were to be espoused in the war because they contributed, if only in small measure, to a reduction in the suffering brought by war to all mankind, and

[58] *Journal de Moscow,* Janvier 7, 1936, p. 1.

[59] Litvinov, Speech to the League of Nations, September 21, 1938, quoted in Pope, *Maxim Litvinov* (1943) pp. 20–21.

[60] Note of Molotov dated November 25, 1941, on the German atrocities against Soviet prisoners of war, 1 *Soviet Foreign Policy During the Patriotic War: Documents and Materials,* Andrew Rothstein, translator (no date, c. 1944) p. 108.

[61] Korovin, *Kratkii Kurs Mezhdunarodnogo Prava, Chast II Pravo Voiny* [*Short Course in International Law, Part 2, The Law of War*] (1944) p. 10.

especially to the workmen and peasants in whose name the revolution in Russia had been fought.

Immediately after the war high Soviet legal scholars proposed revision of the Hague Conventions, particularly to afford protection to guerrillas fighting behind the lines.[62] It was argued that the Hague Conventions had been unduly harsh on such fighters because of the influence of the German professional army men who had assisted in their negotiation. Revision in the light of the experience of the Soviet civilians who had served effectively as guerrillas in the occupied Ukraine was demanded. The matter of guerrilla warfare was related to revolutionary aims by another Soviet speaker who argued before the Soviet Academy of Social Sciences that guerrilla warfare had become a form of national struggle against the exploitation of imperialist powers in Greece, Spain, South Korea, Indonesia, Malaya and the Philippines. Consequently, in the speaker's opinion 'the task of Soviet jurists was to establish a scientific base in law for guerrilla warfare in territories occupied by imperialist aggressors'. This was to be done by placing the problem within the pattern of thought expressed by Lenin and Stalin with relation to just and unjust wars. A consideration of the manner in which such a position could be developed, in the speaker's opinion within the principles of the Hague Convention of 1907, was then set forth in outline.[63]

With the years bringing a close to the war the U.S.S.R. entered into the agreements which have been much in dispute in more recent times, namely those of Teheran, Yalta and Potsdam, in which the western powers thought they had outlined a pattern of organisation for Central and Eastern Europe which would result in the reassertion of democratic principles of government and the re-emergence of a group of sovereign States. The U.S.S.R. seems to have conceived of them as providing a means of obtaining a free hand in the affairs of its neighbours. These measures were accompanied by Soviet participation in the negotiations at Dumbarton Oaks and San Francisco leading to the organisation of the United Nations. The U.S.S.R. even agreed to participation in the new International Court of Justice

62 Trainin, 'Questions of Guerrilla Warfare in the Law of War' (1946) 40 *American Journal of International Law* 534.

63 Mankovsky, 'Vladimir Ilich Lenin and the Partisan Character of Research', [1950] 7 Sov. Gos. i Pravo 68 at pp. 69–70.

and presented Soviet citizens as nominees for election. This it had never consented to do with the Permanent Court of International Justice even after it had adhered to the Covenant of the League of Nations.

Yet there were signs after the war that the U.S.S.R. was beginning to reinterpret its position on international law and to avoid being placed in a position in which other States could outvote it in interpreting that law. The veto was demanded as a price of Soviet participation in the United Nations, and there was no acceptance of the clause providing for compulsory jurisdiction of the International Court of Justice.

POWER BRINGS CHANGES

The power position had been altered greatly by the war, as the Soviet leaders seem to have appreciated even before the war's end. From a position of weakness, the U.S.S.R. had grown to the stature of one of the Great Powers. Not only had there been military victory, but this victory had been accompanied by the development of Soviet industrial potential sufficient, even after the destruction of the war, to assure the Soviet Union an industrial base to support her military forces in the kind of war she might expect during the foreseeable future. The selection process to which Soviet post-war authors of international law textbooks had referred became more apparent. Principles of international law were re-examined with care to see whether they might become a restraint upon Soviet post-war efforts to take advantage of the devastation in Europe and Asia to further the cause of communism.

Cracks in the position which Soviet diplomacy had developed in the immediate pre-war years to afford protection in international law against aggressive members of the capitalist world began to appear even before the Japanese had surrendered. One of the first was in the relatively unpublicised 1945 negotiation of a charter under which the Nazi war criminals were to be tried at Nuremberg. The negotiator for the United States, Mr. Justice Robert Jackson of the United States Supreme Court, has recounted an incident.[64] The representatives of France, the

[64] Address of Mr. Justice Robert H. Jackson at Institute in the Teaching of Comparative Law, August 25, 1948, Proceedings of the Institute (mimeographed, 1948), summarized in the *New York Times*, August 26,

United Kingdom, the United States and the U.S.S.R. were meeting in London from June 26 to August 8, 1945.

The Soviet delegation wished to limit the jurisdiction of the tribunal to the specific Axis situation. The Soviet proposal was to phrase jurisdiction in these words:

'The Tribunal shall have the power to try any person who has in any capacity whatever directed or participated in the preparation or conduct of any or all of the following acts, designs or attempts, namely: (1) Aggression against or domination over other nations carried out by the European Axis in violation of the principles of international law and treaties'.

The Soviet draft was the subject of objection by the United States on the ground that it limited the declaration that a war of aggression was a crime to a war perpetrated by the Axis Powers. Mr. Justice Jackson reports that the United States stood ready to break up the conference without argument rather than accept a definition so conditioned, and ultimately the Soviet delegation yielded.

Further, the Soviet delegation later opposed any definition in the Nuremberg Charter of what was to be meant by aggression, even though the United States delegation presented the very definition which the U.S.S.R. had incorporated in its treaty of 1933 defining aggression, to which reference has already been made. The issue was not pressed and became academic, because the captured documents demonstrated that the German attack upon Poland had been so calculated and blatant an aggression by any permissible formula that the omission caused no serious embarrassment to the negotiators.

Another shift in policy became apparent subsequently when a definition of aggression was before a committee of the United Nations in connection with the Korean war. The U.S.S.R's delegation was prepared to withdraw from the position they had taken on the Nuremberg Charter against any definition of aggression. Yet, they wanted such definition as might be adopted limited to the obvious types of military attack by the army of a State. They would accept no clause like that in their

1948. Referred to briefly in preface to Report of Robert H. Jackson, United States Representative to the International Conference on Military Trials, London, 1945. Department of State Publication 3080 (1949) p. vii.

1933 treaty defining aggression, including within the definition 'support to armed bands' which move from the territory of one State on to the territory of another.

Foreign Minister Vyshinsky spoke in the General Assembly of the United Nations on December 6, 1950, in defence of the government of Mao-tse-tung, saying that there had been no aggression when an army of Chinese who called themselves 'volunteers' marched on to Korean soil to participate in the war.[65] He quoted in support of his position Article 6 of the Hague Convention of 1907, to which reference has already been made, saying that it was not unneutral to permit the crossing of a State's frontier by persons offering their services to one of the belligerents.

The conclusion could have been drawn, and was in some quarters, that the U.S.S.R. had reached a position of such strength that she felt that international legal protection from such bands coming from beyond her borders was no longer necessary, as she could cope with them effectively with her own troops. In consequence the basis for selection of principles of international law could be altered. It was not felt necessary longer to espouse some principles previously deemed necessary to the protection of the U.S.S.R. Some doors could now be left open since they could be used effectively in furtherance of Soviet policy. They opened out upon a 'capitalist encirclement' which seemed, apparently, to Soviet leaders to be ripe for revolution and for the assistance of 'volunteers' to help native elements prepared to fight.

The selection of paragraphs to be included in a definition of aggression was a discriminating one, however, since the U.S.S.R. was prepared to continue those provisions of the definition which would have made illegal the moving of forces with which she did not, apparently, feel prepared to cope. She wanted it made clear that the marching of an army, or the sailing of a navy across frontiers when they were sent as the official army of a State and not as armed bands was to be illegal. It is not improbable that she had been much impressed by the success of the amphibious attack of United Nations forces at Inchon in Korea. It suggested the possibilities open to strong

65 United Nations General Assembly, Fifth Session, December 6, 1950, A/PV. 319, p. 590 at p. 592.

naval powers like Britain or the United States in any theatre of war.

Those seeking to determine the relationship between the Soviet position on international legal principles and the international situation were provided with further evidence of the influence of events when the Soviet delegates at the United Nations switched back to their 1933 stand on the definition of aggression. This occurred in the Legal Committee of the United Nations in January, 1952, when the U.S.S.R. again espoused a definition of aggression including the provision relating to the succouring of armed bands.[66] Many western observers related the change in attitude to the growing strength of western trained subversive elements along the borders of Eastern European States and the provision of a special fund in the budget of the United States to help refugees from Eastern European areas. It seemed that the U.S.S.R. had decided that it was more necessary to preserve for herself what protection she could gain in international law from saboteurs and even possible military attack than to keep open the door in international law for such efforts when mounted from Soviet territory.

PUBLIC OPINION AND THE KOREAN WAR

The Korean war presented other opportunities for the U.S.S.R. to indicate its position on elements of international law. Soviet lawyers claimed immediately in 1950 upon entrance into Korea of troops carrying the flag of the United Nations that their presence was illegal under international law. In order to make such a claim, two steps would seem to have been necessary. First it seems necessary to argue that the war in Korea was a civil war and not a war between sovereign States, so that the provisions of the Charter of the United Nations prohibiting intervention in matters of domestic jurisdiction might be called upon. Secondly, it seems necessary to argue that even if this were not so, the decision in the United Nations, having been taken without the presence of the U.S.S.R. in the Security Council, was not legal under the Charter.

Soviet authors seem to have found no reason to argue the question of whether the war in Korea was a civil war or a war

[66] United Nations General Assembly, Sixth Committee, January 5, 1952, A/C. 6/SR. 278, pp. 149–150.

between sovereign States. They have not faced the argument, presented by the legal adviser to the Secretary-General of the United Nations, that the war was not a civil war because the United Nations had already recognised the Republic of Korea as having a *de facto* boundary on the 38th parallel, and the marching of troops across that boundary was an act of aggression against a sovereign State.[67] Soviet authors merely have declared that it is a civil war.[68] They move from that assertion to argue that any armed participation by other States in the war becomes intervention in a civil war and illegal under the provisions of Article 2, paragraphs 4 and 7 of the Charter, and also against the law established by the judgment at Nuremberg that aggressive war is a crime.

The second question as to whether a decision taken without the presence of the Soviet Union in the Security Council of the United Nations, because of its boycott of the proceedings, can become a legally adopted decision of the United Nations, must seem to Soviet lawyers to have been pushed to the background by the answer they have given to the first question. If the troops flying the United Nations flag have intervened in a civil war, it would seem unimportant legally how the decision to intervene was reached since the whole action must be illegal. Yet, Soviet authors have continued to publicise their refusal to recognise the legality of the decision of the Security Council to sanction the use of troops in Korea. They must feel that such publicity has value.

The position taken by the U.S.S.R. on the illegality of participation of some non-Korean armies in the war in Korea, and the legality of participation of the Chinese suggests the reasons why the U.S.S.R. finds comfort in international law. Certainly, in view of the expressed opinion of Soviet leaders that international law is not the essence of Divine wisdom, reason or a body of changeless rules of social intercourse derived from experience, but an instrument of State policy, just like municipal law, the Soviet appeal for respect of international law cannot be designed to obtain for the U.S.S.R. the protection of some

67 Feller, 'The United Nations, International Law and Korea' (1950) *Proceedings of the Section of International and Comparative Law, American Bar Association*, p. 21.

68 Durdenevsky and Ladyzhensky, 'Aggression and Intervention in the Far East in the Light of International Law', [1951] 2 Sov. Gos. i Pravo 53.

superior force above the nation State. The appeal must rest on some reason of less philosophical character. All evidence provided by Soviet practice suggests that the Soviet leadership has reached the conclusion that the peoples of the world revere legality in international relations and, consequently, support of peoples is most likely for the State which makes the best legal case before the bar of public opinion.

War in the mid-twentieth century has often been declared to be possible only for coalitions of powers. No single State is thought by military experts strong enough to mount the gruelling offensive, requiring years for its success, which modern war involves. In consequence, it is possible that Soviet leaders reason that if the U.S.S.R. can by an appeal to public opinion prevent the coalition of a sufficiently powerful group of States against it, it can reduce the danger of being overcome. It may even free its own hands for the taking of steps designed to reduce the 'capitalist encirclement' to which its leaders lay the necessity of preserving vigorously repressive measures in Soviet municipal law.

That this is not an idle surmise is suggested by the ardent wooing of public opinion by the U.S.S.R. with policies designed to claim such sanctity as international law may provide at the bar of world public opinion. The allegations of germ warfare by United Nations' troops in Korea; the allegations of United Nations' mistreatment of prisoners under the Geneva Convention: the allegations of United Nations' atrocities committed on the civilian population—all have their apparent basis in an attempt to arouse world public opinion against those powers who oppose the position which is accorded Soviet support. An indication of Soviet appreciation of the value in public opinion of a position claiming the sanctity of international law is dramatised by such propaganda practices as those utilised in the 'Stockholm appeal' of 1950 calling for the outlawing of the atomic bomb, and the frequent presentation in the United Nations of a proposal that an international convention be negotiated for the purpose.[69]

[69] See speeches of Vyshinsky in the General Assembly of the United Nations, given on October 1, 1948, October 7, 1948, October 12, 1948, November 11, 1948, November 13, 1948, November 19, 1948, November 10, 1949, November 12, 1949, published in Vyshinsky, *Voprosy Mezhdunarodnogo Prava i Mezhdunarodnoi Politiki* [*Questions of International Law and International Politics*] (1951) pp. 60, 75, 192, 220, 246, 611 and 622.

Yet, with the espousal of an extension of international law into the atomic field, the U.S.S.R. has again been carefully selective. It seems not prepared to accept such a convention if it is tied with international control of atomic energy, or with inspection by international teams of scientists as these procedures have been formulated by the majority in the United Nations.[70] Such provisions would constitute, apparently, concessions of too grave a nature. It is not hard to imagine that the Soviet mind, tutored as it has been in the theory of the economic source of political power, would resist to the end any measure which would convey to others, even an international body of which the U.S.S.R. was a member, the right to control an important economic factor such as motive power. It would expect this control to be utilised in ways harmful to Soviet development.

To the Soviet mind international control of atomic energy would open the door to international control over its economic plans, for since the time of Lenin's 1920 pronouncement concerning the key role in planning played by electricity, it has been a matter of Soviet doctrine that motive power is the key to the whole edifice of economic planning. International inspection well beyond the influence of the inspected power, with the information it would give not only on military movements but also on economic potential, which the U.S.S.R. places on a par with *matériel* and manpower, is equally to be resisted. In consequence, world public opinion, valuable as its support is thought to be, is not to be courted with such proposals, lest the more important element of continued Soviet economic and political growth be endangered in the process.

'WORLD LAW'

There are other points on which public opinion is not courted, even though the U.S.S.R. might make many friends throughout the world by doing so. One such point has become increasingly apparent since the second world war. It is 'world law'. All demands for world law, whether they come from the elements

[70] Kozhevnikov declares that the USSR's position is to establish strict international control and strict inspection, but in such a way that the latter will not lead to interference in those spheres of production not linked with atomic energy. Kozhevnikov, *Sovetskoe Gosudarstvo i Mezhdunarodnoe Pravo* [*The Soviet State and International Law*] (1948) p. 358.

who want the abolition of the sovereign State, or the international lawyers in many lands who have espoused only the international legal protection of human rights, are resisted.

The U.S.S.R. and its small group of supporters abstained from voting on the International Declaration of Human Rights, even though by its terms it was to have no legal force, but was to be a popular appeal. The U.S.S.R. could not, apparently, risk the loss of popular support throughout the world which attached to this immensely popular declaration by voting against it, but it could not bring itself to vote in favour of it. Further, in the committee hearings leading up to the preparation of a Covenant of Human Rights it has found it necessary to participate, but it has opposed at every juncture any provisions which would take out of the hands of each state the decision as to when a violation has occurred.

Many have limited their view of Soviet opposition to international action on human rights to a consideration of whether the U.S.S.R. felt itself vulnerable to international prosecution because of the way it has treated its own citizens. It is possible that the U.S.S.R.'s position is taken for broader reasons, as valid as the narrower analysis may be. It is possible that the U.S.S.R. opposes the development of an international policy, and eventually of an international law, on human rights because it does not want to see a precedent set under which there may come into effect a 'world law' to which all States are subject. It does not want a world law growing out of the demands of the whole articulate mass of mankind outside the area of Soviet influence when that mankind has not been guided, as Soviet leaders guide their own people, to seek goals believed by Soviet leaders to be those required in the progress of mankind towards communism.

There is much evidence to support such a conclusion. Some have seen it in the Soviet campaign within their own country against 'cosmopolitanism', which is a relatively new Soviet term to designate what might elsewhere be called cultural internationalism. So long as the bulk of the peoples of the world are beyond the reach of Soviet influence, any such cultural internationalism would probably follow the dictation of the majority and develop in the image of the non-Soviet world and not of the Soviet world. This the Soviet leaders must avoid at all costs.

Some have seen support for the conclusion that the U.S.S.R. is prepared to resist with all of its strength the move toward 'world law' in the violent verbal attacks upon those who have argued that the individual has come or must soon come to have a place in international law.[71] It is noted by Soviet authors that such men as Philip Jessup of the United States are in the forefront of those pressing the scholarly espousal of the inclusion of the individual among the subjects of international law. It is said by Soviet authors that western scholarly leadership of such a movement is not mere chance.

If individuals obtain a place in international law, Soviet authors seem to fear that their cause may be espoused by enemy States and heard before a hostile international tribunal. In the present power relationship, the U.S.S.R. professes to see a subtle measure of United States policy in the Jessup thesis, in that the United States could claim to intervene legally in the domestic affairs of other States, as it has attempted to do under the peace treaties with Bulgaria and Hungary when it protested the Kotkov and Mindszenty trials.[72] A world law in which individuals have a right to be subjects of the law might be expected to raise to the world level provisions like those incorporated in the peace treaties ending the second world war.

Further concrete evidence of Soviet desire to retain a free hand in the interpretation of international law so that the public opinion of the world may not be mobilised against the U.S.S.R., with the argument that it has acted against the principles of international law, is to be found in the Soviet attitude towards interpretation of the Charter of the United Nations.

Vyshinsky has argued that the Charter cannot be brought to the International Court of Justice for interpretation, because it is not like a constitution of a single State, nor is the court like a supreme court of a State. Vyshinsky goes further to say that even if the Charter and the International Court of Justice were accepted as being analogous to a constitution and a supreme court of a single State, there is no reason to follow the principle of constitutional interpretation found in the Anglo-Saxon world.[73] Continental States, he argues, usually have no legal

[71] Levin, 'The International Law of the American Imperialist Bandits', [1951] 3 Sov. Gos. i Pravo 77.

[72] Trainin, 'Spurious Humanism', [1950] 7 Sots.Zak. 34.

[73] Vyshinsky, 'International Law and International Organisation', [1948] 1 Sov. Gos. i Pravo 1 at p. 13.

tradition of interpretation of constitutions by supreme courts, and it is inappropriate to generalise from the legal traditions of a small part of the world.

SOCIALIST INTERNATIONAL LAW

With the growth in number of States which have been brought under Soviet influence, or have allied themselves with the U.S.S.R. since the war, Sovier international lawyers profess to see new opportunities in international law. They talk of the beginnings of a new 'socialist international law'.[74] By this they mean, presumably, that the relations between these States are the relationships planned by Soviet leaders, or in the case of China, perhaps, concurred in by the Soviet leaders. They are the relationships which those trained in Soviet doctrine believe designed to guide eastern Europe and northern Asia in the direction set by men who advocate the goal of a Soviet-type socialism and communism. They are relationships designed to bring an increasingly large amount of territory and numbers of peoples within the orbit which responds to Soviet leadership.

To the extent that such measures increase Soviet influence they may be presumed to be reducing in Soviet eyes the 'capitalist encirclement'.

As the area expands, the encirclement can become only that part of the world which lies beyond the segment accepting Soviet leadership, or even a single great power with military force sufficient to challenge expansion of the Soviet sphere of influence. There are linguists who argue that the proper translation of the Russian word *okruzhenie,* which all Soviet official translation into English calls 'encirclement', is 'environment', or the French '*milieu*'. If this be so, then the future for the 'withering away' of the State, even assuming the best will in the world on the part of Soviet leadership, an assumption which many in the west are not prepared to make, is remote indeed.

The formulæ of the law and the institutions of the lawyer can be expected under such interpretation to have a lengthy period of further development within the U.S.S.R. as they are manipulated to meet the requirements of a leadership seeking social change.

[74] Kozhevnikov, *Sovetskoe Gosudarstvo i Mezhdunarodnoe Pravo* [*The Soviet State and International Law*] (1948) p. 24.

ACKNOWLEDGMENTS

PERMISSION to use material from parts of papers appearing previously in the following reviews is gratefully acknowledged. *American Society of International Law (Proceedings), Columbia Law Review, Cornell Law Quarterly, Harvard Law Review, Illinois Law Review, Michigan Law Review, Soviet Studies, The Political Quarterly, University of Chicago Law Review* and *Wisconsin Law Review.*

The author's former collaborator, Morris L. Weisberg, has graciously consented to the use of materials from *Cases and Readings on Soviet Law,* the copyright to which is held jointly by him and the author.

Many of the judicial decisions reported in this volume were discovered in the unindexed Soviet reports by George I. Krynski, research assistant to the author, under a grant received from the Russian Institute of Columbia University.

SELECTED READINGS

This list has been prepared with two aims in view: (1) indication of sources of such English translations as exist of codes, statutes and diplomatic documents referred to in the text, and (2) designation of works, usually of book length, with which a reader interested in detail may pursue his interest. Material has been arranged under headings which parallel the order of treatment in the text. For the convenience of those readers who wish to read intensively in the field a list of selected bibliographies is included. The table of abbreviations in this volume will indicate the periodicals in the Russian language which are primary sources. Other Russian language sources are listed in the footnote references.

Legal History and Philosophy

Berman. *Justice in Russia: An Interpretation of Soviet Law.* (Harvard University Press. Cambridge, Mass. 1950. pp 322)

Bunyan and Fisher. *The Bolshevik Revolution 1917–1918: Documents and Materials.* (Stanford University Press. Stanford University, California. 1934. pp 735)

Graham. *New Governments of Eastern Europe.* (Henry Holt and Company. New York. 1927. Part II–Select Documents. pp 565–620)

Schlesinger. *Soviet Legal Theory: Its Social Background and Development.* (Kegan Paul. London. 1945. Oxford University Press. New York. 1945. pp 299)

Lenin *et al.* *Soviet Legal Philosophy. 20th Century Legal Philosophy Series:* Vol. 5. Translated by Hugh W. Babb with an introduction by John N. Hazard. (Harvard University Press. Cambridge, Mass. 1951. pp 465)

Lenin. *State and Revolution.* (International Publishers. New York. 1932. pp 103)

Civil Law

Gsovski. *Soviet Civil Law.* (University of Michigan Law School. Ann Arbor, Mich. 1948–1949. 2 vols. pp 909 and pp 907)

Administrative Law

Arnold. *Banks, Credit and Money in Soviet Russia.* (Columbia University Press. New York. 1937. pp 559)

Bienstock, Schwarz and Yugow. *Management in Russian Industry and Agriculture.* (Oxford University Press. New York. 1944. pp 198)

Littlepage and Bess. *In Search of Soviet Gold.* (Harcourt Brace and Company. New York. 1939. pp 310)

Maxwell. *The Soviet State: A Study of Bolshevik Rule.* (Steves & Wayburn. Topeka, Kansas. 1934. pp 383)

Schwarz. *Heads of Russian Factories.* (New School for Social Research. New York. 1942. pp 333)

Scott. *Behind the Urals.* (Houghton Mifflin. Boston, Mass. 1942. Secher and Warburg. London. 1942. pp 279)

Simon, Robson and Jewkes. *Moscow in the Making.* (Longmans, Green and Company. London. 1937. pp 253)

Timasheff. 'The Organisation of Industry in Soviet Russia' [1929] *International Labour Review* 338

Webb, Sidney and Beatrice. *Soviet Communism: A New Civilisation?* (Scribners. London and New York. 1936 and 1942. 2 vols. pp 1174)

Constitutional Law

Meisel and Kozera. *Materials for the Study of the Soviet System.* (Wahr Publishing Co. Ann Arbor, Mich. 2nd edition, 1953. pp lxxxiv, 613)

Moore, B., Jr. *Soviet Politics—The Dilemma of Power.* (Harvard University Press. Cambridge, Mass. 1950. pp 503)

Towster. *Political Power in the U.S.S.R.* (Oxford University Press. New York. 1948. pp 443)

Vyshinsky. *The Law of the Soviet State.* (Macmillan. New York. 1948. pp 749)

Criminal Law

Beck and Godin. *Russian Purge and the Extraction of Confession.* (Viking Press. New York. 1951. pp 288)

Callcott. *Russian Justice.* (Macmillan. New York. 1935. pp 265)

Edelman. *G.P.U. Justice.* (Allen and Unwin. London. 1938. pp 231)

Makarenko. *Road to Life.* Translated by S. Garry. (Nott. London. 1936. pp 287)

The Criminal Code of the Russian Socialist Federal Soviet Republic (1922). Translated by H. O. Rayner. (H.M. Stationery Office. London. 1925. pp 58)

The Labour Correction Code of the R.S.F.S.R. (Prisons Code). Translated by Hsinwoo Chao. (Sweet & Maxwell. London. 1936. pp 45)

The Penal Code of the Russian Socialist Federal Soviet Republic. Text of 1926 (with Amendments up to December 1, 1932) with three Appendices. (Foreign Office, July 1934. H.M. Stationery Office. London. 1934. pp 82)

Von Koerber. *Soviet Russia Fights Crime.* (Dutton. New York. 1935. pp 240)

Zelitch. *Soviet Administration of Criminal Law.* (University of Pennsylvania Press. Philadelphia. 1931. pp 418)

Agrarian and Co-operative Law

Barou. *Co-operation in the Soviet Union.* (Gollancz. London. 1946. pp 123)

Blanc. *Co-operative Movement in Russia.* (Columbia University Press. New York. 1924. pp 324)

Fisher. *The Famine in Soviet Russia 1919–1923.* (Macmillan. New York. 1927. pp 609)

Hubbard. *The Economics of Soviet Agriculture.* (Macmillan. London. 1939. pp 316)

Hubbard. *Soviet Trade and Distribution.* (Macmillan. London. 1938. pp 380)

International Labour Office. *The Co-operative Movement in Soviet Russia.* (Geneva. 1925. pp 362)

Robinson. *Rural Russia under the Old Regime: A History of the landlord-peasant world and a prologue to the peasant revolution of 1917.* (Longmans, Green and Co. London and New York. 1932. pp 342) Reprinted. (Macmillan. New York. 1949)

Vucinich. *Soviet Economic Institutions: The Social Structure of Production Units.* (Stanford University Press. Stanford University, California. 1952. pp 150)

Labour and Industrial Law

A Selection of Documents Relative to the Labour Legislation in Force in the Union of Soviet Socialist Republics. (H.M. Stationery Office. London. 1931. pp 200)

Bergson. *The Structure of Soviet Wages.* (Harvard University Press. Cambridge, Mass. 1944. pp 255)

Deutscher. *Soviet Trade Unions: Their Place in Soviet Labour Policy.* (Royal Institute of International Affairs. London and New York. 1950. pp 156)
Gordon. *Workers Before and After Lenin.* (Dutton. New York. 1941. pp 524)
Hubbard. *Soviet Labour and Industry.* (Macmillan. New York. 1942. pp 315)
International Labour Office. *Industrial Life in Soviet Russia 1917–1923.* (Studies and Reports, Series B, No. 14) (Geneva. 1924. pp 256)
International Labour Office. *Labour Code.* (Legislative Series 1922. Russia I) (Geneva. 1922. pp 27)
International Labour Office. *The Trade Union Movement in Soviet Russia* (Studies and Reports, Series A, No. 26) (Geneva. 1927. pp 287)
Konstantinovsky. *Soviet Law in Action: The Recollected Cases of a Soviet Lawyer* (edited by Harold J. Berman). (Harvard University Press. Cambridge, Mass. 1953. pp 77)

Patent Law

Nikonow. 'New Patent Laws of the Soviet Union', 16 *Journal of the Patent Office Society* 285 (1934)
Olkhovsky. 'Principles of Soviet Patent Law and Social Organisation of Inventions in the U.S.S.R.', 17 *Journal of the Patent Office Society* 568 (1935)
Patent Law of the Union of Socialist Soviet Republics. (Russian Information Bureau. Washington, D.C. 1925)
Prince. 'The New Soviet Patent Law'. A translation. 28 *Journal of the Patent Office Society* 261 (1946)
The Soviet Patent Act, 1931. 172 *Law Times* 120, 137 (1931)

Family Law

Kiralfy. 'The Juvenile Law-Breaker in the U.S.S.R.', 15 *Modern Law* Review 472 (1952)
Schlesinger. *Changing Attitudes in Soviet Russia: The Family.* (Kegan Paul. London. 1949. pp 408)
The Code of Laws on Marriage, Family and Guardianship of the R.S.F.S.R. Translated by Hsinwoo Chao. (Sweet & Maxwell. London. 1936. pp 51)

International Law

Barmine. *Memoirs of a Soviet Diplomat: twenty years in the service of the U.S.S.R.* Translated by Gerard Hopkins. (Dickson. London. 1938. pp 360)
Dallin. *Soviet Russia's Foreign Policy 1939–1942.* Translated by Leon Denman. (Yale University Press. New Haven, Conn. 1942. pp 452)
Dégras, editor. *Soviet Documents on Foreign Policy.* (Oxford University Press. London. 1951. 2 vols. pp 501 and pp 560)
Dulles, F. R. *The Road to Teheran. The Story of Russia and America, 1781–1943.* (Princeton University Press. Princeton, N.J. 1944. pp 279)
Fischer. *The Soviets in World Affairs.* (Jonathan Cape-Harrison Smith. London. 1930. Reprinted by Princeton University Press. Princeton, N.J. 1951. 2 vols. pp 892)
Litvinov. *Against Aggression.* (International Publishers. New York. 1939. pp 208)
Malenkov. *Report to the Nineteenth Party Congress on the Work of the Central Committee of the C.P.S.U. (B).* (Foreign Languages Publishing House. Moscow. 1952. pp 147)
Moore, H. *Soviet Far Eastern Policy 1931–1945* (Princeton University Press. Princeton, N.J. 1945. pp 285)

Soviet Foreign Policy During the Patriotic War: Documents and Materials. Vol. 1 (June 22, 1941–December 31, 1943). Translated by Andrew Rothstein. (Hutchinson & Co. London. No date, *c.* 1944. pp 320)

Stalin. *Economic Problems of Socialism in the U.S.S.R.* (Foreign Languages Publishing House. Moscow. 1952. pp 104)

Taracouzio. *The Soviet Union and International Law.* (Macmillan. New York. 1935. pp 530)

Taracouzio. *War and Peace in Soviet Diplomacy.* (Macmillan. New York. 1940. pp 354)

Bibliographies

Grierson. *Books on Soviet Russia 1917–1942. A Bibliography and a Guide to Reading.* (Methuen & Co. London. 1943. pp 354)

Gsovski. *Soviet Civil Law.* (University of Michigan Law School. Ann Arbor, Mich. 1948–1949. Vol. 2. pp 679–709)

Hazard and Stern. *Bibliography of the Principal Materials on Soviet Law.* (American Foreign Law Association. New York. 1945. pp 46)

Library of Congress. *General Reference and Bibliography Division. Guide to Soviet Bibliographies. A Selected List of References.* Compiled by John T. Dorosh. (Washington, D.C. 1950. pp 158)

Library of Congress. *Division of Bibliography. Soviet Russia: A Selected List of Recent References.* (Washington, D.C. 1943. pp 85)

Schwartz. *The Soviet Economy: A Selected Bibliography of Materials in English.* (Syracuse University Press. Syracuse, N.Y. 1949. pp 93)

INDEX

Proper names are indexed, with few exceptions, only when they appear in the text